AAT

Financial Statements of Limited Companies

Level 4

Professional Diploma in Accounting

Course Book

For assessments from September 2017

Third edition 2017

ISBN 9781 5097 1208 3
ISBN (for internal use only) 9781 5097 1227 4

British Library Cataloguing-in-Publication Data
A catalogue record for this book is available from the
British Library

Published by

BPP Learning Media Ltd
BPP House, Aldine Place
142-144 Uxbridge Road
London W12 8AA

www.bpp.com/learningmedia

Printed in the United Kingdom

> Your learning materials, published by BPP Learning Media
> Ltd, are printed on paper obtained from traceable
> sustainable sources.

Introduction to the course

Syllabus overview

This unit is concerned with the drafting, analysis and interpretation of financial statements of limited companies. This builds on Levels 2 and 3, where the emphasis of the financial accounting units is on identifying and recording transactions in accounts and ledgers following the principles of double-entry bookkeeping, and drafting the financial statements of unincorporated organisations from the accounts and records prepared.

On successful completion of the unit, a student could be expected, with little supervision, to be able to draft the financial statements of single limited companies and groups of companies. A student could also analyse and interpret financial statements of limited companies by means of ratio analysis for the purposes of assisting outside user groups in their decision making, thereby fulfilling a useful role within an accounting team.

The unit provides students with the skills and knowledge for drafting the financial statements of single limited companies, and consolidated financial statements for groups of companies. It ensures that students will have a proficient level of knowledge and understanding of international accounting standards, which they will be able to apply when drafting the financial statements, and will have a sound appreciation of the regulatory and conceptual frameworks that underpin the preparation of limited company financial statements.

Finally, the unit will equip students with the tools and techniques that will enable them to analyse and interpret financial statements effectively.

Financial Statements of Limited Companies is a mandatory unit. It builds on the skills and knowledge acquired in the two Level 2 units, *Bookkeeping Transactions* and *Bookkeeping Controls*, and the two Level 3 units *Advanced Bookkeeping* and *Final Accounts Preparation*.

Contents

Test specification for this unit assessment

Assessment method	Marking type	Duration of assessment
Computer based assessment	Partially computer/ partially human marked	2.5 hours

	Learning outcomes	Weighting
1	Demonstrate an understanding of the reporting frameworks and ethical principles that underpin financial reporting	7%
2	Demonstrate an understanding of the key features of a published set of financial statements	18%
3	Draft statutory financial statements for a limited company	27%
4	Draft consolidated financial statements	20%
5	Interpret financial statements using ratio analysis	28%
Total		**100%**

Assessment structure

2½ hours duration

Competency is 70%

*Note that this is only a guideline as to what might come up. The format and content of each task may vary from what we have listed below.

Your assessment will consist of 8 tasks.

The assessment will take the form of a computer-based test, which will include extended writing tasks. The assessment will require both computer and human marking and as such, the results will take approximately 6 weeks to be finalised and published.

Task	Expected content	Approx. marks (per sample)	Chapter ref	Study complete
Task 1 and 2	Draft the statutory financial statements for a limited company Type of question: picklist and gapfill	40	The statement of financial position/ The statements of financial performance /The statement of cash flows	
Task 3	IASB *Conceptual Framework*, the regulatory framework and ethics Type of question: written question	22 (across tasks 3 and 4)	The frameworks and ethical principles	
Task 4	International Financial Reporting Standards Type of question: written question		All chapters (apart from interpreting financial statements)	
Task 5	International Financial Reporting Standards Type of question: multiple choice, picklist and gapfill	15	All chapters (apart from interpreting financial statements)	
Task 6	Consolidated financial statements Type of question: picklist and gapfill	30	Group accounts chapters	
Task 7	Analysis and interpretation of financial statements (ratio formulas and calculations) Type of question: picklist and gapfill	20	Interpreting financial statements	
Task 8	Analysis and interpretation of financial statements Type of question: written question	23	Interpreting financial statements	

Skills bank

Our experience of preparing students for this type of assessment suggests that to obtain competency, you will need to develop a number of key skills.

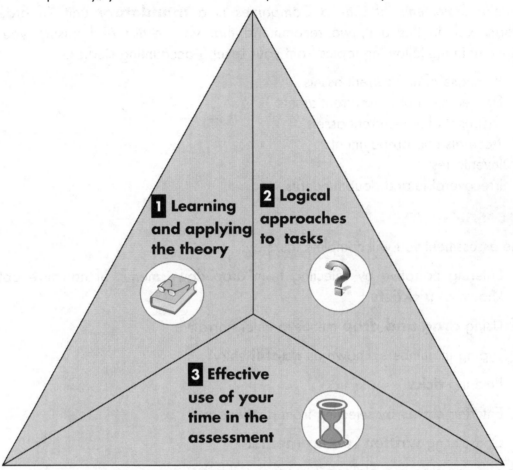

Each of these key skills are analysed on the following pages.

What do I need to know to do well in the assessment?

This unit is one of the mandatory Level 4 units. *Financial Statements of Limited Companies* is a broad syllabus that is examined by a mixture of written questions, computational questions that require the application of knowledge, multiple choice questions and true/false type questions. The questions are both theoretical and application based, which means that you need an overall broad knowledge of the syllabus alongside fairly detailed knowledge for some areas. You will also need an understanding of the techniques involved in approaching the computational questions.

The knowledge that you have to acquire includes the following:

Theoretical knowledge – the fundamental definitions and basic thinking behind different financial statement principles and standards. These will often be tested in narrative questions and are largely non-application in nature.

Practical knowledge – the application of techniques to 'real life' situations, which will be tested mostly in computational questions.

In this section we will look at approaches that you can take to help you learn the key elements of the knowledge in the syllabus and develop your application skills.

Assumed knowledge

Financial Statements of Limited Companies is a **mandatory** unit. In order to perform well in this unit, we recommend that you re-visit and ensure you are competent in the following topics from your Level 3 accounting studies:

- Purchase of non-current assets
- Depreciation of non-current assets
- Disposal of non-current assets
- Accruals and prepayments
- Inventories
- Irrecoverable and doubtful debts

Assessment style

In the assessment you will complete tasks by:

1   Entering narrative by selecting from drop down menus of narrative options known as **picklists**

2   Using **drag and drop** menus to enter narrative

3   Typing in numbers, known as **gapfill** entry

4   Entering **ticks**

5   Entering **dates** by selecting from a calendar

6   Completing **written requirements.**

Each question style is explained in more detail below.

Picklists

Here you need to answer questions by selecting the appropriate wording from a list of options. These options will be given in a drop down box and be presented in alphabetical order.

For example, the following question is an extract which appears in the AAT *Financial Statements of Limited Companies* sample assessment Task 2:

Draft the statement of cash flows for Chicago Ltd for the year ended 31 December 20X1.

	£000
Net cash from operating activities	
Investing activities	
▼	
▼	
Net cash from investing activities	

Picklist:

Adjustment in respect of inventories
Adjustment in respect of trade payables
Adjustment in respect of trade receivables
Bank loans
Depreciation
Finance costs
Interest paid
Proceeds on disposal of PPE
Profits after tax
Profit before tax
Profit on disposal of PPE
Purchases of PPE
Revaluation surplus
Tax paid

In this example, you need to know that 'purchases of PPE' and 'proceeds on disposal of PPE' are investing activities and select these narratives from the drop-down list. This is typical of how you will complete the statement of financial position proformas in the assessment.

Gapfill entry

Many tasks will require you to calculate a specific number and then enter it into the proforma / solution box on-screen. This is known as gapfill entry.

An example is given below:

Draft the statement of financial position for Bookham Ltd as at 30 June 20X1.

	£000
ASSETS	
Non-current assets	
Property, plant and equipment	
Current assets	

To calculate the number to include as non-current assets you must consider both:

- The numbers in the trial balance, given in the scenario; and
- Further information (eg relating to the depreciation charge for the number)

Note that in the assessment, the trial balance and further information will be provided to you through 'pop-up' boxes. It is **very** important to log in to the AAT website are familiarise yourself with the style of the exam, well before you sit the real assessment!

Long computational questions

These can be questions on accounts preparation for a single company, accounts preparation for a group of companies and ratio calculation for the analysis question.

The key to performing successfully in these questions is to have the knowledge (see skill 1) and to know the **technique** for answering each type of long computational question. The techniques are explained in each chapter and it is important that you practise questions until you have perfected the technique.

A good technique in approaching the questions and doing the workings in a logical manner will often mean the difference between a good answer and a very bad one. Stick to your technique!

For the ratio calculation question – know the theory and be very careful when performing the calculations. Carelessness can cost you the question. Ensure you present the answer correctly – days, times or percentages.

What if I do not remember how to do one of the adjustments?

The best approach is to forget about that adjustment and complete the rest of the question without it. Rarely will one wrong (or left out) adjustment mean a declaration of incompetence on a question.

If you have time at the end of the paper, you can go back to that one adjustment and guess!

What if I do not have time to add up the financial statements I am drafting?

Usually very few marks are allocated to adding up. It is better to stick to your timing and move onto another question where you will be able to show the examiner your knowledge and skills.

Workings

Also, for the longer numerical questions where you complete single entity and consolidated statements of financial statements, there will be **on-screen workings** for you to complete.

As we have seen, the information at the start of the assessment will say:

'In Tasks 1, 2 and 6 you will see there are tables that can be used as workings for your proformas. You don't have to use the workings to achieve full marks on the task, but data entered into the workings tables will be taken into consideration if you make errors in the proforma.'

We highly recommend that you complete the on-screen workings as this will maximise your changes of obtaining marks and being successful in the assessment

Where on-screen workings are not provided but a calculation is necessary, it is important that you set out a proper working to calculate the correct answer. This will help you to avoid making unnecessary mistakes. There will be **rough working paper** available on which you can carry out calculations. However, these workings will not be marked.

Entering ticks

Several short-form objective style questions will require you to indicate your answer by entering a tick. For example:

- 'Yes' or 'no'
- 'True' or 'false'
- ticking to indicate your choice of number.

The following question appears in the AAT *Financial Statements of Limited Companies* sample assessment, Task 5 part (d):

How much revenue in total should be recognised in the statement of profit or loss in respect of these transactions?

	✓
£40,000	✓
£48,000	
£50,000	
£58,000	

You may need to read the scenario and requirement several times in order to understand the requirement before you enter a tick in the correct box.

Answering written questions

In your assessment there will be written questions on companies, the regulatory framework, ethics and the financial reporting standards. There will also be a written part in the analysis and interpretation question.

Companies, the regulatory framework, ethics and financial reporting standards

Most of the written questions on companies, the regulatory framework and the financial reporting standards are purely theoretical and quite high level, so the skills learned in skill 1 should be adequate to prepare you for a written question in the exam.

The main verbs used for these type of question requirements are:

Identify – analyse and select for presentation

Explain – set out in detail the meaning of

Discuss – by argument, discuss the pros and cons

STEP 1

READ the question carefully

It is important to read the question carefully to identify exactly what is being asked of you. It is a good idea to highlight key words and all verbs as this will ensure you answer the question that is being asked, not the question you think they should ask!

STEP 2

PLAN your answer

Once you have established the requirement, note down what you know about the topic, **relevant** to what is being asked (key words only). It is a good idea to do this on a piece of paper so you can eliminate irrelevant knowledge and formulate a logical answer when you enter it on screen.

With ethics in particular, do not be tempted to give a vague answer or imagine that common sense alone will earn you the marks. In real life, ethics can be a grey area, but in the assessment, precise answers are required, based on the AAT's *Code of Professional Ethics* and the specific situation described in the question.

Analysis and interpretation

With the **analysis and interpretation questions**, you should:

1. Read the question carefully, identifying the answer format required (eg memo, report etc).

2. Make sure you have scrap paper available so that you can plan your answer.

3. Identify the ratios you are asked to analyse. Note them down on scrap paper to ensure you don't miss any out!

4. For each ratio, you should be commenting on whether it is better / worse than the industry average / prior year / other company; why it is better / worse; what it tells you about the company; and how to improve it (if applicable).

5. If you are asked to give a conclusion or recommendation, you must do this! Marks will be available for this part of the answer

Before answering the question set, you need to carefully review the scenario given in order to consider what questions need to be answered, and what needs to be discussed. A simple framework that could be used to answer the question is as follows:

*   Point – make the point
*   Evidence – use information from the scenario as evidence
*   Explain – explain why the evidence links to the point

For example if an assessment task asked us to explain the Net Profit Margin we could answer as follows:

1. Point – the NPM tell us the amount of net profit earned per pound of revenue

2. Evidence – in this case the company is performing better than the competitor as we have a higher net profit percentage than Company Y

3. Explain – which means that/the consequences are ...

Recommendations are normally also required, to provide guidance on how to proceed:

1. Recommendation – therefore we should invest in the company

This approach provides a formula or framework that can be followed, to answer written questions:

The NPM tells us that (Point) .... in this case the company is (Evidence) ..... which means that (Explain) .... so we should/should not .... (Recommendation).

You must familiarise yourself with the style of the online questions and the AAT software before taking the assessment. As part of your revision, login to the **AAT website** and attempt their **online practice assessments**.

Introduction to the assessment

The question practice you do will prepare you for the format of tasks you will see in the *Financial Statements of Limited Companies* assessment. It is also useful to familiarise yourself with the introductory information you **may** be given at the start of the assessment. For example:

You have 2 hours and 30 minutes to complete this sample assessment.

The assessment contains <u>8 tasks</u> and you should therefore attempt and aim to complete EVERY task. Each task is independent. You will not need to refer to your answers to previous tasks.

Read every task carefully to make sure you understand what is required.

In Tasks 1, 2 and 6 you will see there are tables that can be used as workings for your proformas. You don't have to use the workings to achieve full marks on the task, but data entered into the workings tables will be taken into consideration if you make errors in the proforma.

Where the date is relevant, it is given in the task data.

Both minus signs and brackets can be used to indicate negative numbers UNLESS task instructions say otherwise.

You must use a full stop to indicate a decimal point. For example, write 100.57 NOT 100,57 OR 100 57.

You may use a comma to indicate a number in the thousands, but you don't have to. For example, 10000 and 10,000 are both acceptable.

---

1   As you revise, use the **BPP Passcards** to consolidate your knowledge. They are a pocket-sized revision tool, perfect for packing in that last-minute revision.

2   Attempt as many tasks as possible in the **Question Bank**. There are plenty of assessment-style tasks which are excellent preparation for the real assessment.

3   Always **check** through your own answers as you will in the real assessment, before looking at the solutions in the back of the Question Bank.

Key to icons

 Key term

A key definition which is important to be aware of for the assessment

 Formula to learn

A formula you will need to learn as it will not be provided in the assessment

 Formula provided

A formula which is provided within the assessment and generally available as a pop-up on screen

 Activity

An example which allows you to apply your knowledge to the technique covered in the Course Book. The solution is provided at the end of the chapter

 Illustration

A worked example which can be used to review and see how an assessment question could be answered

 Assessment focus point

A high priority point for the assessment

 Open book reference

Where use of an open book will be allowed for the assessment

Real life examples

A practical real life scenario

AAT qualifications

The material in this book may support the following AAT qualifications:

AAT Professional Diploma in Accounting Level 4, AAT Professional Diploma in Accounting at SCQF Level 8 and Certificate: Accounting (Level 5 AATSA).

Supplements

From time to time we may need to publish supplementary materials to one of our titles. This can be for a variety of reasons, from a small change in the AAT unit guidance to new legislation coming into effect between editions.

You should check our supplements page regularly for anything that may affect your learning materials. All supplements are available free of charge on our supplements page on our website at:

www.bpp.com/learning-media/about/students

Improving material and removing errors

There is a constant need to update and enhance our study materials in line with both regulatory changes and new insights into the assessments.

From our team of authors BPP appoints a subject expert to update and improve these materials for each new edition.

Their updated draft is subsequently technically checked by another author and from time to time non-technically checked by a proof reader.

We are very keen to remove as many numerical errors and narrative typos as we can but given the volume of detailed information being changed in a short space of time we know that a few errors will sometimes get through our net.

We apologise in advance for any inconvenience that an error might cause. We continue to look for new ways to improve these study materials and would welcome your suggestions. Please feel free to contact our AAT Head of Programme at nisarahmed@bpp.com if you have any suggestions for us.

Introduction to limited companies

1

Learning outcomes

1.1	Explain the regulatory framework that underpins financial reporting
	• The purpose of financial statements
	• The different types of business organisation (sole traders, partnerships, limited liability partnerships, corporations and companies, not-for-profit organisations (charities, clubs and societies), public sector organisations (local authorities, central government and the National Health Service and cooperatives)
	• The types of limited company
	• How the financial statements of limited companies differ from those of sole traders and partnerships
	• Forms of equity, reserves and loan capital

Assessment context

This chapter provides background information on companies which sets the scene for the course. The statement of financial position is also introduced, which prepares learners for the accounts preparation questions which are an important part of the assessment.

Qualification context

This chapter includes terminology and information that has been seen in the Level 2 and 3 accounting papers. It also introduces new concepts that will be used and built upon in this course.

Business context

Company directors have a legal duty to ensure that their companies comply with the regulatory framework.

Chapter overview

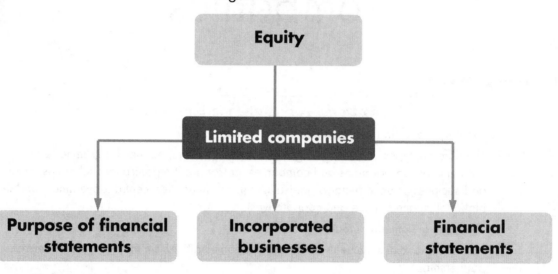

- New shares at nominal value
- New shares at a premium
- Bonus issue
- Rights issue

Equity

Limited companies

Purpose of financial statements

Users need to:
- Make economic decisions
- Assess the performance of management

Incorporated businesses

- Company is a separate legal entity
- Owners are called shareholders
- Directors run the company day to day

Financial statements

Key features for a company:

Statement of profit or loss
- Revenue
- Cost of sales
- Distribution costs
- Administrative expenses

Statement of financial position
- Share capital
- Share premium
- Retained earnings
- Revaluation reserve
- Bank loans
- Tax

Introduction

In this first chapter we look at the reasons why a limited company is different from a **sole trader** or a partnership, before moving on to explain some of the items which appear in limited company accounts. The format of the statement of profit or loss (income statement) and statement of financial position for a limited company are introduced in this chapter and are covered in more detail in Chapters 3 and 4.

1 The purpose of financial statements

The purpose of financial statements is to provide information about an organisation's:

- Financial position (assets and liabilities)
- Financial performance (profit or loss)
- Changes in financial position (cash flows)

Users need this information:

(a) To make economic decisions (eg to assist in deciding whether to invest in the company)

(b) To assess the **stewardship** of the organisation's management (how well the directors have used the company's resources to generate profit)

2 The different types of organisation

There are several broad types of organisation. These can be classified into **profit-making organisations** and **not-for-profit organisations**. You will already have met some of these in your earlier studies. Your focus is on profit-making organisations, specifically limited companies, but we will briefly consider not-for-profit organisations.

2.1 Not-for-profit organisations

These consist of:

Charities, clubs and societies: owned by their members or trustees and created for a specific non-commercial purpose (eg to give grants to the homeless, to enable members to enjoy a particular sport).

Public sector organisations: these are owned by the general public and include central government; local government; the National Health Service; and public corporations.

Their **chief characteristics** are:

- Quality of service provision is often more important than profit.
- Efficiency of use of resources is key.
- Focus is often on small profits or breakeven.
- Need to satisfy a wide group of stakeholders.

IFRS are not always relevant to not-for-profit organisations. The world's capital markets tend to focus on **profit** and **fair value** (buy; hold; sell decisions) which are concepts that are not so relevant to not-for-profit and public sector entities. However, **accountability** is still very important for these entities as they often handle public funds.

Their **approach to performance measurement** is different from that of profit-making organisations. **Profit is clearly not the key objective** of a 'not-for-profit' organisation. However, such organisations produce budgets, which their performance can be assessed against and many of the performance indicators relating to **efficiency** (eg inventory management) will be relevant to a not-for-profit organisation.

Examples of **Key Performance Indicators** (KPIs) relevant to not-for-profit organisations are:

Public sector (hospital):

- Length of waiting lists
- Percentage of patients treated successfully

Private sector (charity):

- Proportion of donations spent on administration
- Humanitarian aid provided

The 'Three Es' (or Value for Money) are often a useful way of assessing performance for not-for-profit and public sector entities:

Economy	The business is conducted with the least expenditure of money, manpower or other resources.
Efficiency	Resources are used in the most advantageous way.
Effectiveness	Policy objectives or other intended effects are achieved.

2.2 Profit-making organisations

These are:

Sole traders: a business owned and managed by one person
Partnerships: a business owned and managed by two or more people
Companies: a business that is a separate legal **entity** from its owners

Later we look more closely at the nature of limited companies and the reasons why they are different from sole traders and partnerships.

For the purpose of preparing financial statements, a business is always treated as being separate from its owners.

Accounts for a sole trader and partnership accounts were studied in the Level 2 and Level 3 accounting papers. You will be familiar with the structure of a statement of profit or loss and statement of financial position for these types of businesses.

In this course, the focus is on preparing and interpreting the financial statements of limited companies.

2.3 Unincorporated businesses

Sole traders and **partnerships** are unincorporated businesses. This means that there is no legal distinction between the business and their owners. Consequently, sole traders and partners have unlimited liability.

Therefore, if the business does not have the resources to pay its liabilities the owners must meet the claims against the business.

Tax does not appear in the accounts of unincorporated businesses as the owners are taxed personally on the profits of the business.

2.4 Incorporated entities

A **company** is a separate legal **entity**. It can enter into contracts, acquire assets and incur liabilities in its own right.

This contrasts with the situation of sole traders and partnerships. For accounting purposes the **business** is treated as a separate entity (the separate entity concept), but the legal position is that it is the owners themselves who enter into contracts and who are personally liable for any debts incurred.

'Limited company' means that the liability of the owners of the company is limited to their investment in the company. As the company is a separate legal entity, should the business fail and be liquidated, the maximum amount that the owners lose is the amount of capital they have agreed to invest in the company.

The owners of a company are called shareholders. Each shareholder must own at least one share in the company.

There are two types of company: public limited companies (plc) and private limited companies (Ltd).

Public limited companies: may raise capital from the public on the stock exchange, although they do not have to.

Private limited companies: cannot invite the general public to invest in their shares through a stock exchange.

As companies are separate legal entities, they are taxed in their own right. Therefore, tax will appear in the financial statements of limited companies.

2.5 Advantages of trading as a limited company

The main advantage is limited liability (see above); however, there are other potential benefits:

(a) It is easier to raise finance:

    (i) There may be any number of shareholders.

    (ii) Investing in a listed company is less risky and therefore more attractive than investing in a partnership or a sole trader (limited liability).

(In practice, shareholders in small companies are often asked to give personal guarantees to lenders, so that the advantage of limited liability no longer applies.)

(b) A limited company continues to operate regardless of the identity of the owners (unlike a partnership, where the old partnership ceases and a new one is formed whenever a partner is admitted or retires).

(c) Limited companies are taxed as separate entities (tax is treated as an appropriation of profits). Partners and sole traders are personally liable for tax on their share of the business profits.

(d) It is reasonably easy to transfer shares from one owner to another.

2.6 Owners and managers

Sole traders and partners normally own and manage their business themselves.

Limited companies (particularly the large ones) are often managed by persons other than their owners.

- **Shareholders** (owners) will invest in the business but are not involved in the day to day running of the company.

- **Directors** are appointed to manage the company on behalf of the shareholders.

As shareholders are not involved in the running of the business day to day, they need a way of evaluating the performance of the directors. The financial statements enable them to assess the way in which the directors are safeguarding the assets of the company and using them to generate profits (stewardship of management).

To assist them in this, the components of a set of financial statements are as follows:

- Statement of financial position
- Statement of profit or loss and other comprehensive income
- Statement of changes in equity
- Statement of cash flows
- Notes to the financial statements

Activity 1: Limited companies

(a) Which of the following statements is correct?

With 'limited liability':

A company may only have a certain prescribed maximum liability on its statement of financial position.	
The shareholders of a company are protected in that they can only lose their investment in the company, should the company fail.	
A company can only enter into transactions involving debt up to a certain limit before gaining express approval from the shareholders in general meeting.	
The shareholders may only invest in a company up to a prescribed limit per shareholder.	

The following terms are used in relation to the preparation of accounts.

(i) Statement of cash flows
(ii) Statement of profit or loss and other comprehensive income
(iii) Directors' report
(iv) Statement of financial position
(v) Statement of changes in equity
(vi) Notes to the financial statements

(b) A complete set of financial statements includes which of the following?

All of the above	
(i), (ii), (iii), (iv) and (v)	
(i), (ii), (iv), (v) and (vi)	
(i), (ii), (iv) and (v)	

3 Financial statements for limited companies

3.1 Comparison with sole traders

The statement of profit or loss provides information about the financial performance of a business. It shows the income generated and the expenditure incurred during an accounting period.

You are familiar with preparing the statement of profit or loss for sole traders and partnerships, and many of the account names you have studied are also relevant when preparing company accounts.

However, certain headings are used when preparing company accounts.

3.2 Proforma – statement of profit or loss

XYZ Ltd
Statement of profit or loss for the year ended 31 December 20X2

	20X2 £000	20X1 £000
Revenue	X	X
Cost of sales	(X)	(X)
Gross profit	X	X
Distribution costs	(X)	(X)
Administrative expenses	(X)	(X)
Profit from operations	X	X
Finance costs	(X)	(X)
Profit before tax	X	X
Tax	(X)	(X)
Profit for the year from continuing operations	X	X

3.3 Proforma – statement of financial position

A statement of financial position shows the assets, liabilities and equity of a business at a stated date.

XYZ Ltd
Statement of financial position as at 31 December 20X2

	20X2 £000	20X1 £000
ASSETS		
Non-current assets		
Intangible assets	X	X
Property, plant and equipment	X	X
	X	X
Current assets		
Inventories	X	X
Trade and other receivables	X	X
Cash and cash equivalents	X	X
	X	X
Total assets	X	X
EQUITY AND LIABILITIES		
Equity		
Share capital	X	X
Share premium	X	X
Retained earnings	X	X
Revaluation reserve	X	X
Total equity	X	X
Non-current liabilities		
Bank loans	X	X
	X	X

	20X2 £000	20X1 £000
Current liabilities		
Trade and other payables	X	X
Short-term borrowings	X	X
Tax liability	X	X
	X	X
Total liabilities	X	X
Total equity and liabilities	X	X

While there are many similarities with the accounts for sole traders and partnerships, you will notice that company financial statements include some additional items.

The *Financial Statements of Limited Companies* syllabus includes:

- Intangible assets
- Share capital
- Share premium
- Retained earnings
- Revaluation reserve
- Bank loans
- Tax

Intangible assets and the revaluation reserve will be studied later in the course. **Share capital**, **share premium**, **retained earnings**, bank loans and tax will be introduced in the next sections.

3.4 Equity

You are familiar with the way the ownership interest is represented in a sole trader/partnership statement of financial position.

It tends to comprise:

Ownership	£
Capital at start of the year	X
Net profit for the year	X
Less drawings	(X)
Capital at end of the year	X

For a **limited company**, the section of the statement of financial position which shows ownership interest consists of **share capital** and reserves.

The ownership interest in a limited company is normally referred to as **equity**. The equity section of the statement of financial position represents the shareholders' interest in the business.

Equity	£
Share capital	X
Share premium	X
Retained earnings	X
Revaluation reserve	X
Total equity	X

Share capital is the capital invested in a company by its owners. The capital of a company is divided into a number of identifiable units, called shares. When a company is formed it issues shares, which are purchased by investors.

Equity shares are an important source of financing for companies. The following terms are important:

Terms	Explanation
Authorised share capital	The maximum number of shares a company may issue.
Nominal/face value	The minimum share issue price.
Issue price	The price the shares are actually issued for.
Share capital account	The nominal value of shares issued is credited to the share capital account.
Share premium account	Where shares are issued at a price above their nominal value, the excess is credited to the share premium account.

Ordinary shares generally carry voting rights. Ordinary shareholders are entitled to the profits of the company after all other claims have been met; however, they do not have a legal right to a dividend.

In the assessment, you may be asked to record share issues. This could take the form of:

- New shares at nominal value
- New shares at a premium (above nominal value)
- **Bonus issue**
- **Rights issue**

Illustration 1 – Issue of new shares at nominal value

Orion Ltd started business on 1 January 20X4 issuing 100,000 ordinary shares with a nominal value of 50p each, for 50p per share.

The double entry to record the issue is:

	Debit £	Credit £
Cash	50,000	
Share capital		50,000

Orion Ltd

Initial statement of financial position (extract) as at 1 January 20X4

	£
Assets	
Cash and cash equivalents (100,000 × 50p)	50,000
Equity	
Share capital	50,000

3.5 Issue of new shares at a premium

Where shares are issued for more than their nominal value, the excess must be credited to a **share premium** account, as only the nominal value may be recorded as share capital.

Illustration 2 – Issue of new shares at premium

A company issues 150,000 50p ordinary shares at 75p each. The shares are fully paid in cash at the time of issue.

For each share purchased, the shareholders have paid the nominal value of 50p and a premium of 25p. The total amount received by the company is:

	£
Nominal value (150,000 × 50p)	75,000
Premium (150,000 × 25p)	37,500
	112,500

The double entry to record the share issue is:

DEBIT Bank £112,500
CREDIT Share capital £75,000
CREDIT Share premium £37,500

In the statement of financial position, the shares will appear as follows:

Equity:

	£
Share capital	75,000
Share premium	37,500

Activity 2: Issue of shares at a premium

On 1 July 20X4 Orion Ltd issued a further 200,000 ordinary shares of 50p each for 80p per share.

Required

Using the information in Illustration 1, complete the statement of financial position (extract) at 1 July 20X4 to reflect this further issue of shares.

Orion Ltd
Statement of financial position (extract) at 1 July 20X4

	£
Assets	
Equity	

Working

The double entry to record the issue is:

	Debit £	Credit £

3.6 Bonus issue

A **bonus issue** is the issue of extra shares to existing shareholders at no cost. A bonus issue does **not** raise any additional finance. It is simply a means of reclassifying reserves as share capital.

The share premium account tends to be used to make the bonus issue.

This will be demonstrated through an example.

Illustration 3 – Bonus issue

A company has the following equity:

	£
Share capital (£1 ordinary shares)	100,000
Share premium	50,000
Retained earnings	350,000
	500,000

It makes a 1 for 4 bonus issue, using the share premium account.

The total number of new shares issued is 25,000 (100,000 ÷ 4).

The double entry to record the bonus issue is:

DEBIT	Share premium	£25,000	
CREDIT	Share capital		£25,000

Equity now appears as follows:

	£
Share capital (£1 ordinary shares)	125,000
Share premium	25,000
Retained earnings	350,000
	500,000

Activity 3: Bonus issue

Dark Ltd has the following equity:

	£
Equity	
Share capital (£1 ordinary shares)	100,000
Share premium	40,000
Retained earnings	200,000
	340,000

Dark Ltd makes a 1 for 5 bonus issue, using the share premium account.

Required

Complete the equity section of Dark Ltd's statement of financial position.

Dark Ltd

Statement of financial position (extract)

	£
Equity	

Working

The double entry to record the bonus issue is:

	Debit £	Credit £

3.7 Rights issue

A **rights issue** is an issue of shares to existing shareholders at below market value. The shares are offered to shareholders in proportion to their existing shareholdings. The shareholders can choose whether or not to take the shares offered to them.

A rights issue is a relatively cheap way of raising extra capital.

Again, the accounting treatment of a rights issue will be demonstrated through an example.

Illustration 4 – Rights issue

A company has the following equity:

	£
Share capital (£1 ordinary shares)	50,000
Share premium	10,000
Retained earnings	90,000
	150,000

It makes a 1 for 5 rights issue at £1.10 per share. All the existing shareholders take up the new shares for cash.

The total number of new shares issued is 10,000 (50,000 ÷ 5).

The double entry to record the rights issue is:

DEBIT	Bank (10,000 × £1.10)	£11,000	
CREDIT	Share capital		£10,000
CREDIT	Share premium		£1,000

Equity now appears as follows:

	£
Share capital (£1 ordinary shares)	60,000
Share premium	11,000
Retained earnings	90,000
	161,000

Activity 4: Rights issue

Light Ltd has the following equity:

	£
Equity	
Share capital (£1 ordinary shares)	200,000
Share premium	50,000
Retained earnings	300,000
	550,000

Light Ltd makes a 1 for 4 rights issue at £1.20 per share. All the existing shareholders take up the new shares for cash.

Required

Complete the equity section of Light Ltd's statement of financial position.

Light Ltd

Statement of financial position (extract)

	£
Equity	

Working

The double entry to record the rights issue is:

	Debit £	Credit £

3.8 Retained earnings

The objective of the companies considered in this course is to generate a profit. Where companies succeed in making a profit, this can be:

- Distributed (by way of a dividend to shareholders)
- Retained in the business

Profits which are retained within the business are included in the **'retained earnings'** account.

3.9 Dividends

A company's profit for the year (ie profit after tax) is available for distribution to shareholders in the form of **dividends**. Dividends can be viewed as the equivalent of drawings in a sole trader or partnership.

Dividends are not shown in the statement of profit or loss and other comprehensive income, as they are not an expense. Instead, they are a distribution to the shareholders.

Consequently, they are deducted from retained earnings. (This will be shown in the statement of changes in equity, which is considered later in the course.)

In accounts preparation questions, the additional data may say 'X Ltd had paid a dividend of £10,000 on 7 July 20X1'. Alternatively, the dividend payment may be shown in the trial balance. This information is important when calculating retained earnings.

3.10 Calculating retained earnings

Accounts preparation questions will require you to calculate retained earnings. An on-screen working is provided in the assessment and then you will include the closing balance in the statement of financial position.

The next example provides the necessary practice at this skill.

Activity 5: Retained earnings

On 1 January 20X5 Orion Ltd had retained earnings of £50,000. In the year to 31 December 20X5 a profit of £20,000 was generated.

A dividend of £5,000 was paid during the year.

Required

What is the balance on the retained earnings account to be included in the statement of financial position at 31 December 20X5?

Orion Ltd
Statement of financial position (extract) as at 31 December 20X5

	£
Equity	

Working

Retained earnings	£

3.11 Revaluation reserve

Where assets are revalued, the gain is included in the revaluation reserve account. This will be explained in Chapter 6.

The company may have other reserves within its equity that are not distributable (cannot be paid out as a dividend to shareholders). A revaluation reserve is not distributable.

4 Preference shares

Preference shares are shares which carry the right to a fixed rate of dividend.

(a) The preference dividend must be paid out of available profits before any ordinary dividend is paid.

(b) In the event of liquidation, preference shareholders normally have the right to the return of their capital before any capital is returned to ordinary shareholders.

(c) Preference shares do not carry the right to vote.

Most types of preference share are actually liabilities of the company, rather than part of equity. This is because the company has an obligation to pay the dividend and may eventually have an obligation to redeem the shares.

If this is the case, the preference shares are not included in share capital, but presented as non-current (long-term) liabilities in the statement of financial position. Dividends relating to redeemable preference shares are recorded as a finance cost in the statement of profit or loss.

5 Bank loans

As well as issuing shares, a company may raise finance by taking out a bank loan or by issuing **loan stock**. Loan stock can also be known as debentures, debenture stock, loan capital or loan notes.

Unlike share capital, bank loans are a liability of the company. The company has a contractual obligation to repay the amount borrowed, plus any interest owed.

Bank loans often carry a fixed rate of interest. The interest must be paid, regardless of whether the company has generated profits.

Illustration 5 – Finance charge

A company has a 5% £100,000 bank loan. The finance charge has not been paid by the year end.

The double entry to record the annual interest is:

	Debit £	Credit £
Finance charges (SPL)	5,000	
Trade and other payables (SOFP)		5,000

Activity 6: Bank loan

On 1 January 20X6 Orion Ltd has an 8% bank loan of £200,000. Interest of £8,000 has been paid during the year ended 31 December 20X6. No entries have been included in respect of interest on the bank loan.

Required

Complete the extracts below to show the entries required in respect of the bank loan and interest on the bank loan as at 31 December 20X6.

Orion Ltd
Statement of financial position (extract) as at 31 December 20X6

	£
Non-current liabilities	
Current liabilities	

Orion Ltd
Statement of profit or loss (extract) for the year ended 31 December 20X6

	£

Working

The double entry to record the finance charge is:

	Debit £	Credit £

6 Tax (introduction)

Current tax is the amount of tax payable or recoverable in respect of taxable profit or loss for a period.

At the end of the year entities **estimate** the tax due on their profits.

A tax charge is shown as an expense in the statement of profit or loss and a current liability in the statement of financial position.

The journal to include tax in the financial statements is:

	Debit £	Credit £
Tax (SPL)	X	
Tax liability (SOFP)		X

Tax will be studied in more detail later in the course. However, it is important to be aware of this journal at an early stage, as it is relevant to the accounts preparation questions which follow.

- The purpose of financial statements is to provide information, about an entity's financial performance and financial position, that is useful to a wide range of users for making economic decisions and assessing the stewardship of the entity's management.

- There are several broad types of organisation:

  Not for profit

  - Charities, clubs and societies
  - Public sector, eg central and local government or the NHS

  Profit making

  - Sole traders
  - Partnerships
  - Companies

  A limited company:

  - Has a separate legal personality from those of its owners
  - Gives its shareholders (owners) limited liability

- Limited liability means that the owners' liability is limited to the amount that they have paid for their shares. This is the maximum amount that they can lose if the company is wound up.

- Limited companies are owned by shareholders and managed by directors.

- There are two types of limited company:

  - Public companies
  - Private companies

- The advantages of trading as a limited company are:

  - Limited liability
  - It is easier to raise finance
  - The company continues even if the owners change
  - There may be tax advantages
  - It is easy to transfer shares

- The disadvantages of trading as a limited company are:

  - Publication of annual accounts

  - Legal and administrative formalities (including compliance with accounting standards)

  - Restrictions on issuing shares and reducing capital

- Limited companies pay tax, which is deducted from net profit in the statement of profit or loss.

- The ownership interest of a limited company is called equity and consists of:
  - Share capital
  - Reserves
- Share capital is reported in the statement of financial position at its nominal ('face') value.
- If a company issues shares at a premium (above their nominal value), a sum equal to the premium is transferred to a share premium account.
- A company's retained earnings reserve is its cumulative profits after tax, less dividends paid to shareholders.
- Reserves are either:
  - Distributable (including retained profits); or
  - Non-distributable (including share premium and revaluation reserve).
- Loan stock is used to raise finance. Loan stock holders are creditors. They receive a fixed rate of interest, which is an expense in the statement of profit or loss.
- The statement of profit or loss and statement of financial position of a limited company must follow a specific format.
- To adjust for the tax expense for the period:

  DEBIT   Tax expense (statement of profit or loss)   X
  CREDIT Tax payable (statement of financial position)   X

- **Bonus issue:** An issue of extra shares to existing shareholders at no cost, made to shareholders in proportion to their existing shareholdings

- **Company:** A business that is a separate legal entity from its owners

- **Dividends:** Amounts paid to shareholders from profits or distributable reserves

- **Entity:** Any organisation (whether profit making or not for profit) that prepares accounts as a separate entity from its owners

- **Equity:** Ownership interest. A company's equity is its ordinary share capital and its reserves

- **Loan stock (debentures):** Long-term loans made to a company, which normally carry a fixed rate of interest

- **Ordinary shares:** Shares which entitle the holders to share in profits after all prior claims have been satisfied

- **Partnership:** A business jointly owned and managed by two or more people

- **Preference shares:** Shares which carry the right to a fixed rate of dividend

- **Private companies:** Companies that cannot invite members of the general public to invest in their shares

- **Retained earnings:** The cumulative total of the company's retained profits

- **Rights issue:** An issue of shares to existing shareholders at below market value, offered to shareholders in proportion to their existing shareholdings

- **Share capital:** The capital invested in a company by its owners, divided into a number of identifiable shares

- **Share premium:** A non-distributable reserve consisting of the difference between consideration received for shares and the nominal value of the shares issued

- **Sole trader:** A business owned and managed by one person

- **Stewardship:** The accountability of management for the resources entrusted to it by the owners of an entity

Test your learning

1   If a limited company becomes insolvent, the maximum amount that the shareholders can lose is the amount that they have invested in the company.

   Is this statement true or false?

True	
False	

2   In a company's statement of financial position, the amount shown as 'Share capital' represents the total market value of the company's shares.

   Is this statement true or false?

True	
False	

3   **Which ONE of the following items is included in the statement of financial position of a limited company but not in the statement of financial position of a partnership or a sole trader?**

Accruals	
Drawings	
Loan stock	
Sales	

4   Diamond Ltd made a profit from operations of £140,000 for the year ended 31 December 20X5. Throughout the year the company has had 250,000 £1 ordinary shares and £150,000 9% loan stock. Tax has been estimated at £74,000 for the year. During the year, Diamond Ltd paid a dividend of 5p per ordinary share.

   What is the profit for the year ended 31 December 20X5?

£40,000	
£52,500	
£66,000	
£126,500	

5 The trial balance of Hearts Ltd at 31 December 20X2 is shown below:

	£000	£000
Bank		420
Bank loan		2,100
Loan interest	105	
Retained earnings reserve		3,955
Operating expenses	3,912	
Purchases	10,493	
Revaluation reserve		1,365
Sales		16,100
Share capital (£1 ordinary shares)		840
Inventories (at 1 January 20X2)	4,515	
Property, plant and equipment (net carrying amount)	5,852	
Trade payables		3,675
Trade receivables	3,578	
	28,455	28,455

Inventories were £5,292,000 at 31 December 20X2.

Tax on profits for the year is estimated to be £280,000.

(a) Draft the statement of profit or loss for Hearts Ltd for the year ended 31 December 20X2.

Hearts Ltd
Statement of profit or loss for the year ended 31 December 20X2

	£000
Revenue	
Cost of sales	
Gross profit	
Operating expenses	
Profit from operations	
Finance cost	
Profit before tax	
Tax	
Profit for the year	

(b) Draft the statement of financial position for Hearts Ltd as at 31 December 20X2.

(Complete the left-hand column by writing in the correct line items from the list provided.)

Hearts Ltd
Statement of financial position as at 31 December 20X2

	£000	£000
Assets		
Non-current assets:		
▼		
Current assets:		
▼		
▼		
Total assets		
Equity and liabilities		
Equity:		
▼		
▼		
▼		
Non-current liabilities:		
▼		
Current liabilities:		
▼		
▼		
▼		
Total liabilities		
Total equity and liabilities		

Picklist:

Bank loan
Bank overdraft
Inventories
Property, plant and equipment
Receivables
Retained earnings
Revaluation reserve
Share capital
Tax payable
Trade payables

6   Knave Ltd issues 200,000 50p ordinary shares at a market price of 80p. All shares are fully paid in cash as soon as they are issued.

Show the double entry to record the share issue.

Journal

Account name	Debit £	Credit £

The frameworks and ethical principles

2

Learning outcomes

1.1	**Explain the regulatory framework that underpins financial reporting**
	The reasons for the existence of a regulatory framework
	• Sources of regulation: international accounting standards and company law (Companies Act 2006)
	• The purpose of accounting standards
	• The duties and responsibilities of the directors in respect of financial statements
1.2	**Explain the International Accounting Standards Board (IASB) Conceptual Framework that underpins financial reporting**
	• The concepts that underlie the preparation and presentation of financial statements for external users, as detailed in the guidance notes
1.3	**Discuss the ethical principles that underpin financial reporting in accordance with the AAT Code of Professional Ethics**
	• Explain fundamental principles
	• Identify the threats
	• Apply the safeguards to resolve ethical conflict.

Assessment context

The information in this chapter will be tested in short-form or written tasks.

Qualification context

This chapter sets out the principles around which the standards are based and, therefore, a good understanding of this chapter will aid your understanding of the standards discussed in later chapters. You have studied ethics at Level 3, but possibly under a previous syllabus or version of the AAT Code.

Business context

When a transaction arises and is not covered by an existing accounting standard, the framework is used as a basis to determine how to account for the transaction. This chapter is therefore key to accountants in business.

Ethics are very important in business life. The AAT *Code of Professional Ethics* (2014) notes that: 'the decisions you make in the everyday course of your professional lives can have real ethical implications'.

Chapter overview

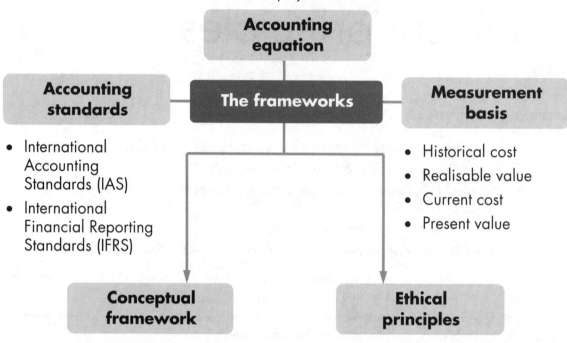

- Shows the relationship between the elements of the financial statements
- Assets = Equity + Liabilities

Accounting equation

Accounting standards

The frameworks

Measurement basis

- International Accounting Standards (IAS)
- International Financial Reporting Standards (IFRS)

- Historical cost
- Realisable value
- Current cost
- Present value

Conceptual framework

Ethical principles

Elements of financial statements

- Assets
- Liabilities
- Equity
- Income
- Expenses

Underlying assumption

- Going concern

Fundamental qualitative characteristics

- Relevance
- Faithful representation

Enhancing qualitative characteristics

- Comparability
- Verifiability
- Timeliness
- Understandability

Fundamental principles

- Integrity
- Objectivity
- Professional competence and due care
- Confidentiality
- Professional behaviour

Threats

- Self-interest
- Self-review
- Familiarity
- Intimidation

Safeguards

- Created by the profession
- In the work environment

Introduction

In this chapter we put the drafting of limited company financial statements in context by considering why we prepare financial statements, who uses them and what makes them useful. We also look at several important ideas that underpin the preparation of financial statements. These ideas are set out in the IASB's *Conceptual Framework for Financial Reporting*.

Limited companies have to publish their financial statements and, unlike sole traders and partnerships, are obliged to comply with company law and **accounting standards** when preparing them. We begin this chapter by briefly explaining these.

In the final section of the chapter, we consider the fundamental principles of ethical behaviour as they apply in the general context of the UK accountancy profession, and the framework set out by the AAT's *Code of Professional Ethics* and the regulatory environment.

1 Generally accepted accounting principles (GAAP)

Limited companies are required to observe various rules and regulations when preparing financial statements. There are established national accounting procedures which are referred to as generally accepted accounting principles (GAAP).

In most countries GAAP does not have any statutory or regulatory authority or definition, but the major components are normally:

- Accounting standards (eg International Financial Reporting Standards)

- National company law (eg Companies Act 2006 in the UK)

- Stock exchange requirements (for companies quoted on a recognised stock exchange)

2 Accounting standards

Recent decades have seen a dramatic rise in global trade and cross-listing on the world's capital markets. This has led to significant demand for consistent international financial information.

Organisations set up in response to this demand are:

Organisations	Standards
International Accounting Standards Committee (IASC) Founded in 1973	Issued International Accounting Standards (IAS)
International Accounting Standards Board (IASB) Formed in 2001 and replaced the IASC	Adopted existing IAS Issues International Financial Reporting Standards (IFRS)

Accounting standards state how particular transactions and events should be reflected in the financial statements.

During this course you will study a range of:

- International Accounting Standards (IAS)
- International Financial Reporting Standards (IFRS)

You do not need to learn the IFRS/IAS reference numbers for the assessment. The focus is on the practical application of the standards.

Assessment focus point

In your assessment, you will be expected to prepare financial statements that comply with **International Financial Reporting Standards and International Accounting Standards**, not UK GAAP.

2.1 Purpose of accounting standards

The main benefits of accounting standards are credibility, comparability and discipline.

Credibility	Financial statements would lose credibility if companies carrying out similar transactions disclosed markedly different results simply because they could select accounting policies.
	Therefore, accounting standards are necessary to ensure financial reports give a true and fair view of the company.
Comparability	By having financial statements prepared on a consistent basis, inter-company comparisons can be made.
Discipline	Accounting standards detail how transactions are recognised in the financial statements, meaning there is less scope for manipulation.
	Consequently, the directors must ensure the financial statements give a true and fair view, rather than presenting the company in a favourable light.

2.2 'Principles-based' approach

IFRS are written using a 'principles-based' approach. This means that they are written based on the definitions of the elements of the financial statements, recognition and measurement principles, as set out in the *Conceptual Framework for Financial Reporting*. This will be studied later in the chapter.

In IFRS, the underlying accounting treatments are these 'principles', which are designed to cover a wider variety of scenarios without the need for very detailed scenario by scenario guidance, as far as possible.

Other GAAP, for example US GAAP, are 'rules based', which means that accounting standards contain rules which apply to specific scenarios.

3 Companies Act 2006

All UK-registered companies must comply with the Companies Act 2006.

The Companies Act contains many provisions relating to the formation, governance and administration of a company. For this course, you are only required to know the provisions relating to the duties and responsibilities of directors.

The **Companies Act** is legally binding in the UK. Therefore, contravening it is a criminal offence which may result in the directors or other responsible parties receiving penalties in the form of a fine and/or imprisonment.

3.1 Companies Act accounts

The Companies Act 2006 states that the following items must be filed with the Registrar of Companies. These are often referred to as **published accounts**:

- A **profit and loss account** (statement of profit or loss) showing the profit or loss for the accounting period

- A **balance sheet** (statement of financial position) showing the state of the company's affairs on the last day of the accounting period

- A directors' report

- An auditors' report

- **Group accounts** (if the company has subsidiaries)

(Companies Act, 2006)

The profit and loss account and balance sheet are supported by notes, which analyse the figures in the main statements and may disclose additional information.

3.2 Duties and responsibilities of the directors

The directors are responsible for keeping proper company accounting records.

They are also responsible for preparing the company's annual financial statements, having them audited (if the company is of a certain size) and presenting them to the shareholders in a general meeting.

The shareholders must approve the financial statements at the general meeting and then the directors are responsible for filing them with the Registrar of Companies. You may have heard this organisation referred to as Companies House.

The directors must ensure the accounts are filed with the Registrar of Companies within the prescribed period after year end.

3.3 True and fair view

The financial statements must show a true and fair view of the company's results for the period and its **assets** and liabilities at the end of the period.

'True and fair' is not formally defined. The concept evolves over time in accordance with changes in the business environment.

However, if financial statements are prepared in accordance with generally accepted accounting practices they will give a true and fair view (also referred to as a 'fair presentation').

Activity 1: Duties and responsibilities of the directors

The following statements refer to actions that may be required in relation to companies.

(i)   Enter into contracts on behalf of the company
(ii)   File the financial statements on time
(iii) Prepare proper accounting records
(iv)   Present the financial statements to be audited (if applicable)

Required

Which of the above statements are duties of a director?

(ii), (iii) and (iv)	
(i), (ii), (iii) and (iv)	
(i), (iii) and (iv)	
(i), (ii) and (iii)	

4 Conceptual Framework

The **Conceptual Framework** is produced by the International Accounting Standards Board (IASB). The main objectives of this financial reporting framework is to provide the basis for:

- The development of consistent and logical accounting standards; and
- The use of judgement in resolving accounting issues.

(IASB, 2010)

This means that the principles of the *Conceptual Framework* are used by the IASB as a guide when producing a new accounting standard and this minimises inconsistencies between standards.

The *Conceptual Framework* is also used to resolve accounting issues that are not addressed directly in an accounting standard. In the absence of a standard or interpretation, management must use their judgement to determine how to account for a transaction so that the financial information remains relevant and reliable. The *Framework* should be used by management in exercising their judgement.

The *Framework* is not a financial reporting standard and as such will be overridden if there is a conflict between it and a financial reporting standard.

The *Conceptual Framework* covers the following topics:

- The objective of financial reporting

- The qualitative characteristics of useful financial information (the qualities that make financial information useful)

- The definition, recognition and measurement of the elements from which financial statements are constructed

(Conceptual Framework: Scope, 2010)

Many of the IASB's standards have been strongly influenced by the ideas set out in the *Conceptual Framework*.

4.1 Users of financial statements and their information needs

The *Conceptual Framework* states that:

'The objective of general purpose financial reporting is to provide financial information about the reporting entity that is useful to existing and potential investors, lenders and other creditors in making decisions about providing resources to the entity.'

(Conceptual Framework, Chapter 1: para. 2)

The *Conceptual Framework* focuses on two primary users of financial statements:

- Existing and potential investors
- Existing and potential lenders and other creditors

(Conceptual Framework, Chapter 1: para. 2)

Existing and potential investors need to make decisions that involve buying, selling or holding equity (shares) or debt instruments (loan stock and debentures). They need information about the returns that they expect from an investment (dividends, interest, repayment of the principal amount of a debt instrument or market price increases).

Existing and potential lenders and other creditors need to make decisions about providing or settling loans and other forms of credit. They need information about the returns they can expect from lending (interest payments and the eventual repayment of the principal amount of the loan).

Consequently, investors and lenders need information about the amount, timing and uncertainty of future net cash inflows to the entity. This in turn means that they need information about:

- The resources of an entity (assets)

- The claims against an entity (liabilities)

- How efficiently and effectively the entity's management have discharged their responsibilities relating to the entity's resources (stewardship)

(Conceptual Framework, Chapter 1: para. 2)

Activity 2: Users of the financial statements

Why will investors and lenders (both existing and potential) use the financial statements?

Investors	Lenders

The *Conceptual Framework* also mentions several other, secondary, users that are interested in the financial information (*Conceptual Framework*, Chapter 1: para. 4).

This includes:

- Management
- Regulators
- Employees
- Individuals

These users will be interested in:

- An entity's resources (assets)

- Claims against the entity (liabilities)

- How efficiently and effectively the entity's management have discharged their responsibility to use the entity's resources (stewardship)

While users may gain most of their information from the financial statements, it is important that they obtain relevant information from other sources too.

4.2 Qualitative characteristics of useful financial information

The qualitative characteristics of useful financial information identify the types of information that are likely to be most useful to existing and potential investors, lenders and other creditors for making decisions about the reporting entity on the basis of information in its financial report (financial information).

They are categorised into:

- Fundamental qualitative characteristics (*Conceptual Framework*, Chapter 3: QC 5–18)

- Enhancing qualitative characteristics (*Conceptual Framework*, Chapter 3: QC 19–32)

In addition, the *Conceptual Framework* requires consideration of 'the cost constraint on useful financial reporting' (IASB, 2010).

Fundamental qualitative characteristics

Relevance

Relevant financial information is capable of making a difference in the decisions made by users, ie if it has:

- Predictive value; and/or
- Confirmatory value.

Materiality

Information is material if omitting it or misstating it could influence decisions that users make on the basis of financial information

Faithful representation

To be useful, financial information must faithfully represent the phenomenon it purports to represent.

A perfect faithful representation would be:

- Complete;
- Neutral; and
- Free from error.

Enhancing qualitative characteristics

Comparability

Information is more useful if it can be compared with similar information about:

- Other entities; and
- Other periods.

Consistency helps achieve comparability

Verifiability

Assures users that information faithfully represents the economic phenomenon it purports to represent

Verification can be direct or indirect

Timeliness

Having information available to decision makers in time to be capable of influencing their decisions

Understandability

Classifying, characterising and presenting information clearly and concisely

---

The cost constraint on useful financial reporting

Consideration of whether the benefits of reporting particular information justify the costs incurred to provide and use that information

BigCo has net income of £100,000,000. The company owned a building which was destroyed in a fire and, after a lengthy battle with the insurance company, the company reported a loss of £100,000 in respect of the building. The materiality concept states that this loss is immaterial because the average financial statement user would not be concerned with something that is only 0.1% of net income.

SmallCo has net income of £500,000. SmallCo also owned a building which was destroyed in a fire, reporting a loss of £100,000.

Required

Is the loss material for:

BigCo?	
SmallCo?	

4.3 The Framework (1989): remaining text

4.3.1 Underlying assumption

Going concern

The financial statements are normally prepared on the assumption that an entity is a going concern and will continue in operation for the foreseeable future. Hence, it is assumed that the entity has neither the intention nor the need to liquidate or materially curtail the scale of its operations; if such an intention or need exists, the financial statements may have to be prepared on a different basis and, if so, the basis used is disclosed (*Conceptual Framework*, Chapter 4: para. 4.1).

4.3.2 The elements of financial statements

The *Conceptual Framework* defines elements of financial statements. The definitions reduce confusion over which items ought to be recognised and which should not (if an item is not one of the defined elements of financial statements it should not feature in the financial statements) (*Conceptual Framework*, Chapter 4: para. 4.2–4.36).

The five elements of financial statements and their definitions are:

> **Asset**
> A resource **controlled** by an entity as a result of **past events** and from which **future economic benefits** are expected to flow to the entity.

> **Liability**
> A **present obligation** of the entity arising from **past events**, the settlement of which is expected to result in an **outflow** from the entity of resources embodying economic benefits.

> **Equity**
> The **residual interest** in the assets of an entity after deducting all its liabilities, so EQUITY = NET ASSETS = SHARE CAPITAL + RESERVES.

> **Income**
> Increases in economic benefits during the accounting period in the form of **inflows** or enhancements **of assets or decreases of liabilities** that result in increases in equity, **other than** those relating to **contributions from equity participants**.

> **Expenses**
> Decreases in economic benefits during the accounting period in the form of **outflows** or depletions **of assets or increases of liabilities** that result in decreases in equity, **other than those relating to distributions to equity participants**.

(IASB, 2010)

The *Conceptual Framework* definitions demonstrate that IFRS are based on a statement of financial position approach to recognition, ie **income** and **expenses** are defined as changes in assets and liabilities, rather than the other way round.

4.3.3 Recognition of the elements of financial statements

Recognition is the process of showing an item in the financial statements, with a description in words and a number value.

An item is recognised in the statement of financial position or the statement of profit or loss and other comprehensive income, when:

(a)   It meets the definition of an element of the financial statements;

(b)   It is probable that any future economic benefit associated with the item will flow to or from the entity; and

(c)   The item has a cost or value that can be measured with reliability.

Hence, recognition relies heavily upon a good assessment of probability of whether economic benefits will flow to or from the entity (*Conceptual Framework*, Chapter 4: para. 4.37–4.53).

5 Accounting equation

The relationship between these elements is shown by the accounting equation:

Assets = **Equity** + Liabilities

Rearranged: Assets – Liabilities = Equity

Equity = **Contributions from owners** + Income – Expenses – **Distributions to owners**

Therefore if net assets increase, it is either as a result of income or from a contribution. In the same way, if net assets decrease, it is either an expense or a distribution.

Assessment focus point

Short written questions are often asked on the accounting equation. You may, for example, be asked to define the elements that make up the equation and/or to explain how one element is related to the others. The key is to answer the question set, and not to just state the accounting equation.

You should refer to the Skills Bank at the beginning of this Course Book for advice on tackling written questions.

Activity 4: Elements of the financial statements

A resource controlled by an entity as a result of a past event and from which future economic benefits are expected to flow to the entity.

Required

(a) This statement describes:

An asset	
A liability	
Equity	
Income	
Expenses	

The residual interest in the assets of an entity after deducting all its liabilities.

(b) This statement describes:

An asset	
A liability	
Equity	
Income	
Expenses	

A distribution to equity participants is an expense.

(c)   Is this statement true or false?

True	
False	

6 Measuring the elements of financial statements

Measurement is the process of determining the monetary amounts at which the elements of the financial statements are to be recognised and carried in the statement of financial position and statement of profit or loss and other comprehensive income. There are four key measurement techniques for you to be aware of (*Conceptual Framework*: para. 4.55):

Historical cost (this is the most commonly used) Measured at the amount paid at transaction date	**Current cost** Measured at the amount that would be paid if the transaction occurred today
Realism value (settlement value) Measured at the amount that could be obtained if the asset were sold, or liability realised, today	**Present value** Measured at the discounted value of all future cash flows

Illustration 1 – Current cost

Three years ago, a company purchased equipment for £150,000. The equipment is expected to generate discounted net cash flows of £20,000 per year for the next 3 years. It could be sold for £40,000. An identical piece of equipment would cost the company £225,000.

What is the current cost of the equipment?

£40,000	
£60,000	
£150,000	
£225,000	

Solution

£40,000	
£60,000	
£150,000	
£225,000	✓

The current cost is the amount of cash that would have to be paid if the same or a similar asset was acquired currently.

Activity 5: Measurement bases

A number of different measurement bases are used in the financial statements.

Required

(a) **Match the measurement bases with an appropriate example.**

A company can sell machine A for £9,000.	
If a company had to buy machine B now, it would pay £20,000.	
Machine C will be used by a company to generate sales. It is expected to generate discounted net cash flows of £20,000 over the next 5 years.	
Three years ago, machine D cost the company £15,000.	

Picklist:

Current cost
Historical cost
Present value
Realisable value

An asset was purchased for £20,000. It is estimated that it will generate a net cash inflow of £30,000 for the business, and that it can be sold for £25,000. An identical asset can now be purchased for £22,000.

(b) **Measuring the asset under the historical cost basis, the asset will be recorded at:**

£20,000	
£22,000	
£25,000	
£30,000	

7 Introduction to ethics

Ethics are a set of moral principles that guide behaviour.

Ethical values are assumptions and beliefs about what constitutes 'right' and 'wrong' behaviour.

Individuals have **personal ethics**, often reflecting the beliefs of the families, cultures and educational **environments** in which they developed their ideas.

Organisations also have ethical values, based on the **norms and standards of behaviour** that their leaders believe will best help them express their identity and achieve their objectives.

7.1 Why behave ethically?

(a) Ethical issues may be a matter of **law and regulation**. You are expected to know and apply the **civil and criminal law** of the country in which you live and work – as a basic minimum requirement for good practice. The AAT Code is based on the laws effective in the UK, with which members are expected to comply as a minimum requirement. (It is sometimes said that 'the law is a floor': the lowest acceptable level of behaviour required to preserve the public interest and individual rights.)

(b) The **AAT** (like other professional bodies) requires its members to conduct themselves, and provide services to clients, according to certain professional and ethical standards. It does this, in part, to maintain its own **reputation and standing** – but this is also of benefit to its members and to the accounting profession as a whole.

(c) Professional and ethical behaviour protects the **public interest**. The accountancy profession sees itself as having duties to society as a whole – in addition to its specific obligations to employers and clients.

7.2 Professional ethics

Professional ethics are the views and rules of the professional organisation that an individual is a member of. In the case of an accountant it is usually the rules and views of the organisation that they are a member of, such as the AAT, ACCA, ICAEW or CIMA.

8 AAT Code of Professional Ethics

The AAT requires its members and students to adopt and maintain high ethical standards. To assist with this it has published the **AAT *Code of Professional Ethics***. This is made available on the AAT website (www.aat.org.uk) and AAT members are required to act in accordance with the Code.

The *Code of Professional Ethics* came into effect on 1 September 2011 and the most recent revision of it came into force on 1 January 2014.

8.1 Fundamental principles

You might have your own ideas about what is 'ethical behaviour'. These ideas will be shaped by your personal assumptions and values, and the values of the culture in which you operate (at work and in the country in which you live). However, there are five fundamental principles set out in the AAT Code (Part A, Section 100.5, 2014) that underpin ethical behaviour in an accounting context:

Fundamental principle	Explanation
Integrity	A member shall be straightforward and honest in all professional and business relationships.
Objectivity	A member shall not allow bias, conflict of interest or undue influence of others to override professional or business judgements.
Professional competence and due care	Members must maintain professional knowledge and skill at the level required to ensure that clients or employers receive competent professional service. They must act diligently when providing professional services.
Confidentiality	Members must not disclose information acquired as a result of professional and business relationships and must not use confidential information to advantage themselves or others.
Professional behaviour	Members must avoid any action that may bring disrepute to the profession.

Due care

Due care means that having agreed to perform a task you have an obligation to perform it:

- To the best of your ability

- In the client or employer's best interests

- Within a reasonable timescale

- With regard to the technical and professional standards expected of you as a professional

The fundamental principles are core professional values which must be demonstrated by organisations and individuals.

Assessment focus point

It is **very important** that you understand the meaning of the fundamental principles for the assessment. It is not enough to write in general terms about ethical behaviour – you need a precise definition and the ability to apply it to the task set.

The next Activity provides an opportunity to consider the meaning of each of them in practical scenarios.

Activity 6: Fundamental principles

Required

Using the choices below indicate the fundamental principle which is illustrated.

Illustration	Fundamental principle
Professional judgements should be made fairly so they are free from all forms of prejudice and bias.	▼
A member must not bring the profession into disrepute by making disparaging references to the work of others.	▼
Members shall not agree to carry out a task if they lack the competence to carry it out to a satisfactory standard.	▼
A member shall not be associated with reports, communications or other information where they believe that the information contains a false or misleading statement.	▼
The need to comply with the principle of confidentiality continues even after the end of the relationship between a member and a client or employer.	▼

Picklist:

Confidentiality
Integrity
Objectivity
Professional behaviour
Professional competence and due care

Illustration 2 – Principles in practice

Incident one

You are asked to produce an aged receivables' listing for your manager as soon as possible. However, you do not have up to date figures because of a problem with the computer system. A colleague suggests that to get the report done in time you use averages for the missing figures.

There is an **integrity** issue here. Using averages instead of actual figures will almost certainly result in an inaccurate listing. You should report the problem to your manager and ask for an extension to your deadline in order to provide an accurate listing.

Incident two

You have received a letter from an estate agent, requesting financial information about one of your company's customers that is applying to rent a property. The information is needed as soon as possible, by fax or email, in order to secure approval for the rent agreement.

There is a **confidentiality** issue here. You need the customer's authority to disclose the information; you may also need to confirm the identity of the person making the request. You should also take steps to protect the confidentiality of the information when you send it: for example, not using fax or email (which can be intercepted), and stating clearly that the information is confidential.

Incident three

While out to lunch, you run into a friend at the sandwich bar. In conversation, she tells you that she expects to inherit from a recently deceased uncle, and asks you how she will be affected by inheritance tax, capital gains tax and other matters.

There are issues of **professional competence and due care** here. You are not qualified to give advice on matters of taxation. Even if you were qualified, any answer you give on the spot would risk being incomplete or inaccurate with potentially serious consequences.

Incident four

A client of the accountancy practice you work in is so pleased with the service you gave him this year that he offers you a free weekend break in a luxury hotel, just as a 'thank you'.

There is an **objectivity** issue here, as the gift is of significant value. Think about how it looks: a third-party observer is entitled to wonder what 'special favours' deserve this extra reward – and/or how such a gift may bias you in the client's favour in future.

8.2 Conflict and AAT's 'problem-solving approach'

It is impossible to give guidelines on every possible situation that may arise in the course of your work which conflicts with the fundamental ethical principles. The AAT Code (Section A, para. 100.6–100.11) therefore sets out a basic **problem-solving procedure**, which you can use in any situation, to give yourself the best chance of complying with the principles. This procedure forms the ethics **'conceptual framework'** which requires the following:

(a)   Identify where there may be a **threat** to a fundamental principle.

(b)   **Evaluate the threat**: how significant is it?

(c)   For any significant threat **apply safeguards** that will eliminate the threat or reduce it to an acceptable level (so that compliance with the fundamental principle is not compromised).

(d)   If safeguards cannot be applied, **decline or discontinue** the specific action or professional service involved or, where necessary, **resign** from the client (if you are a member in practice) or the employing organisation (if you are a member in business).

8.3 Threats

Many of the threats that may create a risk of compromising the fundamental principles will fall into one of the following five categories (AAT Code: Section A, para. 100.12).

Threat	Explanation	Examples
Self-interest	Financial or other interests may inappropriately influence the member's judgement or behaviour	Undue fee dependence on one particular client
Self-review	A previous judgement needs to be re-evaluated by the member responsible for that judgement	Tax and accountancy work carried out by the same engagement team
Advocacy	A member promotes a position or opinion to the point that subsequent objectivity may be compromised	Acting on behalf of an assurance client which is in litigation or dispute with a third party

Threat	Explanation	Examples
Familiarity	Due to close or personal relationships, a member becomes too sympathetic to the interests of others	A senior member undertaking an assurance engagement for a number of years for the same client
Intimidation	A member may be deterred from acting objectively by threats (actual or perceived)	Threatened withdrawal of services by a dominant client

8.4 Safeguards

The AAT Code defines safeguards as '**actions or other measures that may eliminate threats or reduce them to an acceptable level**'. The Code identifies two broad categories of safeguards that you might use to reduce or eliminate the threats we have described above (AAT Code: Section A, para. 113, 114).

(a) **Safeguards created by the profession and/or legislation and regulation. These include:**

   (i)   Education, training and experience, as requirements for entry into the profession

   (ii) CPD

   (iii) Corporate governance regulations

   (iv) Professional standards

   (v) Professional or regulatory monitoring and disciplinary procedures

   (vi) External review of financial reports, returns, communications or information produced by members

(b) **Safeguards in the work environment**, which increase the likelihood of **identifying or deterring unethical behaviour**, include:

   (a)   Quality controls, and internal audits of quality controls

   (b)   Mechanisms to empower and protect staff who raise ethical concerns ('whistleblowers')

   (c)   Involvement of, or consultation with, independent third parties (eg non-executive directors or regulatory bodies)

   (d)   Rotation of personnel to avoid excessive familiarity and opportunities for collusion in fraud

   (e)   Opportunities to discuss ethical dilemmas (eg with an ethics officer, committee or forum)

Activity 7: Which threat?

Jake has been put under significant pressure by his manager to change the conclusion of a report he has written which reflects badly on the manager's performance.

Required

Which threat is Jake facing?

	✓
Self-interest	
Advocacy	
Intimidation	

Activity 8: Objectivity

Which of these might (or might be thought to) affect the objectivity of providers of professional accounting services?

	✓
Failure to keep up to date on CPD	
A personal financial interest in the client's affairs	
Being negligent or reckless with the accuracy of the information provided to the client	

Activity 9: Problem solving

Required

Put the four steps of the problem-solving methodology or 'conceptual framework' for ethical conduct into the correct order:

Apply safeguards to eliminate or reduce the threat to an acceptable level	▼
Evaluate the seriousness of the threat	▼
Discontinue the action or relationship giving rise to the threat	▼
Identify a potential threat to a fundamental ethical principle	▼

Picklist:

1
2
3
4

Assessment focus point

Students often dislike written questions, and ethics is likely to be tested in a written question. Practice is the key to overcoming the fear factor, so you should try **all** the ethics questions in Chapter 2 of the BPP Question Bank.

You should refer to the Skills Bank at the beginning of this Course Book for advice on tackling written questions.

Chapter summary

- Financial information must be presented fairly if it is to be useful. This normally means that it must comply with all applicable regulations.

- Regulation ensures that:
  - Users are able to compare the financial statements of different companies and of the same company over time
  - Users are not deliberately misled by the financial statements
  - Financial statements provide the information that users need

- The most important sources of regulation in the UK are:
  - The Companies Act 2006
  - Accounting standards

- International Accounting Standards (IAS) and International Financial Reporting Standards (IFRS) are issued by the International Accounting Standards Board (IASB).

- The Companies Act 2006 states that the directors of a limited company must file annual accounts with the Registrar of Companies.

- Every shareholder in a limited company is entitled to receive a copy of the company's annual accounts.

- These can be either 'Companies Act accounts' or 'IFRS accounts'.

- Published IFRS accounts consist of:
  - A statement of financial position
  - A statement of profit or loss and other comprehensive income
  - A statement of changes in equity
  - A statement of cash flows
  - Notes

- Directors have a legal duty to keep proper accounting records.

- The published accounts must show a true and fair view/fair presentation: they must comply with the requirements of the Companies Act and applicable accounting standards.

- The *Conceptual Framework for Financial Reporting* sets out the principles and concepts that the IASB believes should underlie the preparation and presentation of financial statements.

- The objective of general purpose financial reporting is to provide financial information about the reporting entity that is useful to existing and potential investors, lenders and other creditors in making decisions about providing resources to the entity.

- Useful financial information has two fundamental qualitative characteristics:
  - Relevance
  - Faithful representation

- The enhancing qualitative characteristics of useful financial information are:
  - Comparability
  - Verifiability
  - Timeliness
  - Understandability

- Going concern is regarded as a fundamental accounting concept/underlying assumption.

- The elements of financial statements are:
  - Assets
  - Liabilities
  - Equity
  - Income
  - Expenses

- The elements restate the accounting equation:
  - Assets – Liabilities = Equity

  - Equity = Contributions from owners + Income – Expenses – Distributions to owners

- An item that meets the definition of an element should be recognised if:
  - It is probable that any future economic benefit associated with the item will flow to or from the entity

  - The item has a cost or value that can be measured with reliability

- A number of different measurement bases are used in financial statements:
  - Historical cost
  - Current cost
  - Realisable value
  - Present value

- Ethical values are assumptions and beliefs about what constitutes 'right' and 'wrong' behaviour. Individuals, families, national cultures and organisation cultures all develop ethical values and norms.

- Ethical behaviour is necessary to comply with law and regulation; to protect the public interest; to protect the reputation and standing of a professional body and its members; and to enable people to live and work together in society.

- The AAT's *Code of Professional Ethics* (2014) notes that: 'the decisions you make in the everyday course of your professional lives can have real ethical implications'.

- The five fundamental principles described in the AAT Code are:

  - Integrity
  - Objectivity
  - Professional competence and due care
  - Confidentiality
  - Professional behaviour

- The AAT's Code sets out a basic problem-solving procedure for unethical action (the 'conceptual framework'):

  - Identify the threat to the fundamental principles that the action represents
  - Evaluate the threat
  - Apply safeguards to eliminate or reduce the threat
  - If safeguards cannot be applied, decline or discontinue the action

- **AAT Code of Professional Ethics:** The AAT requires its members and students to adopt and maintain high ethical standards. To assist with this it has published the AAT *Code of Professional Ethics*

- **Accounting standards:** Authoritative statements of how particular types of transactions and other events should be reflected in financial statements

- **Asset:** Resource controlled by an entity as a result of a past event from which future economic benefits are expected to flow to the entity

- **Companies Act accounts:** Published accounts that comply with the accounting rules in the Companies Act 2006 and with the requirements of UK accounting standards

- **Conceptual framework:** A set of concepts and principles that underpin the preparation of financial statements

- **Contributions from owners:** Increases in ownership interest resulting from transfers from owners in their capacity as owners

- **Current cost:** Assets are carried at the amount of cash that would have to be paid if the same or a similar asset was acquired currently

- **Distributions to owners:** Decreases in ownership interest resulting from transfers to owners in their capacity as owners

- **Equity:** The residual amount found by deducting all of an entity's liabilities from all of an entity's assets

- **Ethical values:** Assumptions and beliefs about what constitutes 'right' and 'wrong' behaviour

- **Ethics:** A set of moral principles that guide behaviour

- **Expenses:** Decreases in economic benefits during the accounting period in the form of decreases of assets or increases of liabilities that result in decreases in equity other than distributions to owners

- **Going concern:** Financial statements are prepared on the basis that an entity will continue in operational existence for the foreseeable future

- **Historical cost:** Assets are recorded at the amount of cash paid or the fair value of the consideration given to acquire them at the time of the acquisition

- **Income:** Increases in economic benefits in the form of increases of assets or decreases of liabilities that result in increases in equity other than contributions from owners

- **Liability:** A present obligation of an entity arising from past events, the settlement of which is expected to result in an outflow of economic benefits

- **Materiality:** Information is material if omitting it or misstating it could influence decisions that users make on the basis of financial information about a specific reporting entity

- **Present value:** Assets are carried at the present discounted value of the future net cash inflows that the item is expected to generate in the normal course of business

- **Published accounts/financial statements:** The financial statements of limited companies that are circulated to shareholders and filed with the Registrar of Companies (also referred to as statutory accounts)

- **Realisable value:** Assets are carried at the amount of cash that could currently be obtained by selling the asset

- **Recognition:** Including an item in the financial statements

1   In the UK, limited companies must observe the requirements of the Companies Act 2006 and of accounting standards when preparing financial statements.

   Explain why accounting regulation is needed.

2   The Companies Act 2006 sets out the duties and responsibilities of directors of limited companies.

   Which of the following is NOT a legal responsibility of the directors?

To prepare and approve the annual accounts	
To file the accounts with the Registrar of Companies	
To keep accounting records that are neutral, complete and free from error	
To ensure that the accounts show a true and fair view	

3   The IASB's *Conceptual Framework for Financial Reporting* is an accounting standard.

   Is this statement true or false?

True	
False	

4   **State the objective of general purpose financial reporting.**

5   **According to the IASB's *Conceptual Framework*, who are the most important users of financial statements? Choose TWO.**

Employees	
Government	
Investors	
Lenders	

6   **According to the IASB's *Conceptual Framework*, which ONE of the following items is the most important assumption underlying financial statements?**

Accruals	
Consistency	
Going concern	
Reliability	

7 **According to the IASB's *Conceptual Framework*, which ONE of the following is a FUNDAMENTAL qualitative characteristic of useful financial information?**

Consistency	
Going concern	
Relevance	
Timeliness	

8 **List the elements that appear in financial statements, according to the *Conceptual Framework for Financial Reporting*.**

9 A business has signed a contract to pay its managing director £200,000 per year for the next 5 years. He has agreed to work full time for the business over that period.

The business should recognise a liability in respect of the contract.

Is this statement true or false?

True	
False	

10 Stevens Ltd uses an item of plant. The directors have calculated that the total sales revenue from the goods produced over the remaining life of the plant, less the costs of operating it, will be £200,000 after adjusting the amounts to reflect the time value of money.

This amount of £200,000 is the plant's:

Current cost	
Fair value	
Historical cost	
Present value	

11 Only individuals can have 'ethical values'.

Is this statement true or false?

True	
False	

12 **The AAT needs to protect its reputation and standing by maintaining standards of conduct and service among its members in order to be able to:**

	✓
Enhance the reputation and standing of its members	
Limit the number of members that it has	
Make sure that its members are able to earn large salaries	

13 A client asks you a technical question about accounting standards which you are not sure you are able to answer correctly. 'You are supposed to be an accountant, aren't you?' says the client. 'I need an answer now.'

What should you do first?

	✓
Say that you will get back to him when you have looked up the answer.	
Give him the contact details of a friend in your firm who knows all about accounting standards.	
Clarify the limits of your expertise with the client.	

14 **Why are professional standards important?**

	✓
It is in the public interest that employees who fail to comply with standards are prosecuted.	
It is in the public interest that services are carried out to professional standards.	

The statement of financial position

3

Learning outcomes

1.1	Explain the regulatory framework that underpins financial reporting
	• The purpose of financial statements
	• Forms of equity, reserves and loan capital
2.1	Examine the effect of international accounting standards on the preparation of financial statements
	• Explain the effect of international accounting standards on the presentation, valuation and disclosure of items within the financial statements
	• Make any supporting calculations
3.2	Draft a statement of financial position
	• Make appropriate entries in the statement in respect of information extracted from a trial balance and additional information

Assessment context

Drafting a statement of financial position may feature as a significant task in the assessment.

Qualification context

The Level 2 and 3 AAT courses explained the process of recording year-end adjustments and preparing financial statements for sole traders and partnerships. These skills are now developed as you prepare a statement of financial position for companies.

Business context

All registered companies must prepare a set of financial statements on an annual basis. The statement of financial position is one of the primary components of a set of financial statements.

Chapter overview

Set of financial statements

- Statement of financial position
- Statement of profit or loss and other comprehensive income
- Statement of changes in equity
- Statement of cash flows
- Notes to the financial statements

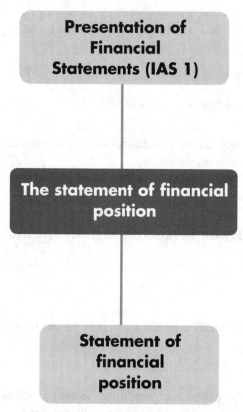

Presentation of Financial Statements (IAS 1)

The statement of financial position

Statement of financial position

- Share capital
- Share premium
- Retained earnings
- Revaluation reserve

Principles

- Accruals
- Materiality and aggregation
- Offset
- Comparative information
- Consistency of presentation

Introduction

In Chapter 1 we introduced the limited company statement of profit or loss and statement of financial position. In the next three chapters we look at the financial statements in more depth. This chapter explains the general requirements of IAS 1 *Presentation of Financial Statements*. It then focuses on the statement of financial position: the required format and the information that must be disclosed. The best way to master the drafting of financial statements for limited companies is to practise on as many questions and past assessment tasks as possible.

The chapter also revises some knowledge brought forward from earlier studies by working through activities.

1 IFRS financial statements

1.1 Presentation of financial statements (IAS 1)

As has been seen, IAS 1 applies to the preparation and presentation of general purpose financial statements in accordance with IFRS.

This standard emphasises the general objectives of financial statements which are also outlined in the *Conceptual Framework*:

'The objective of general purpose financial reporting is to provide financial information about the reporting entity that is useful to existing and potential investors, lenders and other creditors in making decisions about providing resources to the entity'   (IASB, 2010)

IAS 1 *Presentation of Financial Statements* states that a complete set of financial statements should be prepared at least annually (IAS 1: para. 1.9).

A complete set of financial statements comprises:

- A statement of financial position
- A statement of profit or loss and other comprehensive income
- A statement of changes in equity
- A statement of cash flows
- Notes, comprising a summary of significant accounting policies and other explanatory information

In addition, the entity must clearly display:

- The name of the company
- The date of the financial statements
- The currency in which the financial statements are presented
- The level of rounding (eg £000 or £ million)

1.2 Fair presentation

The financial statements must present fairly the financial transactions and balances of an entity. This means that all transactions and other events are recorded faithfully, in accordance with the recognition criteria and definition of the elements listed in the *Conceptual Framework*.

Financial statements are required by law (Companies Act 2006) to present fairly the assets, liabilities, financial position and profit or loss of a company. The application of the financial reporting standards results in financial statements that give a fair presentation (true and fair view) of the company.

2 Accounting principles

2.1 Going concern

Financial statements must be prepared on a going concern basis, unless the entity is not a going concern (*Conceptual Framework:* para. 4.1).

(a)   Management must make an assessment of the entity's ability to continue as a going concern.

(b)   Any material uncertainties about the entity's ability to continue as a going concern must be disclosed.

(c)   If financial statements are not prepared on a going concern basis, this must be disclosed, together with the reason why the entity is not regarded as a going concern.

The *Conceptual Framework* explains that 'going concern' is the underlying assumption when financial statements are prepared.

2.2 Accruals

The **accruals** principle means that a transaction is recognised in the financial statements when it meets the definition of an asset, liability, income or expense and it meets the recognition criteria as set out in the *Conceptual Framework*. IAS 1 requires financial statements to be prepared using the accrual basis of accounting (IAS 1: para. 1.27).

This is not necessarily the same time as settlement (payment) takes place. Cash flow information is exempt from the accruals principle.

Activity 1: Accruals

Required

Give two examples of the use of the accruals concept in accounts.

1	
2	

2.3 Materiality and aggregation

IAS 1 (para. 1.29) states that each **material** (significant) class of similar items must be displayed separately. They may only be aggregated if they are immaterial.

For example, inventories, receivables and cash are all shown as separate classes of items on the statement of financial position, grouped together under the heading of current assets. They are not shown as one line titled 'current assets' as they are separate classes of assets.

This means users will be able to identify them separately.

2.4 Offset

Assets, liabilities, income and expenses should not be offset unless this is permitted by a standard (IAS 1: para. 1.32).

For example, suppose a company has two bank accounts with different banks, one of which is overdrawn. The bank account which is not overdrawn is shown as a current asset and the overdrawn account is shown as a current liability. In other words, the net balance is not shown.

2.5 Comparative information

Comparative information should be disclosed in respect of the previous period for all amounts reported in the financial statements (IAS 1: para. 1.38).

2.6 Consistency of presentation

A company must present and classify items in the financial statements in the same way from one period to the next, unless (IAS 1: para. 1.45):

- There has been a significant change in the company's operations which means that a different presentation is now more appropriate; or

- A new IFRS has been issued, which requires a different presentation.

3 Statement of financial position

Earlier in the course, we looked at a statement of financial position and saw that it shows the assets, liabilities and equity of a business at a stated date.

3.1 Proforma – statement of financial position

XYZ Ltd
Statement of financial position as at 31 December 20X2

	20X2 £000	20X1 £000
ASSETS		
Non-current assets		
Intangible assets	X	X
Property, plant and equipment	X	X
	X	X
Current assets		
Inventories	X	X
Trade and other receivables	X	X
Cash and cash equivalents	X	X
	X	X
Total assets	X	X
EQUITY AND LIABILITIES		
Equity		
Share capital	X	X
Share premium	X	X
Retained earnings	X	X
Revaluation reserve	X	X
Total equity	X	X
Bank loans	X	X
	X	X

	20X2	20X1
	£000	£000
Current liabilities		
Trade and other payables	X	X
Short-term borrowings	X	X
Tax liability	X	X
	X	X
Total liabilities	X	X
Total equity and liabilities	X	X

3.2 Further analysis

Items in the statement of financial position should be analysed further when necessary.

The analysis is often shown in notes to the financial statements.

Examples of items which are often analysed are:

- Property, plant and equipment
- Inventories
- Trade and other receivables
- Trade and other payables

3.3 Assumed knowledge

You will be familiar with many of the items in the financial statements from your previous studies, such as:

- Inventories
- Depreciation
- Accruals and prepayments
- Irrecoverable and doubtful debts

Assessment focus point

In the *Financial Statements of Limited Companies* assessment the above items are likely to be included as part of the accounts preparation question. Additional notes to this chapter are provided in Section 5 to recap the key entries you need to know.

4 Assessment tasks

4.1 Approach to preparing the statement of financial position

(1) Read the requirement(s) and scan the task.

(2) Review the 'further information' carefully. Click ➤ (highlighter on the left-hand side of the trial balance) on any rows where the number will change.

(3) Work methodically down the trial balance, identifying items relating to assets, liabilities and equity. Enter the relevant figures:

- In a financial statement proforma (if they require no further adjustment)

- In an on-screen working (if they require adjustment and an on-screen working is provided)

- On scrap paper (if they require adjustment and an on-screen working is not provided)

(4) Complete the workings and include your totals in the proforma.

(5) Review your answer carefully, checking you have dealt with all the items. Does it make sense?

4.2 Preparation question

Now that we have considered the knowledge and techniques required to be successful in this topic, we will work through a full accounts preparation question.

This question is in the **style** of the tasks you will see in your assessment. However, there are further accounting adjustments which may be tested. These will be studied (and practised) later in the course.

Activity 2: Dalmatian Ltd

You have been asked to help prepare the statement of financial position of Dalmatian Ltd for the year ended 31 March 20X1. The company's trial balance as at 31 March 20X1 is shown below. Further information relating to the financial statements is also provided.

Dalmatian Ltd

Trial balance at 31 March 20X1

	Debit £000	Credit £000
Share capital		10,000
Trade and other payables		2,000
Property – cost	32,000	
Property – accumulated depreciation at 1 April 20X0		6,400
Plant and equipment – cost	9,500	
Plant and equipment – accumulated depreciation at 1 April 20X0		4,156
Trade and other receivables	750	
Accruals		50
5% bank loan repayable in 20X9		5,000
Cash and cash equivalents	1,250	
Retained earnings at 31 March 20X1		16,544
Inventories at 31 March 20X1	650	
	44,150	44,150

Further information:

- The share capital of the company consists of ordinary shares with a nominal value of £1.

- Inventories at close of business consist of the following items at cost. Their comparative net realisable values are as follows:

	Cost £000	NRV £000
Furs	500	600
Products	100	75
Toys	50	60
	650	735

- Depreciation is to be provided for the year ended 31 March 20X1 as follows:

Property	10% per annum	Straight line basis
Plant and equipment	25% per annum	Diminishing balance basis

- Trade receivables include a debt of £75,000 that is to be written off in full. A general allowance of 5% of the remaining debt is required.

- Annual insurance of £12,000 has been paid in full for the year ended 31 December 20X1. This payment is included in retained earnings in the trial balance.

- All of the operations are continuing operations.

Required

Draft the statement of financial position for Dalmatian Ltd as at 31 March 20X1.

Dalmatian Ltd
Statement of financial position (extract) as at 31 March 20X1

	£000
ASSETS	
Non-current assets	
▼	
Current assets	
▼	
▼	
▼	
Total assets	
EQUITY AND LIABILITIES	
Equity	
▼	
▼	

	£000
Non-current liabilities	
▼	
Current liabilities	
▼	
Total liabilities	
Total equity and liabilities	

Picklist:

Bank loan
Cash and cash equivalents
Inventories
Property, plant and equipment
Retained earnings
Share capital
Trade and other payables
Trade and other receivables

Workings (will not be provided in the assessment)

Property, plant and equipment	Property £000	Plant and equipment £000	Total £000

Inventories	£000

Prepayments	£000

LEARNING MEDIA

Workings (will be provided in the assessment)

Property, plant and equipment	£000

Inventories	£000

Trade and other receivables	£000

Retained earnings	£000

Note. In the assessment, picklists for the narrative entries are provided for the on-screen workings.

5 Accounting adjustments

Accounts preparation questions will test your knowledge of a range of bookkeeping issues, some of which are brought-forward knowledge from your previous studies.

If it has been a while since you studied the previous accounting papers, you may like to work through the information which follows.

5.1 Depreciation of non-current assets

There are two main methods for calculating depreciation:

(a)   Straight line method
(b)   Diminishing balance method

Under the straight line method, the depreciation charge is the **same every year**:

$$\text{Straight line depreciation} = \frac{\text{Cost} - \text{Residual value}}{\text{Useful life (years)}}$$

This method is suitable for assets which are used up evenly over their useful life.

Under the diminishing balance method, the depreciation charge will be **higher in the earlier years** and reduces over time.

This method is suitable for those assets which generate more revenue in earlier years than in later years; for example, a machine which may become progressively less efficient as it gets older.

Diminishing balance depreciation = depreciation rate (%) x carrying amount

where: carrying amount = cost – accumulated depreciation to date

Note. This method does **not** take account of any residual value, since the carrying amount under this method will never reach zero. The depreciation rate percentage will be provided in the question.

Activity 3: Depreciation

The following is an extract to the trial balance of Silver Ltd as at 31 December 20X2:

Trial balance (extract) as at 31 December 20X2

	£000	£000
Land and buildings – value/cost	100,000	
Accumulated depreciation at 1 January 20X2		30,000
Plant and equipment – cost	32,000	
Accumulated depreciation at 1 January 20X2		8,000
Cost of sales	60,000	
Distribution costs	25,000	
Administrative costs	36,000	

Further information:

- Land, which is not depreciated, is included in the trial balance at a value of £30,000,000.

- Depreciation is to be provided for the year ended 31 December 20X2 as follows:

Buildings	5% per annum	Straight line basis
Plant and equipment	25% per annum	Diminishing balance basis

    Depreciation is to be apportioned as follows:

	%
Cost of sales	60
Distribution costs	30
Administrative expenses	10

Required

Complete the extracts from the statement of profit or loss and statement of financial position for the year to 31 December 20X2.

Silver Ltd
Statement of profit or loss (extract) for the year ended
31 December 20X2

		£000
	▼	
	▼	
	▼	

Statement of financial position (extract) as at 31 December 20X2

		£000
ASSETS		
Non-current assets		
	▼	

Picklist:

Administrative expenses
Cost of sales
Distribution expenses
Property, plant and equipment

Workings (will not be provided in the assessment)

Depreciation	£000

Workings (on-screen proforma provided in the assessment)

Cost of sales	£000

Distribution expenses	£000

Administrative expenses	£000

Property, plant and equipment	£000

5.2 Inventory

Accounting standards state that:

Inventory should be measured at the **lower of cost** and net **realisable value**.

(IAS 2: para. 2.9)

The 'lower of cost and net realisable value' rule must be applied on an item by item basis. In other words, it is applied to each product line.

Cost	Net realisable value
Cost comprises purchase costs and costs of conversion.	Net realisable value is calculated as:
	£
	Estimated selling price X
	Less estimated costs of completion (X)
	Less estimated selling and distribution costs (X)
	X

In the *Financial Statements of Limited Companies* assessment you may be required to calculate closing inventory (as has been described above). Alternatively, you may simply be given the inventory figure.

You will need to read the scenario carefully. For example:

• The trial balance may state the **opening inventories** figure
• The further information may give the **closing inventories** figure

Opening and closing inventory must be included in the financial statements.

Statement of financial position (extract) for the year to 31 December 20X2

	£
Current assets	
Inventories	X

Note. This is **closing inventory** ie the inventory a business has in its warehouse at the year end.

Statement of profit or loss (extract) for the year to 31 December 20X2

	£
Opening inventories	X
Purchases/cost of goods manufactured	X
Closing inventories	(X)
Cost of sales	X

Note. Total cost of sales is included in the statement of profit or loss, below the revenue line.

Methods of costing inventories at the year end will be studied later in the course.

Activity 4: Inventories

The following is an extract to the trial balance of Hudson Ltd as at 31 December 20X2:

Trial balance (extract) as at 31 December 20X2

	£000	£000
Inventories as at 1 January 20X2	5,000	
Purchases	6,000	

Further information:

Inventories at the close of business on 31 December 20X2 were valued at £6,600,000. On 3 January 20X3, goods included in this total at a value of £800,000 were found to be damaged and sold for £300,000.

Required

Complete the extract below to show inventories in the statement of financial position for the year to 31 December 20X2. Then, complete the cost of sales working.

Hudson Ltd
Statement of financial position (extract) as at 31 December 20X2

	£000
ASSETS	
Current assets	
▼	

Picklist:

Inventories
Receivables
Bank

Workings (will not be provided in the assessment)

Closing inventories	£000

Workings (on-screen proforma provided in the assessment)

Cost of sales	£000

5.3 Irrecoverable and doubtful debts

If a debt is definitely **irrecoverable**, it should be **written off** to the statement of profit or loss as an irrecoverable debt.

	Debit £	Credit £
Irrecoverable debt expense (SPL)	X	
Trade receivables (SOFP)		X

If a debt is **possibly** irrecoverable, an **allowance** for the potential irrecoverability of that debt should be made. A new account is created, called the **allowance for doubtful debts account**.

This account is offset against trade receivables in the statement of financial position and the expense taken to the statement of profit or loss.

	Debit £	Credit £
Allowance for doubtful debts adjustment account (SPL)	X	
Allowance for doubtful debts account (SOFP)		X

Activity 5: Irrecoverable and doubtful debts

The following is an extract to the trial balance of Jude Ltd as at 31 December 20X4:

Trial balance (extract) as at 31 December 20X4

	£000	£000
Trade receivables	16,000	
Allowance for doubtful debts		500
Administrative expenses	12,000	

Further information:

Trade receivables includes a debt of £1,000,000 to be written off. An allowance of 5% is required for remaining trade receivables.

Irrecoverable and doubtful debts are to be classified as administrative expenses.

Required

Complete the extract below to show trade receivables in the statement of financial position as at 31 December 20X4. Then, complete the administrative expenses working.

Jude Ltd
Statement of financial position (extract) as at 31 December 20X4

	£000
ASSETS	
Current assets	

Administrative expenses for the year ended 31 December 20X4

Administrative expenses	£000

Picklist:

Administrative expenses
Allowance for doubtful debts
Irrecoverable debt
Trade receivables

Workings (will not be provided in the assessment)

Movement in allowance for doubtful receivables	£000

Workings (on-screen proforma provided in the assessment)

Trade receivables	£000

5.4 Accruals and prepayments

Accruals are expenses incurred by the business during the accounting period but not yet paid for, ie expenses in **arrears**.

Typical examples of items which need to be accrued for at the year end are electricity and interest payable on a loan.

The journal to record an accrual is:

	Debit £	Credit £
(Relevant) expense account (SPL)	X	
Accruals (SOFP – current liabilities)		X

Prepayments arise when expenses are paid for before they have been used, ie expenses in **advance**.

A typical example of an item which is prepaid at the year end is an insurance premium.

The journal to record a prepayment is:

	Debit £	Credit £
Prepayments (SOFP – current assets)	X	
(Relevant) expense account (SPL)		X

Activity 6: Accruals and prepayments

The following is an extract to the trial balance of Nate Ltd as at 31 December 20X2:

Trial balance (extract) as at 31 December 20X2

	£000	£000
Trade and other payables		1,000
Administrative expenses	5,400	
Trade and other receivables	6,000	

Further information:

- Administrative expenses of £800,000 relating to December 20X2 have not been included in the trial balance.

- The company paid £1,200,000 insurance costs in March 20X2, which covered the period from 1 April 20X2 to 31 March 20X3. This was included in the administrative expenses in the trial balance.

Required

Complete the extract from the statement of financial position as at 31 December 20X2. Then, complete the administrative expenses working.

Nate Ltd
Statement of financial position (extract) as at 31 December 20X2

	£000
ASSETS	
Current assets	
▾	
LIABILITIES	
Current liabilities	
▾	

Administrative expenses for the year ended 31 December 20X2

Administrative expenses	£000
▾	
▾	
▾	

Picklist:

Accruals
Administrative expenses
Prepayments
Trade and other payables
Trade and other receivables

Chapter summary

- Financial statements must comply with all the requirements of IFRSs that apply.

- Financial statements must be prepared on a going concern basis and on the accruals basis.

- Each material class of similar items must be presented separately in the financial statements.

- Assets and liabilities, and income and expenses, should not be offset.

- Financial statements should be prepared at least annually.

- An entity must present and classify items consistently from one period to the next.

- IAS 1 sets out the line items which should be disclosed in the statement of financial position.

- The statement of financial position classifies assets and liabilities as either current or non-current.

- An asset or a liability is normally current:

    - If it is held primarily for the purpose of being traded; and

    - If it is expected to be received or paid within 12 months after the end of the reporting period.

- **Accrual accounting:** Financial statements show the effects of transactions and other events on a reporting entity's economic resources and claims in the periods in which those effects occur, even if the resulting cash receipts and payments occur in a different period

- **Consistency:** A company must present and classify items in the financial statements in the same way from one period to the next

- **Going concern:** Financial statements are prepared on the basis that an entity will continue in operational existence for the foreseeable future

- **Materiality:** Information is material if omitting it or misstating it could influence decisions that users make on the basis of financial information about a specific reporting entity

- **Offset:** Assets, liabilities, income and expenses should not be offset unless this is permitted by a standard

Test your learning

1   A company cannot change its reporting date (its year end).

Is this statement true or false?

True	
False	

2   **List the items that appear in the statement of financial position under 'Current assets'.**

3   **Which ONE of the following items need NOT be disclosed as a separate line item in the statement of financial position?**

Financial liabilities	
Investment properties	
Prepayments	
Trade and other payables	

4   You are provided with the following balances relating to a company:

	£000	£000
Trade receivables	4,294	
Bank overdraft		474
Retained earnings		4,503
Allowance for doubtful debts		171
Land and buildings: cost	7,724	
Plant and machinery: cost	6,961	
Inventories	3,061	
Trade payables		1,206
Tax payable		1,458
Buildings: accumulated depreciation		468
Plant and machinery: accumulated depreciation		2,810
Prepayments	94	
Accruals		169
Bank loan		5,400
Ordinary share capital		3,000
Share premium		1,950
Revaluation reserve		525
	22,134	22,134

Draft a statement of financial position in accordance with the requirements of IAS 1.

(Complete the left-hand column by writing in the correct line items from the list provided.)

Statement of financial position as at ...

	£000
ASSETS	
Non-current assets:	
▼	
Current assets:	
▼	
▼	
Total assets	
EQUITY AND LIABILITIES	
Equity:	
▼	
▼	
▼	
▼	
Total equity	
Non-current liabilities:	
▼	
Current liabilities:	
▼	
▼	
▼	
Total liabilities	
Total equity and liabilities	

Picklist:

Bank loan
Bank overdraft
Inventories
Property, plant and equipment
Retained earnings
Revaluation reserve
Share capital
Share premium
Tax payable
Trade and other payables
Trade and other receivables

Workings

(Complete the left-hand column of each working by writing in the correct narrative from the list provided.)

(1)   Property, plant and equipment

	£000
▼	
▼	
▼	
▼	

Picklist:

Accumulated depreciation: Buildings
Accumulated depreciation: Plant and machinery
Land and buildings: Cost
Plant and machinery: Cost

(2)   Trade and other receivables

	£000
▼	
▼	
▼	

Picklist:

Accruals
Allowance for doubtful debts
Prepayments
Trade payables
Trade receivables

(3) Trade and other payables

		£000
	▼	
	▼	

Picklist:

Accruals
Allowance for doubtful debts
Prepayments
Trade payables
Trade receivables

The statements of financial performance

4

Learning outcomes

1.1	**Explain the regulatory framework that underpins financial reporting**
	• The purpose of financial statements
	• Forms of equity, reserves and loan capital
2.1	**Examine the effect of international accounting standards on the preparation of financial statements**
	• Explain the effect of international accounting standards on the presentation, valuation and disclosure of items within the financial statements
	• Make any supporting calculations
3.1	**Draft a statement of profit or loss and other comprehensive income**
	• Make appropriate entries in the statement in respect of information extracted from a trial balance and additional information
3.3	**Draft a statement of changes in equity**
	• Make appropriate entries in the statement in respect of information extracted from a trial balance and additional information or other financial statements provided

Assessment context

Drafting the statements of financial performance will be important in the assessment.

Qualification context

The Level 2 and 3 AAT courses explained the process of recording year-end adjustments and preparing financial statements for sole traders and partnerships. These skills are now developed as you prepare a statement of profit and loss and other comprehensive income for companies.

Business context

All registered companies must prepare a set of financial statements on an annual basis. The statements of financial performance are two of the primary components of a set of financial statements.

Chapter overview

Set of financial statements

- Statement of financial position
- Statement of profit or loss and other comprehensive income
- Statement of changes in equity
- Statement of cash flows
- Notes to the financial statements

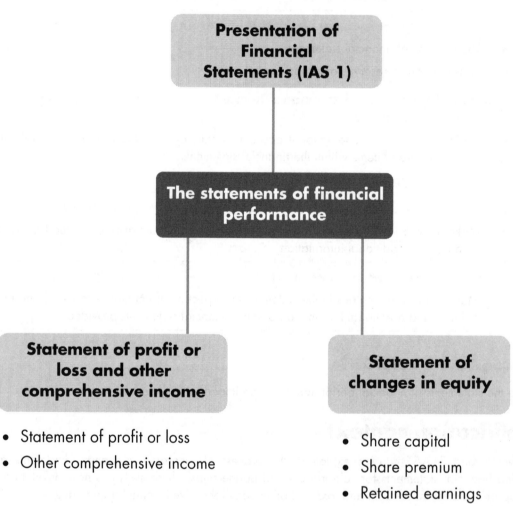

Presentation of Financial Statements (IAS 1)

The statements of financial performance

Statement of profit or loss and other comprehensive income

- Statement of profit or loss
- Other comprehensive income

Statement of changes in equity

- Share capital
- Share premium
- Retained earnings
- Revaluation reserve

Introduction

In this chapter we concentrate on an entity's performance and the way in which it is presented in the financial statements. In particular, we look at the statement of **profit or loss** and **other comprehensive income** and at the statement of changes in equity.

Shareholders and other users of the financial statements need information about the financial performance of an entity.

But what exactly is financial performance? The simple view is that it is the amount that is available for distribution to the shareholders; in other words, profit before dividends, or profit after tax.

An alternative view is that financial performance is wider than profit. It is the total return that an entity obtains on the resources that it controls. It includes all gains and losses, whether or not they have actually been received (realised) in the form of cash or are likely to be received in the near future. It can be expressed using the accounting equation:

Performance (income − expenses) =

closing equity − opening equity; or

net gains/(losses) =

change in net assets in the accounting period.

The IASB has adopted this second, wider view of performance.

1 Presentation of financial statements (IAS 1)

IAS 1 *Presentation of Financial Statements* (para. 1.10) states that a complete set of financial statements should be issued at least annually. A complete set of financial statements comprises:

- A statement of financial position
- **A statement of profit or loss and other comprehensive income**
- **A statement of changes in equity**
- A statement of cash flows
- Notes, comprising a summary of significant **accounting policies** and other explanatory information

In this chapter we will cover the two statements of financial performance: the statement of profit or loss and other comprehensive income and the statement of changes in equity.

1.1 Total comprehensive income

The statement of profit or loss and other comprehensive income required by IAS 1 shows an entity's **total comprehensive income** for the period (IAS 1: para. 1.7).

Total comprehensive income can be thought of as the difference between opening and closing equity (or net assets) other than changes resulting from transactions with owners in their capacity as owners (for example, the payment of dividends).

An entity's total comprehensive income is:

- Its profit or loss for the period; plus
- Its other comprehensive income.

2 Statement of profit or loss and other comprehensive income

IAS 1 (para. 1.10) allows income and expenses to be presented either:

(a) In a single statement of profit or loss and other comprehensive income; or

(b) In two statements: a separate statement of profit or loss and statement of other comprehensive income.

The *Financial Statements of Limited Companies* assessment requires you to prepare a single statement of profit or loss and other comprehensive income only.

2.1 Proforma – statement of profit or loss and other comprehensive income

XYZ Ltd

Statement of profit or loss and other comprehensive income for the year ended 31 December 20X2

	20X2	20X1
	£000	£000
Revenue	X	X
Cost of sales	(X)	(X)
Gross profit	X	X
Distribution costs	(X)	(X)
Administrative expenses	(X)	(X)
Profit from operations	X	X
Finance costs	(X)	(X)

	20X2	20X1
	£000	£000
Profit before tax	X	X
Tax	(X)	(X)
Profit for the year from continuing operations	X	X
Other comprehensive income for the year	X	X
Total comprehensive income for the year	X	X

The part of the statement of comprehensive income from '**revenue**' to '**profit for the year**' is referred to as the statement of profit or loss.

2.2 Expenses

Expenses may be classified by:

- Function (cost of sales, distribution costs, administrative expenses, etc); or
- Nature (raw materials, employee costs, depreciation, etc).

The presentation which provides the most reliable and relevant financial information must be followed.

However, classification by function is the most common form of presentation for companies in the UK and the format which will be used in the assessment.

2.3 Unusual items

Material items of income and expense should be disclosed separately (IAS 1: para. 1.98). Examples of items which may need to be disclosed separately include:

- Losses on inventories, which is written down
- Gains or losses on the disposal of property, plant and equipment

This information is relevant to users as it helps them predict an entity's future performance. For example, a gain on the sale of property, plant and equipment may not occur in future years.

However, such items arise from events or transactions that fall within the ordinary activities.

Companies may not present any item of income or expense as an **extraordinary item**. If any items of income or expense are individually material, they should be disclosed separately, with a short description of their nature in the notes.

2.4 Other comprehensive income

Other comprehensive income is items of income and expense that are not recognised in profit or loss (IAS 1: para. 1.82). For example, when a non-current asset is revalued, the difference between its original cost less depreciation and its fair or market value is not included in profit or loss for the period. Instead, it is recognised as part of other comprehensive income.

In *Financial Statements of Limited Companies*, revaluation gains or losses relating to non-current assets will be the only item included in other comprehensive income.

Activity 1: Other comprehensive income

A company has revalued one of its buildings during the year, resulting in a significant gain.

Required

Are the following statements true or false?

	True	False
The gain is part of the company's performance.		
The gain should be recognised in profit or loss.		

3 Statement of changes in equity

The statement of changes in equity shows the movement in the equity section of the statement of financial position during the year (IAS 1: para. 1.106).

3.1 Proforma – statement of changes in equity

XYZ Ltd
Statement of changes in equity for the year ended
31 December 20X2

	Share capital £000	Share premium £000	Revaluation reserve £000	Retained earnings £000	Total equity £000
Balance at 1 January 20X2	X	X	X	X	X
Changes in equity					
Total comprehensive income			X	X	X

	Share capital	Share premium	Revaluation reserve	Retained earnings	Total equity
	£000	£000	£000	£000	£000
Dividends				(X)	(X)
Issue of share capital	X	X			X
Balance at 31 December 20X2	X	X	X	X	X

When shares are issued, the nominal amount of the issued shares is credited to the share capital account and any excess is credited to share premium.

The total comprehensive income figures come from the statement of profit or loss and other comprehensive income. The profit/(loss) for the year is included in the **retained earnings** column, whilst other comprehensive income is allocated to the **revaluation reserve**.

3.2 Dividends

As you have seen, dividends are not an item of expense and therefore they do not appear in the statement of profit or loss and other comprehensive income.

Instead, they appear in the statement of changes in equity as a reduction in retained earnings, in the year they are declared.

Illustration 1 – Statement of profit or loss and other comprehensive income and statement of changes in equity

Chickpea Ltd made a profit of £609,000 for the year ended 31 December 20X3.

During the year:

(a)   Freehold properties were revalued, resulting in a gain of £125,000

(b)   The company issued 200,000 new £1 ordinary shares at a price of £1.50 each

(c)   A dividend of £100,000 was paid to equity shareholders

Total equity at 1 January 20X3 was £2,020,000.

Draft a statement of profit or loss and other comprehensive income (starting from 'profit for the year') and a statement of changes in equity (total column only) for the year ended 31 December 20X3.

Statement of profit or loss and other comprehensive income for the year ended 31 December 20X3 (extract)

	£000
Profit for the year	
Other comprehensive income for the year	
Total comprehensive income for the year	

Statement of changes in equity for the year ended 31 December 20X3 (extract)

	Total equity £000
Balance at 1 January 20X3	
Changes in equity for 20X3	
Balance at 31 December 20X3	

Solution

Statement of profit or loss and other comprehensive income for the year ended 31 December 20X3 (extract)

	£000
Profit for the year	609
Other comprehensive income for the year	
Gain on property revaluation	125
Total comprehensive income for the year	734

Statement of changes in equity for the year ended 31 December 20X3 (extract)

	Total equity £000
Balance at 1 January 20X3	2,020
Changes in equity for 20X3	
Total comprehensive income	734
Dividends	(100)
Issue of share capital (200,000 × 1.50)	300
Balance at 31 December 20X3	2,954

Activity 2: Mayer Ltd SOCE

You have been asked to help prepare the statement of changes of equity of Mayer Ltd for the year ended 31 December 20X7. An extract from the company's trial balance as at 31 December 20X7 is shown below. Further information relating to the financial statements is also provided.

Mayer Ltd
Trial balance (extract) as at 31 December 20X7

	Debit £	Credit £
Share capital		100,000
Retained earnings, 1 January 20X7		35,000
Revaluation reserve, 1 January 20X7		40,000
Dividend paid	10,000	

Further information:

- Share capital of £20,000 was issued in the year at nominal value. This has not yet been accounted for.
- Profit for the year was £20,000.
- Revaluation gains for the year were £5,000.

Required

Draft the statement of changes in equity for Mayer Ltd for the year ended 31 December 20X7.

Mayer Ltd
Statement of changes in equity for the year ended
31 December 20X7

		Share capital £	Revaluation reserve £	Retained earnings £	Total equity £
	▼				
Changes in equity					
	▼				
	▼				
	▼				
	▼				

Picklist:

Balance at 1 January 20X7
Balance at 31 December 20X7
Dividends
Issue of share capital
Total comprehensive income

4 Summary of the financial statements

This diagram summarises the way that the main financial statements and the elements of the financial statements interrelate.

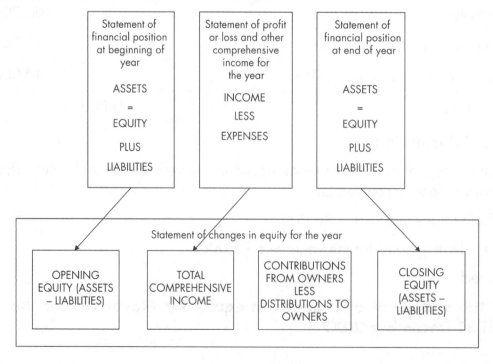

5 Notes to the financial statements

Notes provide or disclose information which is not presented in the statement of profit or loss and other comprehensive income, the statement of financial position, the statement of changes in equity or the statement of cash flows:

- Where it is required by other IFRS
- Where additional information is relevant to understand any of the financial statements

Typically, many of the notes provide a further analysis of the totals shown in the main financial statements. For example, the note to 'trade and other payables' provides an analysis of this balance, and will show amounts arising from trade payables, accruals and other payables.

5.1 Accounting policies

Accounting policies are the specific principles, conventions and practices applied by an entity in preparing and presenting the financial statements.

The notes to the financial statements will also disclose the accounting policies adopted by the directors of the financial statements. For example, they will disclose whether property, plant and equipment is held at cost or revaluation.

5.2 Expenses

Where expenses have been classified by function in the statement of profit or loss and other comprehensive income (showing cost of sales, distribution costs and administrative expenses), additional information is required on the nature of expenses, including:

- Depreciation and amortisation
- Employee benefit expense

6 Assessment tasks

6.1 Approach to preparing the statements of financial performance

(1) Read the requirement(s) and scan the task.

(2) Review the 'further information' carefully. Identify the items which require adjustment.

(3) Work methodically down the trial balance, identifying items relating to income, expenses and equity. Enter the relevant figures in the trial balance:

- In a financial statement proforma (if they require no further adjustment)

- In an on-screen working (if they require adjustment and an on-screen working is provided)

- On scrap paper (if they require adjustment and an on-screen working is not provided)

(4) Complete the workings and include your totals in the proforma.

(5) Review your answer carefully, checking you have dealt with all the items. Does it make sense?

6.2 Assessment Tasks 1 and 2

In the assessment, the financial statement preparation questions will be split across two tasks.

For example, the first task may ask you to prepare a statement of profit or loss and other comprehensive income (SPLOCI) and statement of changes in equity (SOCE). The requirement in the next task could be to prepare a statement of financial position.

The task information may be the same for both tasks. If so, you only need to read it in detail once.

Assessment focus point

You are advised to do assessment Tasks 1 and 2 together, rather than completing Task 1 and then moving on to Task 2. This is because the same piece of information may affect both the SPLOCI and the statement of financial position. By doing both tasks together, you can keep the double entry going, as you will see in the next Activity.

6.3 Using the task information

Task 1 may say: 'You will be asked to draft a statement of financial position in Task 2 using the same data. The data will be repeated.'

Task 2 may say: 'This task is a continuation of the scenario in Task 1 and uses the same data.'

You need to know how to treat the data in the primary statements.

For example, property, plant and equipment is treated as follows:

- Non-current asset in the statement of financial position
- Depreciation charge in the statement of profit or loss
- Revaluation gain/loss to other comprehensive income (in the SPLOCI)
- Revaluation gain/loss in the SOCE

The next example is exam standard in respect of style and format; however, assessment accounting adjustments will be more challenging. These will be practised after studying:

- Property, plant and equipment
- Intangible assets and inventories
- Liabilities

Activity 3: Brindley Ltd SPLOCI and SOCE

You have been asked to help prepare the financial statements of Brindley Ltd for the year ended 31 March 20X9. The company's trial balance as at 31 March 20X9 is shown below. Further information relating to the financial statements is also provided.

Brindley Ltd
Trial balance as at 31 March 20X9

	Debit £	Credit £
Revenue		206,500
Purchases	138,750	
Administration expenses	7,650	
Distribution costs	10,000	
Directors' remuneration	25,000	
Bank interest paid	162	
Interim dividend paid	1,260	
Land and buildings, at valuation	80,000	
Motor vans, at cost (used for distribution)	2,500	
Accumulated depreciation at 1 April 20X8		1,000
Inventories at 1 April 20X8	12,000	
Bank overdraft		12,970
Trade and other receivables	31,000	
Trade and other payables		23,000
Share capital		42,000
Retained earnings, 1 April 20X8		17,852
Revaluation reserve, 31 March 20X9		5,000
	308,322	308,322

Further information:

(a) All the motor vans were purchased on 1 April 20X6. Depreciation is on a straight line basis at 20% per annum from the date of purchase. It has not been calculated in the current year and will be included in distribution costs.

(b) The estimated tax liability for the year to 31 March 20X9 is £12,700.

(c) It is proposed to pay a final dividend of £2,000 for the year to 31 March 20X9.

(d) Inventories at close of business on 31 March 20X9 cost £16,700.

(e) On 7 April 20X9, Brindley Ltd received a telephone bill for £363 relating to the period 1 March 20X9 to 31 May 20X9. No accrual has yet been made, and telephone bills are treated as administration expenses.

(f) Included in administration expenses is an invoice for insurance of £984. The invoice related to the period 1 January 20X9 to 31 December 20X9, yet the whole invoice has been expensed in the draft accounts.

(g) At the year end, the land and buildings were revalued for the first time, resulting in a revaluation reserve of £5,000. This has been credited to the revaluation reserve.

Required

Task 1:

(a) Draft the statement of profit or loss and other comprehensive income for Brindley Ltd for the year ended 31 March 20X9.

(b) Draft the statement of changes in equity for Brindley Ltd for the year ended 31 March 20X9.

Task 2:

Draft the statement of financial position for Brindley Ltd as at 31 March 20X9.

Note. Additional notes and disclosures are not required. You do not need to use the workings tables to achieve full marks on the task but the data entered into the workings tables will be taken into consideration if you make errors in the proformas.

Task 1:

(a) Brindley Ltd

Statement of profit or loss and other comprehensive income for the year ended 31 March 20X9

		£
	▼	
	▼	
	▼	
	▼	
	▼	
Profit from operations		
	▼	
Profit before tax		
	▼	
Profit for the year from continuing operations		
	▼	
Total comprehensive income for the year		

Picklist:

Administrative expenses
Cost of sales
Distribution costs
Finance costs
Gross profit
Other comprehensive income for the year
Revenue
Tax

(b) Brindley Ltd

Statement of changes in equity for the year ended 31 March 20X9

	Share capital £	Revaluation reserve £	Retained earnings £	Total equity £
▼				
Changes in equity				
▼				
▼				
▼				

Picklist:

Balance at 1 April 20X8
Balance at 31 March 20X9
Dividends
Issue of share capital
Total comprehensive income

Task 2:

Brindley Ltd

Statement of financial position as at 31 March 20X9

	£
ASSETS	
Non-current assets	
▼	
Current assets	
▼	
▼	
Total assets	

	£
EQUITY AND LIABILITIES	
Equity	
▼	
▼	
▼	
Current liabilities	
▼	
▼	
▼	
Total liabilities	
Total equity and liabilities	

Picklist:

Bank loan
Bank overdraft
Cash and cash equivalents
Inventories
Property, plant and equipment
Retained earnings
Revaluation reserve
Share capital,
Tax liability
Trade and other payables
Trade and other receivables

Workings (will not be provided in the assessment)

Motor vehicles – depreciation	£

Taxation	Debit £	Credit £

Workings (will be provided in the assessment)

Property, plant and equipment	£

Trade and other receivables	£

Trade and other payables	£

Cost of sales	£

Distribution costs	£

Administrative expenses	£

Note. In the assessment, picklists for the narrative entries are provided for the on-screen workings.

Chapter summary

- Users of the financial statements need information about the financial performance of an entity.

- Financial performance (Income – Expenses) = Closing equity – Opening equity (change in net assets in the accounting period).

- The statement of profit or loss and other comprehensive income shows the profit or loss for the year and items such as revaluation gains and losses which are not recognised in profit or loss.

- IAS 1 sets out the line items which should be disclosed in the statement of profit or loss and other comprehensive income.

- All items of income and expense recognised in a period must be included in profit or loss unless a standard requires otherwise.

- The statement of changes in equity shows the movements in share capital and in each reserve for the year:
  - Changes in accounting policies
  - Correction of prior period errors
  - Total comprehensive income for the year
  - Issues of share capital
  - Dividends paid

Keywords

- **Accounting policies:** The specific principles, bases, conventions, rules and practices applied by an entity in preparing and presenting financial statements

- **Extraordinary items:** Material items possessing a high degree of abnormality which arise from events or transactions that fall outside the ordinary activities of an entity and which are not expected to recur

- **Other comprehensive income:** Items of income and expense that are not recognised in profit or loss

- **Profit or loss:** Income less expenses

1 A gain on revaluation of non-current assets must always be included in profit or loss.

   Is this statement true or false?

True	
False	

2 During the year ended 31 December 20X6 Sycamore Ltd incurred general administrative expenses of £155,000. Depreciation of office furniture was £76,000.

   Included in general administrative expenses was a payment for rent of £24,000 for the 3 months from 1 November 20X6 to 31 January 20X7.

   What are total administrative expenses for the year ended 31 December 20X6?

£147,000	
£215,000	
£223,000	
£239,000	

3 The directors of Tarragona plc have asked you to draft a statement of profit or loss and other comprehensive income for the year ended 30 September 20X3.

   They have given you the trial balance of the company which is set out below.

   Tarragona plc: Trial balance as at 30 September 20X3

	Debit £000	Credit £000
Property, plant and equipment at cost	24,492	
Accumulated depreciation on property, plant and equipment		7,604
Trade receivables	4,150	
Long-term loan		3,780
Distribution costs	6,165	
Administration expenses	3,386	
Ordinary share capital		5,400
Share premium		1,800
Sales		33,202
Inventories as at 1 October 20X2	8,570	

	Debit £000	Credit £000
Cash at bank	256	
Accruals		97
Interest	517	
Trade payables		2,435
Purchases	19,480	
Retained earnings		12,698
	67,016	67,016

Further information:

- The company is proposing a final dividend of 20 pence per share. No interim dividend was paid during the year.

- The inventories at the close of business on 30 September 20X3 were valued at cost at £10,262,000.

- The tax charge for the year has been estimated at £1,333,000.

- Land that had cost £4,800,000 has been revalued by professional valuers at £5,800,000. No adjustment has yet been made to the trial balance. The revaluation is to be included in the financial statements for the year ended 30 September 20X3.

Draft a statement of profit or loss and other comprehensive income for Tarragona plc for the year ended 30 September 20X3.

Tarragona plc
Statement of profit or loss and other comprehensive income for the year ended 30 September 20X3

	£000
Revenue	
Cost of sales	
Gross profit	
Distribution costs	
Administrative expenses	
Profit from operations	
Finance costs	
Profit before tax	
Tax	

	£000
Profit for the period from continuing operations	
Other comprehensive income	
Gain on revaluation of land	
Total comprehensive income for the period	

Working

Cost of sales	£000

4   **Complete the sentence below by writing in the appropriate words.**

[   ] are the specific principles, bases, conventions, rules and practices applied by an entity in preparing and presenting financial statements.

5   The following information relates to Light Ltd:

Equity at 1 January 20X5

	£000
Share capital (£1 ordinary shares)	1,000
Share premium	300
Retained earnings	700
	2,000

The following transactions and events took place during the year:

On 31 December 20X5 a freehold property was revalued to £500,000 and this valuation was incorporated into the financial statements. The property had previously been carried at historical cost less depreciation and had a carrying amount of £350,000 immediately before the revaluation.

On 1 July 20X5 the company issued a further 100,000 £1 ordinary shares at a market price of £1.20.

On 31 December 20X5 the company paid a dividend of £50,000.

Profit for the year ended 31 December 20X5 was £300,000.

Draft a statement of changes in equity for Light Ltd for the year ended 31 December 20X5.

Statement of changes in equity for the year ended 31 December 20X5

	Share capital £000	Share premium £000	Revaluation reserve £000	Retained earnings £000	Total equity £000
Balance at 1 January 20X5					
Changes in equity for 20X5					
Total comprehensive income					
Dividends					
Issue of shares					
Balance at 31 December 20X5					

The statement of cash flows

5

Learning outcomes

1.1	**Explain the regulatory framework that underpins financial reporting**
	• The purpose of financial statements
	• Forms of equity, reserves and loan capital
2.1	**Examine the effect of international accounting standards on the preparation of financial statements**
	• Explain the effect of international accounting standards on the presentation, valuation and disclosure of items within the financial statements
	• Make any supporting calculations
3.4	**Draft a statement of cash flows**
	• Make appropriate entries in the statement, using the indirect method, in respect of information extracted from a statement of profit or loss and other comprehensive income for a single year, and statements of financial position for two years, and any additional information provided

Assessment context

Drafting a statement of cash flows may feature as a significant question in your exam. This topic can also be tested in short-form, objective-style tasks.

Qualification context

This topic is new to the Level 4 *Financial Statements of Limited Companies* course.

Business context

All registered companies must prepare a set of financial statements on an annual basis. The statement of cash flows is one of the primary components of a set of financial statements.

Chapter overview

IAS 1: Set of Financial Statements
- Statement of financial position
- Statement of profit or loss and other comprehensive income
- Statement of changes in equity
- Statement of cash flows
- Notes to the financial statements

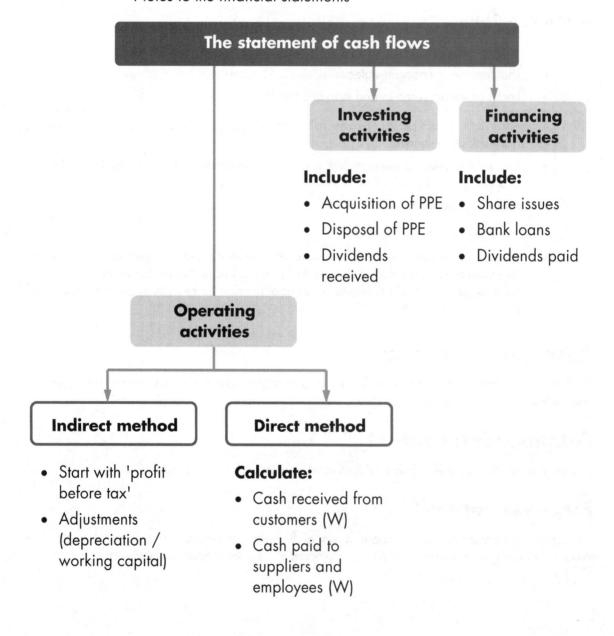

The statement of cash flows

Investing activities

Include:
- Acquisition of PPE
- Disposal of PPE
- Dividends received

Financing activities

Include:
- Share issues
- Bank loans
- Dividends paid

Operating activities

Indirect method
- Start with 'profit before tax'
- Adjustments (depreciation / working capital)

Direct method

Calculate:
- Cash received from customers (W)
- Cash paid to suppliers and employees (W)

Introduction

In this chapter we introduce the **statement of cash flows** (sometimes called the cash flow statement). The statement of profit or loss and other comprehensive income and the statement of financial position provide information about an entity's performance and financial position. The statement of cash flows, as its name suggests, shows the way in which an entity has generated and spent cash. IAS 7 *Statement of Cash Flows* requires companies to include a statement of cash flows in their financial statements and sets out the way in which the statement should be prepared and presented (IAS 7: para. 1).

1 The importance of cash

However profitable a business may appear to be, it will not survive without adequate cash. Businesses need cash to pay suppliers and employees, to pay dividends to shareholders, to repay debt to lenders and to purchase property, plant, equipment and inventories to enable them to go on producing goods or providing services.

The purpose of a statement of cash flows is to show the effect of a company's commercial transactions on its cash balance.

It is thought that users of accounts can readily understand statements of cash flows, as opposed to statements which are subject to manipulation by the use of different accounting policies.

The period in which an item is recognised in the statement of profit or loss or the statement of financial position may depend on:

- The accounting policies adopted and the estimates used by the entity
- The judgement of management (where estimates have to be made)

Cash flow is a matter of fact (it can be verified by looking at the entity's bank statement). It is difficult to manipulate and is less likely to be distorted by 'creative accounting'.

As the statement of profit or loss and other comprehensive income and statement of financial position are prepared under the accruals concept, they do not indicate the cash which has been received or paid at the reporting date. Therefore, the statement of cash flows facilitates an assessment of a company's liquidity.

It also shows how the company uses cash and its ability to generate cash.

Key term

Cash comprises cash on hand and demand deposits, less any bank overdrafts.

Cash equivalents are short-term, highly liquid investments that are readily convertible to known amounts of cash and which are subject to an insignificant risk of changes in value (for example, treasury bills and current asset investments). (IAS 7: para. 7.7–8)

If a current asset investment is a cash equivalent, this will be made clear in the assessment.

The statement of cash flows identifies cash flows from three types of activity (IAS 7: para. 7.10):

- **Operating activities**
- **Investing activities**
- **Financing activities**

Operating activities

This is a key part of the statement of cash flows because it shows whether the business has generated cash from its operations. Do the operating activities result in a net cash inflow?

IAS 7 (para. 7.14) defines operating activities as the principal revenue-producing activities of the entity and other activities that are not investing or financing activities.

Cash flows from operating activities consist of:

- Cash received from customers (receipts from the sale of goods or the rendering of services)

- Cash paid to suppliers for goods and services

- Cash paid to and on behalf of employees

In other words, the **cash generated from operations** can be thought of as profit before tax, adjusted for non-cash items.

Investing activities

This section shows the extent to which there has been investment in the business.

For example, there may be investment in property, plant and equipment resulting in a net cash outflow to acquire new non-current assets.

Also, some older items of property, plant and equipment may have been disposed of in return for cash proceeds. This will result in a cash inflow.

Financing activities

There are two main options here – equity and loan financing.

If the business issues shares for cash or borrows money from a bank then there is a cash inflow. The cash proceeds enable the business to survive long term and fund investment.

Conversely, if the business repays a bank loan, for example, then there is a cash outflow.

1.1 Indirect and direct method

IAS 7 (para. 7.18) permits a choice of methods for reporting cash flows from operating activities:

Indirect method –   Profit before tax is adjusted for the effects of any non-cash items and movement in working capital.

Direct method – Major classes of **gross cash flows**, ie gross cash receipts and gross cash payments, are disclosed.

Note that the indirect and direct methods are only relevant to the cash flows from operating activities. Cash flows from investing activities and cash flows from financing activities are always reported in the same way.

We will consider both methods in turn.

2 Statement of cash flows – indirect method

With the indirect method of preparing a statement of cash flows we start with the profit before tax figure, and adjust it to arrive at the net cash generated from operating activities.

In the assessment, the statement of cash flows is normally drafted in two parts, as is illustrated in the proforma below.

2.1 Proforma – statement of cash flows

XYZ Ltd

Reconciliation of profit before tax to net cash from operating activities for the year ended 31 December 20X2

	£000
Profit before tax	20,500
Adjustments for:	
Depreciation	2,500
Loss on disposal of property, plant and equipment	400
Finance costs	200
Dividends received	(100)
(Increase)/decrease in inventories	(3,000)
(Increase)/decrease in trade receivables	(6,500)
Increase/(decrease) in trade payables	1,000
Cash generated from operations	15,000
Interest paid	(200)
Tax paid	(400)
Net cash from operating activities	14,400

XYZ Ltd

Statement of cash flows for the year ended 31 December 20X2

	£000
Net cash from operating activities	14,400
Investing activities	
Purchase of plant	(14,500)
Receipts from sale of non-current assets	400
Dividends received	100
Net cash used in investing activities	(14,000)
Financing activities	
Proceeds from loan	12,000
Issue of share capital	6,000
Dividends paid	(1,200)
Net cash generated from financing activities	16,800
Net increase/(decrease) in cash and cash equivalents	17,200
Cash and cash equivalents at the beginning of the year	500
Cash and cash equivalents at the end of the year	17,700

Illustration 1 – Statement of cash flows using the indirect method

Bishop Ltd has a profit before tax of £20,500 for the year ended 31 December 20X2. The depreciation charge for the year is £4,000. Profit before tax also includes a loss on disposal of £500 on an item of plant.

Extracts from the statement of financial position are shown below:

	20X2	20X1
	£	£
Inventories	17,400	16,100
Receivables	21,500	20,500
Trade payables	18,400	17,600

Ignore interest and tax.

The company's profit is adjusted for non-cash items in order to arrive at cash generated from operations.

Step 1   Add back depreciation

Depreciation has been charged in arriving at profit before tax, but it does not involve the movement of cash. Therefore it is added back to profit before tax.

Step 2   Adjust for any profits or losses on the disposal of assets

The cash received from the sale of an asset is not a cash flow from operating activities. The profit or loss on sale must be removed from profit before tax:

- A profit on disposal is deducted
- A loss on disposal is added back

Step 3   Adjust to **add back interest (finance costs)** (not given in this example)

Step 4   Adjust for changes in working capital **(inventories, receivables and payables)**

The movements in working capital represent the differences between sales and cash received and purchases and cash paid.

Suppose that sales for the year were £100,000. Opening receivables were £20,500 and closing receivables were £21,500. Therefore cash received was £99,000: £1,000 less than the sales figure. The difference between sales and cash inflow is the difference between opening receivables and closing receivables: £1,000.

Suppose that total expenses were £75,000:

- Opening inventories were £16,100 and closing inventories were £17,400. This means that total purchases were £76,300 (75,000 + 17,400 – 16,100).

- Opening payables were £17,600 and closing payables were £18,400. Therefore cash paid was £75,500 (76,300 + 17,600 – 18,400).

- The difference between operating expenses and cash inflow is £500, which is the difference between opening and closing inventories (£1,300 increase) less the difference between opening and closing payables (£800 increase).

In practice, we simply adjust profit for the differences between the opening and closing amounts:

- Increase in inventories: deduct £1,300 (cash outflow)
- Increase in receivables: deduct £1,000 (cash outflow)
- Increase in trade payables: add £800 (cash inflow)

We can now draw up a reconciliation of profit before tax to cash generated from operations:

	£
Profit before tax	20,500
Depreciation	4,000
Loss on disposal of property, plant and equipment	500
Increase in inventories	(1,300)
Increase in receivables	(1,000)
Increase in payables	800
Cash generated from operations	23,500

Interest paid and tax paid (not given in this example) are then deducted from cash generated from operations to give the net cash from operating activities.

This reconciliation helps users of the financial statements to understand the difference between profit and cash flow. It also shows the movements on the individual items within working capital. This enables users to see how successful or otherwise the entity has been in managing inventories, receivables and payables in order to generate cash.

Most UK companies use the indirect method.

3 Statement of cash flows – calculations in the assessment

Assessment tasks will require you to calculate certain numbers (representing a cash inflow or outflow). These figures will then be included in your statement of cash flow proforma.

In some cases you will be provided with an on-screen working. If so, it is important to complete this, as follow-through marks are available – even if the figure you calculate is incorrect, you will be given credit for transferring your number to the correct place in the statement of cash flow proforma.

Other numbers need to be calculated on scrap paper.

The following information is relevant to the preparation examples which follow.

3.1 Preparation examples for Silver Ltd – task information

You have been asked to prepare the statement of cash flows for Silver Ltd for the year ended 31 December 20X2.

The most recent statement of profit or loss and other comprehensive income and statement of financial position (with comparatives for the previous year) of Silver Ltd are set out below.

Silver Ltd
Statement of profit or loss for the year ended 31 December 20X2

	£000
Revenue	2,553
Cost of sales	(1,814)
Gross profit	739
Dividends received	43
Loss on disposal of property, plant and equipment	(13)
Distribution costs	(125)
Administrative expenses	(294)
Profit from operations	350
Finance costs	(66)
Profit before tax	284
Tax	(140)
Profit for the year	144

Silver Ltd
Statement of financial position as at 31 December 20X2

	20X2 £000	20X1 £000
ASSETS		
Non-current assets		
Property, plant and equipment	380	305
Current assets		
Inventories	150	102
Trade receivables	390	315
Cash and cash equivalents	52	1
	592	418

	20X2 £000	20X1 £000
Total assets	972	723
EQUITY AND LIABILITIES		
Equity		
Share capital (£1 ordinary shares)	100	50
Share premium account	60	50
Retained earnings	210	166
	370	266
Non-current liabilities		
Bank loans	100	–
Current liabilities		
Trade payables	227	199
Bank overdraft	85	98
Tax liability	190	160
	502	457
Total liabilities	602	457
Total equity and liabilities	972	723

Further information:

- The total depreciation charge for the year was £90,000.

- Property, plant and equipment costing £85,000 with accumulated depreciation of £40,000 were sold in the year.

- All sales and purchases were on credit. Other expenses were paid for in cash.

- A dividend of £100,000 was paid during the year.

3.2 Operating activities – working capital movement

The movements in working capital represent the differences between sales and cash received, and purchases and cash paid.

When preparing the cash flows from operating activities, the profit before tax figure is adjusted for working capital movement – ie differences between the opening and closing amounts.

Note that the adjustments can be entered in any order. (The computer searches for correct answers and awards marks accordingly.)

Activity 1: Silver Ltd – working capital movement

Required

Show the adjustments in respect of working capital movement in the extract below for Silver Ltd for the year ended 31 December 20X2.

Reconciliation of profit before tax to net cash from operating activities (extract)

	£000
Profit before tax	X
Adjustments for:	
Cash generated from operations	X

3.3 Operating activities – interest paid and tax paid

The amount of the interest expense in respect of bank loans or other financing arrangements will be shown in the statement of profit or loss. It is referred to as 'finance costs'. To prepare the statement of cash flows, interest paid may need to be calculated or simply transferred to the proforma. The interest figure must be removed from (added back to) profit before tax and inserted in the proforma after cash generated from operations.

Tax paid may need to be calculated, as is illustrated in the next example.

Activity 2: Silver Ltd – interest and tax paid

Required

Include the amounts relating to interest paid and tax paid in the extract for Silver Ltd for the year ended 31 December 20X2.

Reconciliation of profit before tax to net cash from operating activities (extract)

	£000
Cash generated from operations	X
Net cash from operating activities	X

Workings (not provided in the assessment)

Tax paid	£000

3.4 Operating activities and investing activities – property, plant and equipment (PPE) and dividends received

Property, plant and equipment (PPE) affects cash flows from operating activities and investing activities.

Operating activities

Depreciation is a non-cash expense which must be added back to profit before tax. Further, profit before tax must be adjusted for any profit or loss arising on the sale of PPE, as this is also a non-cash item.

Investing activities

Tasks will often ask you to calculate cash flows relating to the acquisition or disposal of any non-current assets. These cash flows are included in investing activities.

The following on-screen workings may be provided:

3.4.1 Example working – proceeds on disposal on PPE

Proceeds on disposal of property, plant and equipment	£000
Carrying amount of PPE sold	X
Gain/(loss) on disposal	X/(X)
	X

3.4.2 Example working – purchases of PPE

Purchases of property, plant and equipment	£000
Property, plant and equipment at start of year	X
Depreciation charge	(X)
Carrying amount of property, plant and equipment sold	(X)
Property, plant and equipment at end of year	(X)
	(X)

The business may also receive a dividend from an investment it has made in another company. Dividends received are included in cash flows from investing activities.

Activity 3: Silver Ltd – PPE and dividend received

Required

Include the amounts relating to property, plant and equipment and the dividend received in the extracts for Silver Ltd for the year ended 31 December 20X2.

Reconciliation of profit before tax to net cash from operating activities (extract)

	£000
Profit before tax	284
Adjustments for:	

	£000
Adjustment in respect of inventories (150 – 102)	(48)
Adjustment in respect of trade receivables (390 – 315)	(75)
Adjustment in respect of trade payables (227 – 199)	28
Cash generated from operations	
Interest paid	(66)
Tax paid	(110)
Net cash from operating activities	

Statement of cash flows (extract) for the year ended 31 December 20X2

	£000
Net cash from operating activities	
Investing activities	
Net cash used in investing activities	

Workings

Proceeds on disposal of property, plant and equipment	£000

Purchases of property, plant and equipment	£000

3.5 Financing activities – bank loans, shares and dividends

Financing cash flows comprise receipts from, or repayments to, external providers of finance as well as any changes to the contributed equity of the business. Examples of financing cash flows are:

- Cash proceeds or repayments of bank loans
- Cash proceeds from issuing shares
- Dividends paid to shareholders

The cash proceeds or repayments of bank loans and issues of shares are calculated by comparing the closing statement of financial position figures with the opening position for the same items.

Information relating to dividends paid to the reporting company's own equity shareholders will be provided in the 'further information'.

In assessment questions, dividends paid to equity shareholders should be included in 'financing activities'. However, IAS 7 also permits them to be included in operating activities.

Activity 4: Silver Ltd – financing activities

Required

Include the amounts relating to shares, bank loans and dividend paid in the statement of cash flows extract for Silver Ltd for the year ended 31 December 20X2.

Statement of cash flows (extract) for the year ended 31 December 20X2

	£000
Financing activities	
Net cash from financing activities	

3.6 Cash and cash equivalents

To complete the cash flow, the net increase or decrease in cash and cash equivalents must be calculated.

The opening and closing cash and cash equivalent balances are also included.

Required

Complete the statement of cash flows for Silver Ltd by including cash and cash equivalents at the beginning and end of the period and the net cash increase in cash and cash equivalents for the year ended 31 December 20X2.

Reconciliation of profit before tax to net cash from operating activities

	£000
Profit before tax	284
Adjustments for:	
Depreciation	90
Loss on sale of property, plant and equipment	13
Finance costs	66
Dividends received	(43)
Adjustment in respect of inventories (150 – 102)	(48)
Adjustment in respect of trade receivables (390 – 315)	(75)
Adjustment in respect of trade payables (227 – 199)	28
Cash generated from operations	315
Interest paid	(66)
Tax paid	(110)
Net cash from operating activities	139

Statement of cash flows for the year ended 31 December 20X2

	£000
Net cash from operating activities	139
Investing activities	
Proceeds on disposal of property, plant and equipment (W)	32
Purchases of property, plant and equipment (W)	(210)
Dividends received	43

	£000
Net cash used in investing activities	(135)
Financing activities	
Proceeds of share issue (160 – 100)	60
Proceeds from bank loans (100 – 0)	100
Dividends paid	(100)
Net cash from financing activities	60
Net increase in cash and cash equivalents	
Cash and cash equivalents at the beginning of the year	
Cash and cash equivalents at the end of the year	

4 Assessment tasks

4.1 Format

There is a lot of information provided in this type of task, including:

- Statement of profit or loss and other comprehensive income
- Statement of financial position (including a comparative year)
- Further information

The requirements to prepare a 'reconciliation of profit before tax to net cash from operating activities' and a 'statement of cash flows' may be split into parts (a) and (b). However, you may find it more efficient to work on the proformas together.

4.2 Approach

When you are preparing a statement of cash flows it is important to have a logical technique.

A recommended approach is to:

(1) Read the requirement and the scenario information.

(2) Consider the additional information. Which numbers in the statement of financial position and statement of profit or loss and other comprehensive income are affected by this?

(3) Work down the statement of financial position, transferring numbers to the proformas or a working. Take account of the additional information.

(4) Work down the statement of profit or loss, transferring numbers to the proformas or a working. Take account of the additional information.

(5) Total your statement of cash flows.

(6) If it doesn't balance, don't worry! It is likely you still have enough marks to obtain competency in the task. Time permitting, you could review your workings to see if you can identify any necessary adjustments.

4.3 Assessment-standard question

Now that we have considered the knowledge and techniques required to be successful in this topic we will work through a full *Financial Statements of Limited Companies* assessment-standard question.

Activity 6: Statement of cash flow – Emma Ltd

The summarised accounts of Emma Ltd for the year ended 31 December 20X8 are as follows:

Emma Ltd
Statement of profit or loss for the year ended 31 December 20X8

	£000
Revenue	600
Cost of sales	(319)
Gross profit	281
Dividends received	45
Gain on disposal of property, plant and equipment	15
Distribution costs	(120)
Administrative expenses	(126)
Profit from operations	95
Finance costs	(8)
Profit before tax	87
Tax	(31)
Profit for the year	56

Emma Ltd
Statement of financial position as at 31 December 20X8

	20X8 £000	20X7 £000
ASSETS		
Non-current assets		
Property, plant and equipment	628	514
Current assets		
Inventories	214	210
Trade receivables	168	147
Cash and cash equivalents	7	0
	389	357
Total assets	1,017	871
EQUITY AND LIABILITIES		
Equity		
Share capital (£1 ordinary shares)	250	200
Share premium account	180	160
Retained earnings	314	282
	744	642
Non-current liabilities		
Bank loans	80	50
Current liabilities		
Bank overdraft	0	14
Trade payables	136	121
Tax liability	57	44
	193	179
Total liabilities	273	229
Total equity and liabilities	1,017	871

Further information:

- The total depreciation charge for the year was £42,000.

- Property, plant and equipment costing £33,000 with accumulated depreciation of £13,000 were sold in the year.

- All sales and purchases were on credit. Other expenses were paid for in cash.

- A dividend of £24,000 was paid during the year.

Required

(a) Prepare a reconciliation of profit before tax to net cash from operating activities for Emma Ltd for the year ended 31 December 20X8.

(b) Prepare the statement of cash flows for Emma Ltd for the year ended 31 December 20X8.

Note. You don't need to use the workings tables to achieve full marks on the task but the data entered into the working tables will be taken into consideration if you make errors in the proformas.

Reconciliation of profit before tax to net cash from operating activities

		£000
	▼	
Adjustments for:		
	▼	
	▼	
	▼	
	▼	
	▼	
	▼	
	▼	
Cash generated from operations		
	▼	
	▼	

Picklist:

Adjustment in respect of inventories
Adjustment in respect of trade payables
Adjustment in respect of trade receivables
Depreciation
Dividends received
Gain on disposal of property, plant and equipment
Finance costs
Interest paid
Profit before tax
Profit from operations
Profit for the year
Tax paid

Note. In the assessment picklists will also be provided for the on-screen workings.

Statement of cash flows for the year ended 31 December 20X8

	£000
Net cash from operating activities	
Investing activities	
▽	
▽	
▽	
Net cash used in investing activities	
Financing activities	
▽	
▽	
▽	
Net cash from financing activities	
▽	
▽	
▽	

Picklist:

Cash and cash equivalents at the beginning of the year
Cash and cash equivalents at the end of the year
Dividends paid
Dividends received
Net increase in cash and cash equivalents
Proceeds from bank loans
Proceeds on disposal of property, plant and equipment
Proceeds from issue of share capital
Purchases of property, plant and equipment

Workings (not provided in the assessment)

Tax paid	£000

Workings (on-screen proforma provided in the assessment)

Proceeds on disposal of property, plant and equipment	£000

Purchases of property, plant and equipment	£000

5 Statement of cash flows – direct method

As we have seen, IAS 7 provides a choice in the method used to report cash flows from operating activities. The direct method requires companies to look back to their accounting records and extract information relating to gross cash receipts and gross cash payments.

The IASB encourages use of the direct method where the necessary information is not too costly to obtain, as it provides additional information to users of the financial statements.

However, it is not mandatory under IAS 7 and therefore in practice it is rarely used.

In the assessment you will not be asked to draft a statement of cash flows using this method. However, you do need to understand how cash flows from operating activities are reported under the direct method.

A proforma for the direct method is as follows:

	£
Cash receipts from customers (W)	X
Cash paid to suppliers and employees (W)	(X)
Cash generated from operations	X
Interest paid	(X)
Tax paid	(X)
Net cash from operating activities	X

The figure for 'cash generated from operations' will be exactly the same as under the indirect method. Also, interest paid and tax paid are calculated in exactly the same way as under the indirect method.

The calculation of cash receipts from customers and cash paid to suppliers and employees will be explained through an illustration.

Illustration 2 – Cash generated from operations

Extracts to the financial statements of Jane Ltd for the year ended 31 December 20X1 are as follows:

Jane Ltd
Statement of profit or loss and other comprehensive income (extract) for the year ended 31 December 20X1

	£
Revenue	80,500
Cost of sales	(39,400)
Gross profit	41,100
Other expenses	(23,000)
Profit from operations	18,100

Jane Ltd
Statement of financial position (extract) as at 31 December 20X1

	20X1 £	20X0 £
Current assets		
Inventories	16,000	15,300
Trade receivables	23,250	20,450
Current liabilities		
Trade payables	13,000	11,350

Further information:

- Other expenses includes depreciation of £5,000 and a loss on disposal of a non-current asset of £200.

- Interest paid is £2,000.

- Tax paid is £3,000.

Required

Calculate the cash generated from operations using the direct method for Jane Ltd for the year ended 31 December 20X1.

Step 1 **Calculate cash received from customers by reconstructing the receivables account**

	£
Trade receivables balance b/d	20,450
Revenue	80,500
Trade receivables balance c/d	(23,250)
Cash received	77,700

Step 2 **Calculate purchases**

	£
Cost of sales (SPL)	39,400
Add closing inventories (SOFP)	16,000
Less opening inventories (SOFP)	(15,300)
	40,100
Operating expenses (SPL)	23,000
Less depreciation	(5,000)
Less loss on disposal of non-current assets	(200)
Purchases	57,900

Step 3 **Calculate cash paid to suppliers and employees by reconstructing the trade payables account**

	£000
Trade payables balance b/d	11,350
Purchases (Step 2 – working)	57,900
Trade payables balance c/d	(13,000)
Cash paid	56,250

Step 4   Calculate net cash from operating activities

	£000
Cash receipts from customers (W)	77,700
Cash paid to suppliers and employees (W)	(56,250)
Cash generated from operations	21,450
Interest paid	(2,000)
Tax paid	(3,000)
Net cash from operating activities	16,450

Therefore, where companies use the direct method to calculate net cash from operating activities, this final proforma will replace the **reconciliation of profit before tax to net cash from operating activities** seen under the indirect method.

6 How useful is the statement of cash flows?

6.1 Useful information provided by a statement of cash flows

Most people agree that the statement of cash flows provides useful information. It alerts users to possible liquidity problems by highlighting inflows and outflows of cash.

IAS 7 (para. 4) explains that a statement of cash flows, used together with the rest of the financial statements, can help users to assess:

- The changes in an entity's net assets and its liquidity and solvency
- An entity's ability to generate cash and cash equivalents and to affect the amounts and timing of cash flows in order to adapt to changing circumstances

There are other advantages of presenting a statement of cash flows:

- It shows an entity's ability to turn profit into cash (by allowing users to compare profit with cash flows from operating activities).
- Cash flow is a matter of fact and is difficult to manipulate.
- Cash flow information is not affected by an entity's choice of accounting policies or by judgement.
- The statement may help users to predict future cash flows.
- Cash flow is easier to understand than profit.
- The standard format enables users to compare the cash flows of different entities.

6.2 Limitations of the statement of cash flows

There are some important limits to the usefulness of the statement of cash flows:

(a) Cash balances are measured at a point in time and, therefore, they can be manipulated. For example, customers may be offered prompt payment discounts or other incentives to make early payment, or an entity may delay paying suppliers until after the year end. These are legitimate ways of managing cash flow (which is part of stewardship), but users may not be aware that this is being done, and may believe that the entity's position is better than it actually is.

(b) A high bank balance is not necessarily a sign of good cash management. Entities sometimes have to sacrifice cash flow in the short term to generate profits in the longer term by, for example, purchasing new plant and equipment. A business must have cash if it is to survive in the short term; if it is to survive in the longer term it must also make a profit. Focusing on cash may mean that an entity has a healthy bank balance but makes a loss.

(c) The statement of cash flows is based on historical information and, therefore, it is not necessarily a reliable indicator of future cash flows.

Neither the statement of profit or loss and other comprehensive income nor the statement of cash flows provides a complete picture of an entity's performance or position by itself.

6.3 Interpreting the statement of cash flows

You may wish to come back to this section after you have studied interpretation of financial statements in Chapter 11.

Assessment focus point

You may be asked to interpret a statement of cash flows in the assessment. This can be done by simple observation.

Look at the net cash flow for the period and then at each category of cash flows in turn.

Net cash flow for the period

- Has cash increased or decreased in the period?

- How material is the increase/decrease in cash compared with the entity's cash balances?

- Does the entity have a positive cash balance or an overdraft?

A decrease in cash is not always a bad sign, particularly if the entity has used the cash to finance capital expenditure or has used surplus cash to purchase liquid resources.

Operating activities

- Have inventories, receivables and payables increased or decreased?

A material increase in working capital is a worrying sign, particularly if the entity has a cash outflow from operating activities.

Interest, tax and dividends

Is there enough cash to cover:

- Interest payments?
- Taxation?
- Dividends?

As well as looking at the current period's cash outflows, look at the liabilities in the statement of financial position, if this information is available; these are the next period's cash outflows.

Remember that interest and corporation tax have to be paid when they are due, but the entity can delay payment of equity dividends until the cash is available.

Investing activities

A cash outflow to purchase assets is usually a good sign, because the assets will generate profits (and cash inflows) in future periods.

If there has been capital expenditure, where has the cash come from? Usually it will have come from several sources: operations; issuing shares or loan stock; taking out a loan; taking out an overdraft.

If the entity has taken out or increased an overdraft, this is usually a worrying sign. In theory, a bank overdraft is repayable on demand.

Financing activities

Ask the following questions:

(a) Is debt increasing or decreasing?

(b) Will the entity be able to pay its debt interest?

(c) Will the entity be able to repay the debt (if it falls due in the near future)?

(d) Is the entity likely to need additional long-term finance? (This might be the case if the bank overdraft is rapidly increasing or nearing its limit, or if the entity has plans to expand in the near future.)

Assessment focus point

When writing your answer to a question on interpretation of the statement of cash flows, the same points apply as for ratio analysis. So don't just say that cash has increased, but consider where the cash has come from. If the cash increase has come mainly from operations, that is a healthier source in the long term than if it has come from the one-off sale of a property, for example. Conversely, cash may have decreased or only increased by a small amount because of investment in a new plant, which may well generate profits and future cash flows.

You should refer to the Skills Bank at the beginning of this Course Book for advice on tackling written questions.

Activity 7: Interpreting the statement of cash flows

Norwood Ltd made a profit from operations of £140,000 but cash generated from operations for the same year was £160,000.

Required

Which of the following is a possible reason for this?

A bonus issue of shares	
An increase in inventories	
An increase in trade payables	
An increase in a long-term loan	

Chapter summary

- Businesses need cash in order to survive.

- Users of the financial statements need information about the liquidity, solvency and financial adaptability of an entity: this is provided by a statement of cash flows.

- IAS 7 requires all companies to include a statement of cash flows in their published financial statements.

- Cash inflows and outflows must be presented under standard headings:

  - Cash flows from operating activities
  - Cash flows from investing activities
  - Cash flows from financing activities

- IAS 7 also requires a note analysing changes in cash and cash equivalents.

- There are two methods of calculating net cash flow from operating activities:

  - List and total the actual cash flows: the direct method
  - Adjust profit for non-cash items: the indirect method

- IAS 7 allows either method.

- Main advantages of cash flow information:

  - It shows an entity's liquidity, solvency and financial adaptability.

  - It allows users to compare profit with net cash flow from operating activities.

  - Cash flow is difficult to manipulate.

  - It is not affected by accounting policies or by estimates.

- Limitations of cash flow information:

  - Cash balances can be manipulated.

  - Businesses need to make profits as well as generate cash: short-term cash management may affect profit in the longer term.

  - It is based on historical information.

- To interpret a statement of cash flows: use simple observation; look at the net cash flow for the period and at each category of cash flows in turn.

Keywords

- **Cash equivalents:** Short-term, highly liquid investments that are readily convertible to known amounts of cash and which are subject to an insignificant risk of changes in value

- **Cash flows:** Inflows and outflows of cash and cash equivalents

- **Cash:** Cash in hand and demand deposits (normally) less overdrafts repayable on demand

- **Financing activities:** Activities that result in changes in the size and composition of the contributed equity (share capital) and borrowings of the entity

- **Gross cash flows:** The individual cash flows that make up the net cash flows reported under each of the headings in the statement of cash flows

- **Investing activities:** The acquisition and disposal of long-term assets and other investments not included in cash equivalents

- **Net cash flows:** The total cash flows reported under each of the standard headings in the statement of cash flows

- **Operating activities:** The principal revenue-producing activities of the entity and other activities that are not investing or financing activities

- **Statement of cash flows:** Primary statement that summarises all movements of cash into and out of a business during the reporting period

1 IAS 7 requires all companies to present a statement of cash flows.

Is this statement true or false?

True	
False	

2 **Which of the following items does not meet the IAS 7 definition of cash?**

Bank current account in foreign currency	
Bank overdraft	
Petty cash float	
Short-term deposit	

3 Listed below are four transactions that will result in cash inflows or outflows.
Complete the table to show the way in which each of the cash flows should be classified in the statement of cash flows.

Transactions:

(a) Increase in short-term deposits classified as cash equivalents
(b) Issue of ordinary share capital
(c) Receipt from sale of property, plant and equipment
(d) Tax paid

Classification	Items
Operating activities	
Investing activities	
Financing activities	
Increase/decrease in cash and cash equivalents	

4 (a) Alexander plc has calculated net cash flow from operating activities by listing and totalling the actual cash flows as shown below:

	£000
Cash receipts from customers	32,450
Cash paid to suppliers and employees	(26,500)
Cash generated from operations	5,950
Interest paid	(300)
Tax paid	(800)
Net cash from operating activities	4,850

This method of calculating and presenting net cash from operating activities is called:

The direct method	
The indirect method	

(b)   IAS 7 does not allow the method illustrated above.

Is this statement true or false?

True	
False	

5   The following information relates to the property, plant and equipment of Bromley Ltd:

	20X2	20X1
	£	£
Cost	480,000	400,000
Accumulated depreciation	(86,000)	(68,000)
Carrying amount at 31 December	394,000	332,000

During the year ended 31 December 20X2 an asset, which had originally cost £20,000 and had a carrying amount of £8,000, was sold for £5,600.

(a)   What amount should be included in the statement of cash flows for the year ended 31 December 20X2 under the heading 'investing activities'?

Cash inflow of £5,600	
Cash outflow of £64,400	
Cash outflow of £94,400	
Cash outflow of £100,000	

(b)   What amount of depreciation should be added back to profit before tax in the reconciliation of profit before tax to net cash from operating activities?

£6,000	
£18,000	
£26,000	
£30,000	

6 The statement of financial position of Orion Ltd as at 30 June 20X5 is provided below, together with comparative figures:

| | 20X5 | | 20X4 | |
	£000	£000	£000	£000
ASSETS				
Non-current assets				
Property, plant and equipment		2,030		1,776
Current assets				
Inventories	1,009		960	
Trade and other receivables	826		668	
Cash	25		100	
		1,860		1,728
Total assets		3,890		3,504
EQUITY AND LIABILITIES				
Equity				
Share capital		1,200		1,200
Share premium		200		200
Retained earnings		1,171		1,028
		2,571		2,428
Non-current liabilities				
Long-term loan		610		460
Current liabilities				
Trade and other payables	641		563	
Tax liabilities	68		53	
		709		616
Total liabilities		1,319		1,076
Total equity and liabilities		3,890		3,504

Further information:

(a) No non-current assets were sold during the year. The depreciation charge for the year amounted to £305,000.

(b) The profit before tax for the year ended 30 June 20X5 was £270,000. Interest of £62,000 was charged in the year. The tax charge for the year was £68,000.

(c) A dividend of £59,000 was paid during the year.

(a) Prepare a reconciliation of profit before tax to net cash from operating activities for Orion Ltd for the year ended 30 June 20X5.

(b) Prepare a statement of cash flows for Orion Ltd for the year ended 30 June 20X5.

(Complete the left-hand columns by writing in the correct line item or narrative from the list provided.)

Reconciliation of profit before tax to net cash from operating activities for the year ended 30 June 20X5

		£000
	▼	
	▼	
	▼	
	▼	
	▼	
Cash generated from operations		
	▼	
	▼	
Net cash from operating activities		

Picklist:

Depreciation
Finance costs
Increase/decrease in inventories
Increase/decrease in receivables
Increase/decrease in trade payables
Interest paid
Profit before tax
Tax paid

Statement of cash flows for the year ended 30 June 20X5

	£000	£000
Net cash from operating activities		
Investing activities:		
▼		
Net cash used in investing activities		
Financing activities:		
▼		
▼		
Net cash from financing activities		
Net increase/(decrease) in cash and cash equivalents for the year		
Cash and cash equivalents at the beginning of the year		
Cash and cash equivalents at the end of the year		

Picklist:

Dividends paid
Increase/decrease in long-term loan
Purchase of property, plant and equipment

Working

Property, plant and equipment	£000
▼	
▼	
▼	

Picklist:

Depreciation
Property, plant and equipment at the beginning of the year
Property, plant and equipment at the end of the year

7 The statement of cash flows of Keynes Ltd is shown below.

Reconciliation of profit before tax to net cash from operating activities for the year ended 31 December 20X5

	£000
Profit before tax	3,654
Adjustments for:	
Depreciation	1,400
Finance costs	560
Decrease in inventories	280
Increase in receivables	(910)
Increase in trade payables	32
Cash generated from operations	5,016
Interest paid	(560)
Tax paid	(1,170)
Net cash from operating activities	3,286

Statement of cash flows for the year ended 31 December 20X5

	£000	£000
Net cash from operating activities		3,286
Investing activities		
Purchase of property, plant and equipment	(2,830)	
Proceeds on disposal of property, plant and equipment	96	
		(2,734)
Net cash used in investing activities		
Financing activities		
Repayment of loan stock	(310)	
Dividends paid	(480)	
Net cash used in financing activities		(790)
Net decrease in cash and cash equivalents for the year		(238)

	£000	£000
Cash and cash equivalents at the beginning of the year		240
Cash and cash equivalents at the end of the year		2

Prepare brief notes to answer the questions below.

Do you think that the company is having problems in managing its cash flow? If not, can you explain why?

Property, plant and equipment

6

Learning outcomes

1.1	**Explain the regulatory framework that underpins financial reporting**
	• The purpose of financial statements
2.1	**Examine the effect of international accounting standards on the preparation of financial statements**
	• Explain the effect of international accounting standards on the presentation, valuation and disclosure of items within the financial statements
	• Make any supporting calculations
3.1	**Draft a statement of profit or loss and other comprehensive income**
	• Make appropriate entries in the statement in respect of information extracted from a trial balance and additional information
3.2	**Draft a statement of financial position**
	• Make appropriate entries in the statement in respect of information extracted from a trial balance and additional information

Assessment context

Tangible non-current assets are frequently examined as an adjustment in the accounts preparation tasks. The topic is also tested in short-term, objective-style requirements and in written questions.

Qualification context

IAS 16 *Property, Plant and Equipment* was introduced in the Level 3 accounting papers. The principles of recognising non-current assets, charging depreciation and recording the disposal of non-current assets are assumed knowledge.

Business context

Virtually all businesses own non-current assets. They must be recorded accurately in the financial statements.

Chapter overview

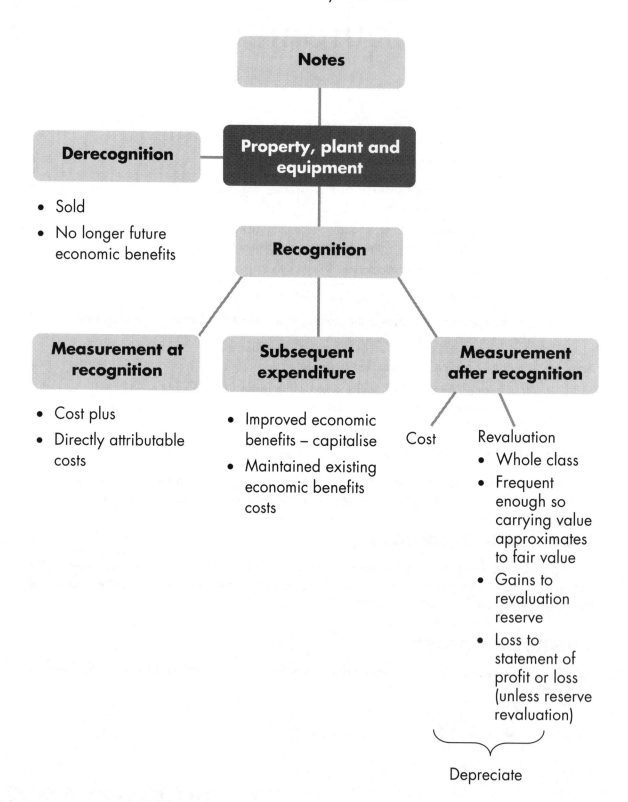

- Policy
- Reconciliation of opening and closing balances by asset class

Notes

Property, plant and equipment

Derecognition

- Sold
- No longer future economic benefits

Recognition

Measurement at recognition

- Cost plus
- Directly attributable costs

Subsequent expenditure

- Improved economic benefits – capitalise
- Maintained existing economic benefits costs

Measurement after recognition

Cost

Revaluation
- Whole class
- Frequent enough so carrying value approximates to fair value
- Gains to revaluation reserve
- Loss to statement of profit or loss (unless reserve revaluation)

Depreciate

Introduction

This is the first of three chapters that deal with the requirements of accounting standards. In this chapter we look at the accounting treatment of tangible non-current assets, as set out in IAS 16 *Property, Plant and Equipment.*

In the assessment, you may be asked to apply the requirements of IAS 16 in making adjustments to the trial balance when drafting financial statements. Another common type of assessment task is to explain the required accounting treatment, often to a non-accountant or someone with limited knowledge of accountancy. The accounting treatment of **property, plant and equipment** is also a popular subject for objective test or short-answer questions (for example, multiple choice or true/false). This means that you must understand the requirements of IAS 16 and be prepared to apply them to a practical situation.

1 Property, plant and equipment (IAS 16)

IAS 16 sets out the way in which items of property, plant and equipment should be treated in the financial statements.

Property, plant and equipment are tangible items that:

- Are held for use in the production or supply of goods or services, for rental to others, or for administrative purposes; and

- Are expected to be used during more than one period (IAS 16: para. 6).

'Tangible' means that the item has physical substance.

The cost of an item of property, plant and equipment should be recognised as an asset if (IAS 16: para. 7):

- It is probable that future economic benefits associated with the item will flow to the entity; and

- The cost of the item can be measured reliably.

2 Initial measurement

2.1 Cost

When an item of property, plant or equipment is first recognised it should be measured at its cost.

The **cost of an asset** is its:

- Purchase price (including any import duties and non-refundable taxes) (IAS 16: para. 16)

- Less any trade discounts (IAS 16: para. 16)

- Plus any directly attributable costs (IAS 16: para. 17)

'Directly attributable costs' are costs incurred to move the asset to the necessary location and to get it ready for use.

Directly attributable costs:

Include	Exclude
• Costs of employees involved in constructing the item • Costs of site preparation • Initial delivery and handling costs • Installation and assembly costs • Costs of testing whether the asset is functioning properly • Professional fees	• Administrative or general overhead costs • Advertising or staff training costs

Activity 1: Purchase of property, plant and equipment

A company purchased a machine at a cost of £28,000. Delivery costs totalled £2,000, the cost of installing the machine was £3,500 and there were also general administrative expenses of £5,200 in connection with the purchase.

Required

According to IAS 16 *Property, Plant and Equipment*, what amount should be recognised as the cost of the machine?

£28,000	
£30,000	
£33,500	
£38,700	

Working

	£

2.2 Subsequent expenditure

During its life, an item of property, plant and equipment may need to be maintained, improved or upgraded. The costs of repairs, maintenance and small parts should be expensed.

Where the expenditure improves the performance of an asset, there will be improved future economic benefit and, therefore, the cost should be added to the cost of the asset.

Examples include:

- The cost of modifying plant to increase its useful economic life
- The cost of upgrading machine parts to achieve a substantial improvement in the quality of output

3 Measurement after recognition

IAS 16 allows a choice of measurement method after an item of property, plant and equipment is first recognised. A company can adopt one of two methods:

- **Cost model**: an item is carried at historical cost less accumulated depreciation (IAS 16: para. 30)
- **Revaluation model**: an item is carried at **fair value** less any subsequent accumulated depreciation (IAS 16: para. 31–42)

Historical cost is the most common measurement after recognition. However, some assets (usually land and buildings) are included in the statement of financial position (SOFP) at their revalued amounts.

3.1 Revaluation

Fair value is defined by IAS 16 (following IFRS 13 *Fair Value Measurement*, Appendix A) as 'the price that would be received to sell an asset or paid to transfer a liability in an orderly transaction between market participants at the measurement date' (para. 6).

Fair value is usually taken to be the market value of the asset. A company can adopt the revaluation model if the fair value of an asset can be measured reliably. This should be done by a professional valuer.

3.2 Frequency of valuation

The frequency of revaluations depends on the changes in the fair values of the items or property, plant and equipment being revalued.

Revaluations should be made with sufficient frequency to ensure that the **carrying amount** of an item does not differ materially from its actual fair value at the year-end date.

IAS 16 (para. 36) states that if an item is revalued then the entire **class** of property, plant and equipment that the asset belongs to must be revalued. For example, if you revalue one building you have to revalue them all.

3.3 Accounting for revaluation gains

If the asset's carrying amount increases as a result of the revaluation the following entries are required:

Account name	Debit	Credit
Non-current asset cost account (to make cost equal to valuation)	✓	
Accumulated depreciation (to cancel all the previous depreciation)	✓	
Revaluation (SOFP/OCI)		✓

3.4 Other comprehensive income (OCI)

When a non-current asset is revalued the gain is unrealised.

In other words, the asset has not been sold, and therefore the gain has not been realised.

This means it is not included in profit or loss. Instead, the credit is included in other comprehensive income (OCI).

When an asset that has been revalued is sold, any remaining balance on the revaluation reserve is recognised in retained earnings as part of the gain on sale.

Illustration 1 – Revaluation gain

Upward Ltd purchased a freehold property for £400,000 on 1 January 20X1. At that date the property had a useful life of 50 years. On 31 December 20X3 the property was valued at £600,000 and the directors decided to incorporate this valuation in the financial statements for the year ended 31 December 20X3.

At 31 December 20X3, the carrying amount of the property (at historical cost) is:

	£000
Cost	400
Less accumulated depreciation (400 × 3/50)	(24)
	376

The double entry to record the revaluation is:

DEBIT	Freehold property: cost/valuation	£200,000	
DEBIT	Freehold property: accumulated depreciation	£24,000	
CREDIT	Revaluation reserve		£224,000

The note to the statement of financial position appears as follows:

	Freehold land and buildings £000
Cost at 1 January 20X3	400
Revaluation	200
Valuation at 31 December 20X3	600
Accumulated depreciation at 1 January 20X3	16
Charge for the year (400/50)	8
Revaluation	(24)
Accumulated depreciation at 31 December 20X3	–
Net carrying amount at 31 December 20X3	600
Net carrying amount at 1 January 20X3	384

The revaluation surplus of £224,000 is recognised in the statement of profit or loss and other comprehensive income as 'other comprehensive income' and in the statement of financial position as a revaluation reserve (revaluation surplus) within equity.

Activity 2: Revaluation gain

Walnut Ltd purchased a freehold property for £250,000 on 1 January 20X1. The useful life of the property was 40 years from that date. On 31 December 20X5 the property was revalued to £350,000.

Required

Show the double entry to record the revaluation.

Journal

Account name	Debit £	Credit £

Activity 3: Pisces Ltd – year ended 31 December 20X3

Pisces Ltd purchased a freehold property for £400,000 on 1 January 20X1. At that date the property had a useful economic life of 50 years.

On 31 December 20X3 the property was valued at £600,000 and the directors decided to incorporate this valuation in the financial statements for the year ended 31 December 20X3.

At 31 December 20X3, the carrying amount of the property at historical cost is:

	£
Cost	400,000
Less accumulated depreciation $(400 \times {}^3/_{50})$	(24,000)
	376,000

Required

Complete the financial statement extracts of Pisces Ltd for the year ended 31 December 20X3.

(a) Pisces Ltd

Statement of profit or loss and other comprehensive income for the year ended 31 December 20X3

	£
Revenue	300,000
Cost of sales	(100,000)
Gross profit	200,000
Distribution costs	(40,000)
Administrative expenses	(60,000)
Profit from operations	100,000
Finance costs	(14,000)
Profit before tax	86,000
Tax	(10,000)
Profit for the year from continuing operations	76,000
Other comprehensive income for the year	
Total comprehensive income for the year	

(b) Pisces Ltd

Statement of changes in equity for the year ended 31 December 20X3

	Share capital £	Revaluation reserve £	Retained earnings £	Total equity £
Balance at 1 January 20X3	100,000	0	30,000	130,000
Changes in equity				
Total comprehensive income				
Dividends			(10,000)	(10,000)
Balance at 31 December 20X3	100,000			

(c) Pisces Ltd

Statement of financial position as at 31 December 20X3

	£
ASSETS	
Non-current assets	
Property, plant and equipment	
EQUITY AND LIABILITIES	
Equity	
Share capital	100,000
Retained earnings	
Revaluation reserve	
Total equity	

Workings (not provided in the assessment)

Account name	Debit £	Credit £

(b)

3.5 Accounting for revaluation losses

If the revaluation decreases the carrying amount of the asset, then the entry should be made directly to the statement of profit or loss, as long as the asset has not previously been revalued (IAS 16: para. 40).

Account name	Debit	Credit
Statement of profit or loss	✓	
Accumulated depreciation (to cancel all the previous depreciation)	✓	
Non-current asset cost account (to make cost equal to valuation)		✓

Activity 4: Ray Ltd

Ray Ltd purchased a freehold property for £200,000 on 1 January 20X6. At that date the property had a useful economic life of 50 years. The asset was held at cost and depreciation is charged to administrative expenses.

At 31 December 20X7 the property was valued at £180,000.

Administrative expenses for the year are £50,000. The depreciation charge and revaluation loss have not yet been accounted for.

Required

Complete the statement of financial position extract and calculate administrative expenses for Ray Ltd for the year ended 31 December 20X7.

Ray Ltd
Statement of financial position (extract) as at 31 December 20X7

	£
ASSETS	
Non-current assets	

Administrative expenses for the year ended 31 December 20X7

	£

Workings

Property, plant and equipment – carrying amount prior to revaluation	£

Revaluation loss	£

Account name	Debit £	Credit £

However, if the asset was previously revalued upwards then the amount should first be debited to the revaluation reserve in the statement of changes in equity and any remaining amount taken directly to the statement of profit or loss.

Account name	Debit	Credit
Accumulated depreciation (to cancel all the previous depreciation)	✓	
Revaluation reserve (with a value equal to the credit balance)	✓	
Statement of profit or loss (balancing figure)	✓	
Non-current asset cost account (to make cost equal to valuation)		✓

Illustration 2 – Revaluation loss

Downward Ltd purchased some land for £500,000 on 1 January 20X1. On 31 December 20X3 the land was valued at £750,000 and the directors decided to incorporate this valuation in the financial statements. On 31 December 20X5 the land was valued at £450,000.

Land is not depreciated, so the double entry to record the upward revaluation on 31 December 20X3 is:

DEBIT   Land: cost/valuation   £250,000

CREDIT   Revaluation reserve   £250,000

A revaluation loss of £300,000 must be recognised in the financial statements for the year ended 31 December 20X5. The loss is first set against the balance of £250,000 on the revaluation reserve and recognised as a loss in other comprehensive income. The remaining £50,000 is recognised as a loss in profit or loss.

The double entry to record the downward revaluation is:

DEBIT   Revaluation reserve   £250,000

DEBIT   Profit or loss   £50,000

CREDIT   Land: cost/valuation   £300,000

Activity 5: Pisces Ltd – year ended 31 December 20X4

On 1 January 20X4 Pisces Ltd has a freehold property carried in the accounting records at £600,000. The asset has previously been revalued, with a gain of £224,000 credited to the revaluation reserve.

Depreciation for the year of £12,766 has already been charged to administrative expenses.

Administrative expenses are £50,000 per the draft financial statements.

At 31 December 20X4, the carrying amount of the property at valuation is:

	£
Freehold property at valuation at 1 January 20X4	600,000
Less depreciation to 31 December 20X4	(12,766)
	587,234

On 31 December 20X4 the property was valued at £350,000. This revaluation has not yet been accounted for.

Required

Complete the financial statement extracts of Pisces Ltd for the year ended 31 December 20X4.

(a) **Pisces Ltd**

Statement of profit or loss and other comprehensive income for the year ended 31 December 20X4

	£
Revenue	400,000
Cost of sales	(200,000)
Gross profit	200,000
Distribution costs	(30,000)
Administrative expenses	
Profit from operations	
Finance costs	(14,000)
Profit before tax	
Tax	(10,000)
Profit for the year from continuing operations	
Other comprehensive (loss)/income for the year	
Total comprehensive (loss)/income for the year	

(b) **Pisces Ltd**

Statement of changes in equity for the year ended 31 December 20X4

	Share capital £	Revaluation reserve £	Retained earnings £	Total equity £
Balance at 1 January 20X4	100,000	224,000	96,000	420,000
Changes in equity				
Total comprehensive income (loss)/(income)				
Dividends			(10,000)	(10,000)
Balance at 31 December 20X4	100,000			

(c) Pisces Ltd

Statement of financial position (extract) as at 31 December 20X4

	£
ASSETS	
Non-current assets	
Property, plant and equipment	
EQUITY AND LIABILITIES	
Equity	
Share capital	100,000
Retained earnings	
Revaluation reserve	
Total equity	

Workings (not provided in the assessment)

Account name	Debit £	Credit £

3.6 Disclosure requirements for revalued PPE

IAS 16 (para. 77) requires certain disclosures for items of PPE stated at revalued amounts:

(a) The effective date of the revaluation

(b) Whether an independent valuer was involved

(c) For each revalued class of property, the carrying amount that would have been recognised had the assets been carried under the cost model

(d) The revaluation surplus, including changes during the period and any restrictions on the distribution of the balance to shareholders

3.7 Depreciation (recap)

Depreciation is covered in depth in the AAT Level 3 courses and is assumed knowledge for Level 4 *Financial Statements of Limited Companies*. The key principles will be recapped, as they may be tested in a short-form or written task.

Depreciation is defined by IAS 16 (para. 6) as 'the systematic allocation of the **depreciable amount** of an asset over its **useful life**'.

The purpose of depreciation is to allocate the cost (or fair value) of an asset to the accounting periods expected to benefit from its use. It is an example of the accruals concept.

Each part of an asset that forms a significant part of the total cost should be depreciated separately.

For example, an aeroplane's engine may have a useful life of 5 years, whereas the other components of the aeroplane have a useful life of 15 years. Therefore, the aeroplane's engine will be depreciated separately.

All tangible non-current assets are to be depreciated (with the exception of land), whether they are held at cost or fair value, unless the **residual value** exceeds the carrying amount (IAS 16: para. 50).

An entity should select a depreciation method that most accurately reflects the manner in which the entity consumes the economic benefit of the asset (IAS 16: para. 62). The two most common methods are straight line and diminishing balance.

The depreciation charge will be recognised in the statement of profit or loss. It will be allocated to cost of sales, distribution expenses and administrative expenses or, depending on the function, to the underlying asset.

When deciding on the useful life of an asset, a company should take into account the expected wear and tear, expected obsolescence, expiry date and expected usage of the asset.

On an annual basis, the company must review the residual values and depreciation methods used for all non-current assets (IAS 16: para. 61).

If a useful life is revised, the carrying amount of the asset at the date of revision should be depreciated over the revised remaining useful life.

A change in estimated residual value should be accounted for prospectively over the asset's remaining useful life.

Illustration 3 – Review of useful life

On 1 January 20X1 Hazel Ltd purchased a machine for £20,000. The machine was depreciated over ten years, using the straight line method.

On 1 January 20X3, the directors reviewed the useful life of the machine and came to the conclusion that it was only five years from that date.

Calculate the depreciation charge for the year ended 31 December 20X3.

£ [   ]

Solution

£ | 3,200

Carrying amount at 1 January 20X3:

	£
Cost	20,000
Accumulated depreciation (£20,000 × 2/10):	(4,000)
	16,000

Depreciation charge for the year ended 31 December 20X3 is £16,000 ÷ 5 = £3,200.

3.8 Changing the method of depreciation

The depreciation methods used should be reviewed at least at each year end. If there has been a significant change in the expected pattern of consumption of the future economic benefits associated with the asset, the method should be changed to reflect the changed pattern.

A change in the method of depreciation is a change in an accounting estimate, not a change in accounting policy.

The carrying amount of the asset is depreciated using the new method over the asset's remaining useful life, beginning in the period in which the change is made.

Activity 6: Changing the method of depreciation

On 1 January 20X1 Hazel Ltd purchased a machine for £20,000. The machine was depreciated over ten years, using the straight line method.

On 1 January 20X3, the directors decided to change the method of depreciation, so that the machine was depreciated at 25% per annum on the reducing balance.

Required

Calculate the depreciation charge for the year ended 31 December 20X3.

£ [   ]

4 Derecognition

A tangible non-current asset should be derecognised (removed from the books) when it is sold, or when there are no more economic benefits to be gained from the asset.

The resulting gain or loss is recognised in cost of sales, administrative or distribution expenses, depending on the function of the underlying asset.

If the asset has previously been revalued and there is still a balance in the revaluation reserve relating to the asset, the balance is transferred out of the revaluation reserve and moved directly into retained earnings.

This transfer will be shown in the statement of changes in equity.

Activity 7: Disposals revision

On 1 January 20X1 Cashew Ltd purchased a building for £300,000. The useful life of the building was 50 years from that date.

On 1 January 20X4, the building was revalued to £500,000. The useful life of the building was deemed to be 50 years from the date of valuation.

On 31 December 20X7, the building was sold for £700,000.

Required

Calculate the gain on disposal.

£	

---

5 Notes to the financial statements

An accounting policy note should disclose the depreciation methods used and whether the company is using the cost model or the valuation model.

They should also disclose a reconciliation of the opening cost and accumulated depreciation to the closing cost and accumulated depreciation, by asset class.

- An item of property, plant and equipment is recognised if it is probable that future economic benefits associated with the item will flow to the entity, and if the cost of the item can be measured reliably.

- An item of property, plant and equipment is initially measured at its cost.

- After an item of property, plant and equipment is first recognised, it is either carried at cost (the cost model) or at fair value (the revaluation model). If an item is revalued, all assets of the same class must be revalued. Valuations must be kept up to date.

- Double entry to record a revaluation:

  DEBIT property, plant and equipment: cost/valuation with the difference between fair value and historical cost/previous valuation

  DEBIT property, plant and equipment: accumulated depreciation with the total depreciation charged on the asset to date

  CREDIT revaluation reserve with the difference between the revalued amount and carrying amount at historical cost/previous valuation

- Revaluation gains are reported in other comprehensive income and in equity (the revaluation reserve).

- The depreciable amount of an asset should be allocated on a systematic basis over its useful life.

- Where an asset has been revalued, the depreciation charge must be based on the revalued amount.

- The gain or loss on the disposal of an item of property, plant and equipment is the difference between the net sale proceeds and the carrying amount (whether this is based on historical cost or on a valuation).

Keywords

- **Carrying amount:** The amount at which an asset is recognised after deducting any accumulated depreciation (amortisation) and accumulated impairment losses

- **Class of assets:** A grouping of assets of a similar nature and use in the entity's operations

- **Cost of an asset:** Purchase price, including import duties and non-refundable purchase taxes, less any trade discounts or rebates, plus any further costs directly attributable to bringing the item to the location and condition necessary for it to be capable of operating in the manner intended by management

- **Depreciable amount:** The cost of an asset (or, where an asset is revalued, the revalued amount) less its residual value

- **Depreciation:** The systematic allocation of the depreciable amount of an asset over its useful life

- **Fair value:** The price that would be received to sell an asset in an orderly transaction between market participants at the measurement date

- **Property, plant and equipment:** Tangible items that are held for use in the production or supply of goods or services, for rental to others, or for administrative purposes; and which are expected to be used during more than one period

- **Residual value:** The estimated amount that an entity would currently obtain from disposal of the asset at the end of its useful life

- **Useful life:** The period over which an asset is expected to be available for use by an entity

1   Tarragon Ltd purchases an item of plant. As well as the purchase price of the plant itself, Tarragon Ltd has to incur the cost of installing the plant and testing it once it has been installed.

This additional expenditure should be included in the statement of financial position as part of the cost of the plant.

Is this statement true or false?

True	
False	

2   Sage Ltd incurs expenditure of £5,000 on repainting the outside of an office building.

This expenditure cannot be capitalised as part of the cost of the building.

Is this statement true or false?

True	
False	

3   Basil Ltd owns three properties. Information about these properties is shown below:

	Cost £000	Accumulated depreciation £000	Fair value £000
Property A	100	10	120
Property B	150	10	140
Property C	120	10	180

The properties are all currently carried in the company's statement of financial position at depreciated historical cost.

(a)   Property A and Property C can be carried at fair value, while Property B can be carried at historical cost.

Is this statement true or false?

True	
False	

(b)   Once the company has adopted a policy of revaluing property, plant and equipment, it must update the valuation annually.

Is this statement true or false?

True	
False	

(c) **Show the journal entry needed to incorporate the revaluations in the financial statements of Basil Ltd.**

Journal

Account name	Debit £	Credit £

4   IAS 16 *Property, Plant and Equipment* states that all entities should use the straight line method of depreciation.

Is this statement true or false?

True	
False	

5   On 1 January 20X1 a freehold property was purchased for £500,000. Its estimated useful life was 25 years at that date. On 1 January 20X6 the property was revalued to £600,000 and this revaluation was recognised in the financial statements. The useful life of the property remained unchanged. The property is depreciated using the straight line method.

What is the depreciation charge for the year ended 31 December 20X6?

£20,000	
£24,000	
£30,000	

6   On 1 January 20X1 Saffron Ltd purchased a building for £450,000. The useful life of the building was 40 years from that date.

On 1 January 20X5, the building was revalued to £540,000. The total useful life of the building was unchanged.

On 31 December 20X5, the building was sold for £575,000.

What is the gain on disposal?

£48,500	
£50,000	
£102,500	
£181,250	

Intangible assets and inventories

7

Learning outcomes

1.1	**Explain the regulatory framework that underpins financial reporting**
	• The purpose of financial statements
2.1	**Examine the effect of international accounting standards on the preparation of financial statements**
	• Explain the effect of international accounting standards on the presentation, valuation and disclosure of items within the financial statements
	• Make any supporting calculations
3.1	**Draft a statement of profit or loss and other comprehensive income**
	• Make appropriate entries in the statement in respect of information extracted from a trial balance and additional information
3.2	**Draft a statement of financial position**
	• Make appropriate entries in the statement in respect of information extracted from a trial balance and additional information
3.3	**Draft a statement of changes in equity**
	• Make appropriate entries in the statement in respect of information extracted from a trial balance and additional information or other financial statements provided

Assessment context

Inventories are frequently examined as an adjustment in the accounts preparation tasks. Intangible assets, impairment and inventories are also tested in short-form, objective-style requirements and in written questions.

Qualification context

Inventory was introduced in the Level 3 AAT accounting papers. Intangible assets and impairments are only examined in this *Financial Statements of Limited Companies* course.

Business context

Most companies (particularly manufacturing and retail businesses) will hold inventory. It needs to be recorded accurately in the financial statements. Many businesses hold intangible assets, and the issues around impairments are relevant to all companies with non-current assets.

Chapter overview

- Measure at lower of cost and net realisable value
- Cost = purchase cost and costs of conversion
- Net realisable value = estimated selling price less selling and distribution costs

Inventories

Intangible assets and inventories

Impairment

- Assets are recorded at lower of cost and recoverable amount
- Impairment loss is the amount by which the carrying amount of an asset exceeds recoverable amount

Intangible assets

- Identifiable non-monetary assets without physical substance

Recognised

- Intangible assets purchased separately
- Development expenditure meeting the PIRATE criteria

Not recognised

- Internally generated goodwill
- Research expenditure

Amortisation

- Amortisation is charged on assets with a finite useful life
- Assets with an indefinite useful life are not amortised

Introduction

This chapter covers the accounting treatment of **intangible assets** and **impairment** (loss of value) of assets and **inventories**.

As with the accounting treatment of property, plant and equipment covered in the previous chapter, you must understand the requirements of each of the accounting standards and be prepared to explain and apply them.

The relevant accounting standards are:

- IAS 38 *Intangible Assets*
- IAS 36 *Impairment of Assets*
- IAS 2 *Inventories*

1 Intangible assets (IAS 38)

An intangible asset is an identifiable, non-monetary asset that has no physical substance (IAS 38: para. 8).

'Identifiable' means that it:

- Can be sold separately without selling the business; or
- Arises from a contractual or legal right.

Examples include:

- **Goodwill**
- **Development** costs
- Brand names
- Licences
- Patents
- Computer software
- Trade marks

The recognition criteria are the same as for other non-current assets (IAS 38: para. 21):

- It is probable that the expected future economic benefits that are attributable to the asset will flow to the entity; and

- The cost of the asset can be measured reliably.

The economic benefits can be in the form of either increased revenue or reduced costs.

Remember, an asset is a resource controlled by the entity as a result of past events and from which future economic benefits are expected to flow to the entity (*Conceptual Framework*: Chapter 4, para. 8).

Activity 1: Staff

A company that develops and markets scientific equipment has several extremely well-qualified and talented members of staff. The company's success is undoubtedly the result of their work.

The company can recognise the staff or their expertise as an asset in the company's statement of financial position.

Required

Is this statement true or false?

True	
False	

1.1 Initial measurement – intangible assets purchased separately

Intangible assets may be **purchased separately** by the entity.

Intangible assets purchased separately are measured at cost (IAS 38: para. 24). For example, a licence to use computer software will be measured at cost.

Cost is the purchase price plus any directly attributable costs.

1.2 Initial measurement – goodwill

Goodwill is the excess of the value of a business over its individual assets and liabilities.

Goodwill may arise as a result of a number of factors, such as the reputation of the business or the skill of its management. It cannot exist independently of the business.

In accounting terms, there is a distinction between goodwill arising on the acquisition of another entity and **internally generated goodwill**.

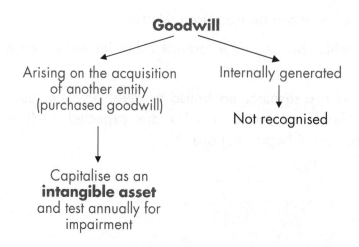

1.3 Goodwill arising on the acquisition of another entity (purchased goodwill)

When an entity acquires the shares or assets and liabilities of another entity it may be prepared to pay more than the entity is currently worth because it anticipates receiving future economic benefits from the acquisition which are over and above the fair value of the net assets acquired.

Goodwill is the excess payment made and can be defined as **the amount paid over and above the fair value of the identifiable net assets and liabilities acquired** (IFRS 3: Appendix A).

Illustration 1 – Goodwill

For example, XYZ Ltd buys an unincorporated business for £200,000. The fair value of its assets and liabilities is as follows:

	£
Property, plant and equipment	110,000
Net current assets	60,000
Non-current liabilities	(20,000)
	150,000

Therefore, as well as acquiring assets and liabilities for £150,000, XYZ Ltd has acquired goodwill worth £50,000.

It is recognised as an intangible asset because it has a cost to the business that has acquired it. It can be measured reliably because there has been a transaction in which it is calculated.

Purchased goodwill is outside the scope of IAS 38. It is governed by the accounting standard IFRS 3 *Business Combinations* and will be studied in the context of group accounts.

1.4 Internally generated goodwill

This is the goodwill a business generates over time. Most businesses will have some internally generated goodwill (eg reputation).

However, it **cannot** be recognised as an asset, because it cannot be measured reliably. It would be impossible to say with any certainty how much the goodwill in a business is worth, as its valuation is so subjective.

1.5 Research and development

Many companies spend large amounts on research and development projects. If these are successful, they result in new products or services that may provide significant income for many years to come.

Research and development expenditure may be an asset, rather than an expense, if it gives access to future economic benefits for the entity. There is an argument for treating it as an asset, capitalising it in the statement of financial position and matching it with the income that it produces in future accounting periods (applying the accruals concept).

On the other hand, it may be impossible to predict whether a project will give rise to future income or to precisely identify the future income if it is received. If this is the case the expenditure must be charged to profit or loss in the period in which it is incurred.

IAS 38 states that an entity should separate a research and development project into a **research phase** and a **development phase**.

Key term

Research is original and planned investigation undertaken with the prospect of gaining new scientific or technical knowledge and understanding. (IAS 38: para. 8)

Development is the application of research findings or other knowledge to a plan or design for the production of new or substantially improved materials, devices, products, processes, systems or services before the start of commercial production or use. (IAS 38: para. 8)

If an entity cannot distinguish between the research phase and the development phase of a project, it should treat the expenditure as if it were incurred in the research phase.

Research activities

IAS 38 gives the following examples:

- Activities aimed at obtaining new knowledge

- The search for, evaluation and final selection of applications of research findings and other knowledge

- The search for alternatives for materials, devices, products, processes, systems or services

- The formulation, design, evaluation and final selection of possible alternatives for new or improved materials, devices, products, processes, systems or services

Development activities

IAS 38 gives the following examples:

- The design, construction and testing of pre-production or pre-use prototypes and models

- The design of tools, jigs, moulds and dies involving new technology

- The design, construction and operation of a pilot plant that is not of a scale economically feasible for commercial production

- The design, construction and testing of a chosen alternative for new or improved materials, devices, products, processes, systems or services

1.6 Initial measurement – research and development

IAS 38 separates a research and development project into a research phase and a development phase. Initially, a project is **researched** (IAS 38: para. 54), and then it moves on to the **development** phase (IAS 38: para. 57).

Internally generated intangible assets

Research:

'costs incurred to gain new scientific or technical knowledge and understanding'

↓

Not recognised as an intangible asset, but shown as an expense in the statement of profit or loss

↓

No certainty of future economic benefits

Development:

'application of research findings to a plan/design for the production of new or substantially improved materials, products or processes prior to commercial production or use'

↓

Must recognise as an intangible asset once all 'PIRATE' criteria are met

↓

Probable future economic benefits will be generated by the asset
Intention to complete and use/sell asset
Resources (technical, financial) adequate to complete asset
Ability to use/sell asset
Technical feasibility of completing asset
Expenditure can be measured reliably

Activity 2: New process

A company has incurred expenditure of £50,000 in investigating a new process. It is hoped that the new process can eventually be adapted and used to manufacture Product Z more efficiently than at present, resulting in considerable cost savings. The project is at a very early stage and the outcome is uncertain.

In the financial statements, this expenditure should be:

Recognised as an intangible asset in the statement of financial position	
Recognised as an expense in profit or loss	

Assessment focus point

Research and development could be tested as a written question, or as a question that requires both explanation and calculations and to **'use the figures [...] to illustrate your answer where possible'**.

You should refer to the Skills Bank at the beginning of this Course Book for advice on tackling written questions.

1.7 Other internally generated intangible assets

IAS 38 (para. 63) states that internally generated brands, mastheads, publishing titles, customer lists and items similar in substance should not be recognised as intangible assets.

Activity 3: Brand

Fifteen years ago, a company developed a brand of self-raising flour. The brand has now become a household name and has captured a substantial share of the market. One of the directors has claimed that it is worth at least £10 million to the company.

The brand cannot be recognised as an intangible asset in the company's financial statements.

Required

Is this statement true or false?

True	
False	

1.8 Amortisation

Amortisation is the equivalent of depreciation, but for intangible assets. It works in the same way as depreciation.

Management need to assess the useful life of intangible assets, which can be finite or indefinite.

Finite life:
- Amortise the intangible asset on a systematic basis over the useful life

Indefinite life:
- No foreseeable limit to the period over which the asset is expected to generate cash inflows for the organisation
- Intangible asset is not amortised
- Useful life reassessed each year
- Impairment review conducted annually

The residual value of the asset is normally zero, as intangibles tend not to have a resale value at the end of their useful life. For example, a ten-year licence which is ten years old cannot really be sold!

Activity 4: Intangible assets

Required

(a) **Internally generated goodwill can be recognised as an intangible asset in accordance with IAS 38 *Intangible Assets*.**

   Is this statement true or false?

True	
False	

(b) **Which of the following are part of the development criteria which must be demonstrated for an asset to be recognised on the statement of financial position?**

Technical feasibility	
Expenditure reliably measured	
Initial investigation suggests the project may generate future economic benefits	
Intention to complete and use/sell asset	
Resources inadequate to complete project	

2 Impairment of assets (IAS 36)

2.1 Definition

An asset is impaired if its **carrying amount** (statement of financial position value) is greater than its **recoverable amount** (IAS 36: para. 18).

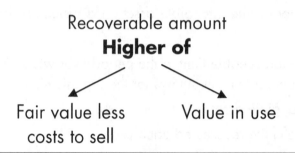

Recoverable amount
Higher of

Fair value less costs to sell   Value in use

Key term

> **Fair value less costs to sell** is the price that would be received to sell an asset in an orderly transaction between market participants, less the costs of disposal.
>
> **Value in use** is the present value of the future cash flows expected to be derived from the asset, as a result of continuing to use it in the business.
>
> For example, the cash flows which will arise from using the asset to produce goods or provide services for sale to customers.

An **impairment loss** is the amount by which the carrying amount of an asset exceeds its recoverable amount.

2.2 Impairment indicators

IAS 36 states that assets should be reviewed for impairment if there is some indication that impairment has occurred.

The standard gives a number of external and internal indicators of impairment (IAS 36: para. 12).

External sources	Internal sources
• A significant fall in the asset's market value	• Obsolescence or physical damage to the asset
• Adverse effects on the company caused by technology, markets, the economy or laws	• Adverse effects on the asset of a significant reorganisation within the company
• Increases in interest rates	• The economic performance of the asset is worse than expected
• The stock market value of the company is less than the carrying amount of net assets	• A fall in profit from operations
	• A fall in the cash flows from operations, or a negative cash flow
	• A fall in budgeted cash flows, or profits from operations

2.3 Recognising an impairment

If the recoverable amount is lower than the carrying amount, an impairment loss is recognised (IAS 36: para. 60).

If the asset is carried at historical cost:

Account name	Debit	Credit
Impairment loss (SPL)	✓	
Asset (SOFP)		✓

If the asset is carried at revalued amount:

Account name	Debit	Credit
Revaluation reserve (any previous revaluation reserve relating to that asset)	✓	
Impairment loss (SPL) (balancing figure)	✓	
Asset (SOFP)		✓

After the impairment, depreciation/amortisation will be recalculated and will continue to be deducted from the carrying amount.

Illustration 2 – Impairment review

Cumin Ltd carries out impairment reviews on three assets, details of which are as follows:

	Carrying amount £000	Fair value less costs of disposal £000	Value in use £000
Asset A	20	18	25
Asset B	25	20	22
Asset C	30	40	38

Step 1   Determine recoverable amount (the higher of **fair value less costs of disposal** and **value in use**)

- Asset A: £25,000 (value in use)
- Asset B: £22,000 (value in use)
- Asset C: £40,000 (fair value less costs of disposal)

Step 2   Compare recoverable amount with carrying amount. If the carrying amount is greater than the recoverable amount, there has been an impairment, and the carrying amount must be written down to the recoverable amount. Asset B is impaired, but not Asset A or Asset C.

Illustration 3 – Calculating impairment loss

Juniper Ltd bought a machine on 1 January 20X1. The machine cost £60,000 and had a useful life of 6 years. It was depreciated using the straight line method.

On 1 January 20X3 an impairment review was carried out, and the recoverable amount of the plant was estimated at £30,000. Its useful life was reviewed and was estimated to be two years at that date.

At 1 January 20X3 the carrying amount of the machine is:

	£
Cost	60,000
Less accumulated depreciation (two years)	(20,000)
	40,000

The recoverable amount of the machine is £30,000 and so an impairment loss of £10,000 is recognised in profit or loss. The double entry is:

DEBIT	Impairment loss	£10,000	
CREDIT	Plant and machinery: accumulated depreciation		£10,000

The remaining useful life of the machine is now 2 years and therefore the annual depreciation charge is now £15,000 (£30,000 ÷ 2).

The total charge to profit or loss for the year ended 31 December 20X3 is £25,000 (impairment loss of £10,000 and depreciation of £15,000).

If the impairment loss is material, it may need to be disclosed separately in a note to the financial statements.

Activity 5: Impairment

The directors of Thomas Ltd considered that a machine with a carrying amount of £30,000 may have become impaired. At present it could be sold for £22,000 and disposal costs would be £500. The directors estimate that the machine will generate cash flows with a net present value of £21,800 over the remainder of its useful life.

Required

(a) **At what amount must Thomas Ltd recognise the machine in its financial statements following the impairment review?**

£21,500	
£21,800	
£22,000	
£30,000	

BPP
LEARNING MEDIA

In July 20X5, Percy Ltd revalued a piece of land from a cost of £500,000 to its market value of £800,000. In July 20X8, due to a decline in the property market, the market value of the land fell to £440,000.

(b) **How much of the impairment loss should be recognised in the company's statement of profit or loss and other comprehensive income for the year ended 31 December 20X8?**

£Nil	
£60,000	
£300,000	
£360,000	

Gordon Ltd has three assets which the directors consider may have become impaired.

Asset	Carrying amount £	Fair value less costs to sell £	Value in use £
(i)	9,000	13,500	7,600
(ii)	7,000	6,500	6,750
(iii)	3,000	1,100	3,230

(c) **Which of the above assets is impaired?**

(ii) only	
(iii) only	
(ii) and (iii)	
(i), (ii) and (iii)	

Sweetie Ltd has four items of plant: sugar mixer, gum press, sweet wrapper and a peppermint maker.

There is a general slump in the sweet market; however, the demand for peppermints has far exceeded the budgeted sales and extra shifts have been introduced on the peppermint maker machine.

Due to the general slump in the sweet market, the financial director must conduct an impairment test on all four items of plant.

(d) **Is this statement true or false?**

True	
False	

2.4 Disclosure

The amount of any impairment loss recognised in the statement of profit or loss and other comprehensive income should be separately disclosed in the notes to the financial statements.

> **Assessment focus point**
>
> Impairment could be tested as a written question, or as a question that requires both explanation and calculation. One of the AAT's sample assessments had the requirement to **'explain, with reasons'** how an impairment should be treated in the financial statement and to **'use the figures [...] to illustrate your answer where possible'**.
>
> You should refer to the Skills Bank at the beginning of the Course Book for advice on tackling written questions.

3 Inventories (IAS 2)

Accounting for inventories was covered extensively in the Level 3 accounting papers (and recapped earlier in this course). The valuation of inventory could be tested as an adjustment to an accounts preparation question or in a short-form task. This will be considered here.

Inventories are current assets that are held for sale.

Companies often have inventories in various forms:

- Raw materials, for use in a manufacturing process
- Work-in-progress
- Finished goods, made by the business and ready for resale to customers
- Finished goods, which have been bought in by the business for resale

IAS 2 states (para. 2.9) that inventories should be valued at the lower of cost and **net realisable value**.

Cost = purchase price plus directly attributable costs

Net realisable value = selling prices less selling costs less costs to complete

Cost cannot include storage costs, abnormal costs (such as wastage) or administrative costs.

3.1 Methods of costing inventories

Where businesses purchase unique items (eg antiques, works of art), each individual item held by the business at the year end will be included in inventories at its actual cost.

However, businesses often purchase large quantities of identical items at regular intervals throughout the year (eg planks of wood). In this situation, it is very unlikely management knows the actual cost of each individual item in inventories at the year end.

There are various costing methods which may be used to establish the cost of closing inventory. Common methods are **first in, first out (FIFO)** and **weighted average (AVCO)**. **Last in, first out (LIFO)** is prohibited by international accounting standards.

Method	Description
First In, First Out (FIFO)	This assumes that items are used in the order in which they were received from suppliers. Therefore, the items in inventory are the most recent purchases.
Last In, First Out (LIFO)	This assumes that the most recent purchases are used first. Therefore, the items in inventory are the earliest purchases.
Weighted Average (AVCO)	After each purchase the weighted average cost of the inventory is calculated. The total cost of the items in inventory is divided by the total number of items in inventory. This average is taken as the cost of each item.

Activity 6: Inventories

Trevor Ltd holds three distinct types of inventory in its warehouse at the end of its accounting year, which are valued as follows:

Product	Cost (FIFO) £	Selling price £	Selling costs £
(i)	2,340	3,500	350
(ii)	1,760	2,250	500
(iii)	1,500	1,100	230
	5,600	6,850	1,080

Required

At what value should inventories be stated in Trevor Ltd's financial statements according to IAS 2 *Inventories*?

£5,600	
£5,770	
£5,200	
£4,960	

Chapter summary

- If an intangible asset is identifiable, either it is separable or it arises from contractual or other legal rights.

- The following internally generated intangible assets are never recognised: goodwill, brands, mastheads, publishing titles, customer lists and similar items.

- Expenditure on research is recognised in profit or loss when it is incurred.

- Development expenditure should be recognised as an asset if all the following can be demonstrated:

  - Probable future economic benefits
  - Intention and ability to complete the asset and to use or sell it
  - Resources available to complete the asset
  - Ability to use or sell it
  - Technical feasibility of completing the asset
  - Expenditure can be measured reliably

- If an intangible asset has a finite useful life, it should be amortised on a systematic basis over its useful life.

- If an intangible asset has an indefinite useful life, it is not amortised. It is reviewed for impairment at least annually.

- To determine whether an asset is impaired, its carrying amount is compared with its recoverable amount.

- If the recoverable amount is less than the carrying amount, the asset is impaired and an impairment loss is recognised.

- Impairment losses are recognised in profit or loss if the asset has not previously been revalued. Otherwise they are treated as downward revaluations.

- Inventories should be stated at the lower of cost and net realisable value.

- The comparison between cost and net realisable value must be made for each individual item of inventory, or each group of similar items.

- Either FIFO or AVCO must be used to arrive at the cost of inventories.

Keywords

- **Amortisation:** The systematic allocation of the depreciable amount of an intangible asset over its useful life

- **Carrying amount:** The amount at which an asset is recognised after deducting any accumulated depreciation (amortisation) and accumulated impairment losses

- **Development:** The application of research findings or other knowledge to a plan or design for the production of new or substantially improved materials, devices, products, processes, systems before the start of commercial production or use

- **Fair value less costs of disposal:** The price that would be received to sell an asset in an orderly transaction between market participants at the measurement date, less the costs of disposal

- **First in, first out (FIFO):** A method of valuing inventories that assumes that items are used in the order in which they were received from suppliers

- **Goodwill:** The excess of the value of a business as a whole over the total value of its individual assets and liabilities

- **Impairment:** A reduction in the recoverable amount of an asset below its carrying amount

- **Impairment loss:** The amount by which the carrying amount of an asset exceeds its recoverable amount

- **Intangible asset:** An identifiable non-monetary asset without physical substance

- **Internally generated goodwill:** The goodwill that a business generates over time

- **Inventories:** Assets held for sale in the ordinary course of business, in the process of production for such sale, or in the form of materials or supplies to be consumed in the production process or in the rendering of services

- **Last in, first out (LIFO):** A method of valuing inventories that assumes that the most recent purchases are used first

- **Net realisable value:** The estimated selling price in the ordinary course of business less the estimated costs of completion and the estimated costs necessary to make the sale

- **Purchased goodwill:** The difference between the cost of an acquired entity and the aggregate of the fair values of that entity's identifiable assets and liabilities

- **Recoverable amount:** The higher of fair value less costs to sell or value in use

- **Research:** Original and planned investigation undertaken with the prospect of gaining new scientific or technical knowledge and understanding

- **Value in use:** The present value of the future cash flows expected to be obtained from an asset as a result of continuing to use it in the business

- **Weighted average cost (AVCO):** A method of valuing inventories which divides the total cost of the items in inventory by the total number of items in inventory, to arrive at the average cost of each item

Test your learning

1 During the year ended 31 December 20X4, a company started two new research and development projects:

Project X: New adhesive

Expected to cost a total of £2,000,000 to complete. Future revenues from the sale of the product are expected to exceed £4,000,000. The completion date of the project is uncertain because external funding will have to be obtained before the work can be completed.

Project Y: New type of cloth

Expected to cost a total of £900,000 to develop. Expected total revenues £2,500,000 once work completed – completion date expected to be early 20X5. Most of the expenditure on the project has now been incurred and the company expects to be able to fund the remainder from its ongoing operations.

On the basis of this information, how should the expenditure on these projects be treated in the financial statements for the year ended 31 December 20X4?

Recognise expenditure on both projects in profit or loss	
Recognise expenditure on Project X in profit or loss Recognise expenditure on Project Y as an intangible asset	
Recognise expenditure on Project Y in profit or loss Recognise expenditure on Project X as an intangible asset	
Recognise expenditure on both projects as an intangible asset	

2 **Indicate which of the following statements are true or false.**

	True	False
An intangible asset may have an indefinite useful life.		
An intangible asset should always be amortised over its useful life.		
Internally generated goodwill should never be recognised.		
No internally generated intangible asset may be recognised.		

3 According to IAS 36 *Impairment of Assets*, all non-current assets should be reviewed for impairment at least annually.

Is this statement true or false?

True	
False	

4 **Prepare brief notes to answer the following questions:**

(a) What is an impairment loss, according to IAS 36 *Impairment of Assets*?

(b) What is an asset's recoverable amount?

(c) When should an impairment loss be recognised in other comprehensive income?

5 **Prepare brief notes to answer the following questions:**

(a) Why is an adjustment made for closing inventories in the financial statements?
(b) What is meant by the cost of inventories, according to IAS 2 *Inventories*?
(c) How should inventories be valued in the financial statements?
(d) Why are inventories an asset?

6 A company started to trade on 1 April and made the following purchases of inventory:

| | Units | Price per unit | |
		£	£
1 April	60	20	1,200
15 April	40	22	880
30 April	50	25	1,250
			3,330

On 30 April 125 units were sold. Total proceeds were £5,000.

The company uses the first in, first out (FIFO) method to arrive at the cost of inventories.

What is the gross profit for April?

£2,170	
£2,225	
£2,295	
£2,670	

Further accounting standards

8

Learning outcomes

1.1	**Explain the regulatory framework that underpins financial reporting** • The purpose of financial statements
2.1	**Examine the effect of international accounting standards on the preparation of financial statements** • Explain the effect of international accounting standards on the presentation, valuation and disclosure of items within the financial statements • Make any supporting calculations
3.1	**Draft a statement of profit or loss and other comprehensive income** • Make appropriate entries in the statement in respect of information extracted from a trial balance and additional information
3.2	**Draft a statement of financial position** • Make appropriate entries in the statement in respect of information extracted from a trial balance and additional information
3.3	**Draft a statement of changes in equity** • Make appropriate entries in the statement in respect of information extracted from a trial balance and additional information or other financial statements provided

Assessment context

This chapter is made up of five different accounting standards. Each standard could be tested in short-form, objective-style tasks or a written question. They could also be examined in the accounts preparation question (common for taxation and events after the reporting period).

Qualification context

All five standards are stand-alone areas of the syllabus that do not affect any other areas of the qualification.

Business context

Most companies will need to be able to account for taxation, leases, provisions and events after the reporting period.

Chapter overview

Accounting treatment

- Adjusting events – changes should be made in the financial statements, if material
- Non-adjusting events – disclose, if material

Events after the reporting period

Provisions, contingent liabilities and contingent assets

Further accounting standards

Income taxes

Accounting treatment

- Provisions are recognised in the financial statements
- Contingent liabilities and contingent assets are disclosed in a note

Leases

Key elements

- Current year tax
- Under-/ overprovision
- Deferred tax

Types

- Finance lease
- Operating lease

Method

- Actuarial method
- Sum-of-digits method

Revenue

Arises from:

- Sale of goods
- Services

Introduction

This chapter deals with the accounting treatment of various liabilities. It begins by looking at the accounting treatment of tax in the financial statements.

It then covers the accounting treatment of **leases** and **provisions, contingent liabilities** and **contingent assets**. We also look at the treatment and disclosure of events that occur after the end of the reporting period (the year end), but before the financial statements are finalised and approved by the directors.

Finally, we explain when and how an entity should recognise sales revenue.

Relevant accounting standards are:

- IAS 12 *Income Taxes*
- IAS 17 *Leases*
- IAS 37 *Provisions, Contingent Liabilities and Contingent Assets*
- IAS 10 *Events After the Reporting Period*
- IAS 18 *Revenue*

1 Income taxes (IAS 12)

IAS 12 outlines the accounting treatment of tax. In the assessment you will be required to account for tax (but not compute it).

1.1 Current tax

Current tax is the amount of tax payable or recoverable in respect of taxable profit or loss for a period (IAS 12: para. 13).

At the end of a year, an entity will **estimate** the tax due on its profits.

A tax charge is shown as an expense in the statement of profit or loss and other comprehensive income (SPLOCI) and a current **liability** in the statement of financial position (SOFP).

The journal to include tax in the accounting records is:

	Debit £	Credit £
Tax (SPLOCI)	X	
Tax liability (SOFP)		X

Activity 1: Oscar Ltd – current year tax

At 31 December 20X0, Oscar Ltd had an estimated current tax liability of £208,000.

Required

Complete the extracts below to show how the above item will be recorded in the statement of profit or loss and other comprehensive income and the statement of financial position for the year to 31 December 20X0.

Oscar Ltd
Statement of profit or loss and other comprehensive income (extract) for the year to 31 December 20X0

	£000

Statement of financial position (extract) as at 31 December 20X0

	£000
Current liabilities	

1.2 Under- or overprovision

Having looked at the current year tax charge, we know that the year-end tax liability is an estimate of the amount due on company profits.

The actual amount payable (or recoverable) is only agreed after the financial statements have been finalised. This means that often the actual amount of tax paid is different from the amount that was recorded in the financial statements.

This over- or underprovision is simply adjusted in the next financial statements.

Therefore, the total tax charge for the year will comprise the current year tax charge and an adjustment in respect of the previous period.

Illustration 1 – Under- or overprovision

Tolkein Ltd estimated the tax charge for the year ended 30 June 20X4 as £45,000. The actual amount payable was £43,000. The estimated tax charge for the year ended 30 June 20X5 is £50,000.

(a)   What is the tax expense for the year ended 30 June 20X5?
(b)   What is the tax liability at 30 June 20X5?

Solution

(a)   Tax charge for the year ended 30 June 20X5:

	£
Tax expense based on profits for the year	50,000
Adjustment in respect of prior period (overprovision)	(2,000)
	48,000

(b)   The tax liability at 30 June 20X5 is £50,000, the estimated tax charge for the year.

Activity 2: Oscar Ltd – under- or overprovision

At 1 January 20X1, Oscar Ltd had an estimated tax liability of £208,000 in respect of the prior year.

In April 20X1 the company paid tax of £220,000 to the tax authorities to settle the amount owed in respect of profits from the previous year.

At 31 December 20X1, the current tax liability for the year has been estimated at £234,000.

Required

What is the tax charge Oscar Ltd will report in the statement of profit or loss and other comprehensive income for the year ended 31 December 20X1?

£208,000	
£220,000	
£234,000	
£246,000	

1.3 Deferred tax

This topic is background knowledge for the assessment. Deferred tax is not an actual tax. It is a way of applying the accruals concept to accounting for current tax.

It arises due to temporary differences (IAS 12: para. 15).

These are differences between the carrying amount of an asset or liability in the statement of financial position and its valuation for tax purposes (tax base).

For example, depreciation is not an allowable expense for tax purposes. Instead, a business claims tax (capital) allowances when assets are purchased. The depreciation rates and tax allowance rates tend to differ.

Due to temporary differences, some items are charged to tax or allowed for tax in a period that is different from the one in which they are recognised in the financial statements.

Illustration 2 – Deferred tax

A company buys an item of equipment on 1 January 20X1 for £1,000,000. It has a useful life of 10 years and is depreciated on a straight line basis.

Tax allowances can be claimed at 20% per annum on a diminishing balance basis.

The tax rate is 30% and the current tax charge for the year has been calculated as £50,000.

Required

Calculate the deferred tax expense to be included in the financial statements for the year ended 31 December 20X1 and the deferred tax liability at that date.

Solution

Accounting depreciation to 31 December 20X1: £1,000,000/0 = £100,000

Tax allowance to 31 December 20X1: £1,000,000 × 20% = £200,000

Deferred tax liability calculation

Date	Accounting carrying value £000	Tax base £000	Temporary differences £000	Deferred tax liability @ 30% £000
Cost at 1.1.X1	1,000	1,000		
Depreciation to 31.12.X1	(100)	(200)		
Carrying amount at 31.12.X1	900	800	100	30

Journal to record deferred tax

	Debit £000	Credit £000
Deferred tax expense (SPLOCI)	30	
Deferred tax liability (SOFP)		30

Statement of profit or loss and other comprehensive income (extract) for the year to 31 December 20X1

	£000
Tax (50 + 30)	80

Statement of financial position (extract) as at 31 December 20X1

	£000
Non-current liabilities	
Deferred tax	30

	£000
Current liabilities	
Tax liability	50

2 Leases (IAS 17)

2.1 Introduction to leases

A lease is a contract between a lessor and a lessee for the hire of a specific asset.

IAS 17 requires companies to account for leases in accordance with the commercial reality (substance) of the arrangement rather than its legal form.

Legal form	The lessor retains ownership of the asset
Substance of the arrangement	The lessee has the right to use the asset for an agreed period of time, in return for rental payments

A key objective of this accounting standard is to resolve the problems of 'off balance sheet financing' which became evident during the 1980s. In that period, a number of complex arrangements were developed that, if accounted for in accordance with their legal form, resulted in accounts that did not report the commercial effect of the arrangement.

For example, lease agreements were introduced by financing organisations that were made to look like rental agreements, when in fact the **substance** of the transaction was actually a purchase on credit.

This meant that in substance liabilities and finance charges were understated. In the assessment you could be asked to:

(a) Distinguish between a finance and an operating lease

(b) Demonstrate knowledge of finance lease calculations, using the actuarial method (payments in arrears or advance)

(c) Demonstrate knowledge of finance lease calculations, using the sum-of-digits method (payments in arrears or advance)

(d) Perform operating lease calculations

(e) Discuss the above in a written task

2.2 Finance lease – definition

A **finance lease** is a lease that transfers **substantially all the risks and rewards of ownership** of an asset to the lessee (IAS 17: para. 4). Title may or may not be eventually transferred.

IAS 17 identifies (para. 10) five situations which would normally lead to a lease being classified as a finance lease.

(a) The lease **transfers ownership** of the asset to the lessee at the end of the lease term.

(b) The lessee has the **option to purchase** the asset at a price sufficiently below fair value at exercise date for it to be **reasonably certain** the option will be exercised.

(c) The lease term is for a **major part** of the asset's economic life, even if title is not transferred.

(d) Present value of **minimum lease payments** (PVMLP) amounts to substantially all of the asset's fair value at inception.

(e) The leased asset is so specialised that only the lessee can use it without major modifications.

Essentially, under a finance lease, the lease is really a loan for the sum of money the lessee would need to buy the asset outright.

Terms	Explanation
Lease term	The **non-cancellable period** for which the lessee has contracted to lease the asset
Minimum lease payments (MLP)	The payments over the lease term that the lessee is required to make
Fair value	The amount for which an **asset could be exchanged (or a liability settled)**, between knowledgeable, willing parties in an **arm's-length transaction** In the assessment, the fair value of the leased asset will be the same as the purchase price of the asset
Interest rate implicit in the lease (lessees)	The discount rate which, at the inception of a lease, causes the present value of the minimum lease payments to be equal to the fair value of the leased asset In other words, the interest charge takes account of the time value of money
Depreciation	The asset is depreciated over the shorter of the lease term and the useful life of the asset

An **operating lease** is a lease other than a finance lease (IAS 17: para. 4). An operating lease is similar to a rental agreement.

IAS 17 requires entities to account for the substance of a lease contract rather than its legal form. This means that finance leases and operating leases are treated differently in the financial statements. We will come back to this later.

2.3 Finance leases disclosure in the financial statements of lessees

Under a finance lease, the financial statements will show:

Statement of financial position (extract)

	£
Non-current assets	
Property, plant and equipment	X
Non-current liabilities	
Lease liability	X
Current liabilities	
Lease liability	X
	X

Statement of profit or loss and other comprehensive income (extract)

	£
Depreciation charge (in relevant expense category)	X
Finance charges	X

The calculations will be considered through activities.

2.4 Finance leases – actuarial method

At the start of the lease

(a) The leased asset is recognised in the lessee's statement of financial position at its **fair value** or, if this is lower, the **present value of the minimum lease payments**.

(b) The lessee also recognises a liability for the loan. This is the same amount as the value of the asset.

(c) To arrive at the present value of the minimum lease payments, the payments are discounted using the **interest rate implicit in the lease** or, if this is not possible, the lessee's **incremental borrowing rate**.

(d) The idea here is that the lease is really a loan for the sum of money that the lessee would need to buy the asset outright (its fair value). The fair value of the asset is the capital amount of the loan and the lessor charges interest on this at a rate that takes account of the time value of money.

Over the term of the lease

(a) The asset is depreciated over its **useful life**. The depreciation rate and method used must be the same as those used for similar assets that are owned by the entity.

(b) The useful life of a leased asset is the shorter of the normal useful life of a similar asset and the lease term. IAS 17 defines the useful life of a leased asset more formally as 'the estimated remaining period over which the economic benefits embodied in the asset are expected to be consumed by the entity'. (IAS 17: para. 4)

(c) The total payments under the lease are usually more than the value of the leased asset in the statement of financial position. The difference is the lease interest.

(d) The lease payments are split between capital and interest. As each instalment is paid, the capital portion reduces the outstanding liability, while the interest is charged to profit or loss.

The next illustration looks at the calculations required where interest is charged using the actuarial method and lease payments are made in **arrears**.

Illustration 3 – Actuarial method

Turnmill Ltd leases a machine under a finance lease.

- The lease runs for four years from 1 January 20X1.
- The company pays £40,000 on 31 December each year.
- The present value of the lease payments is £126,800.
- The rate of interest implicit in the lease is 10%.
- The machine would have cost £127,000 if the company had been able to purchase it outright.
- The useful life of the machine is four years.

At the start of the lease term

We are actually told that the lease is a finance lease. In addition, there are two indications that this is the case:

- The term of the lease is the same as the useful life of the machine: four years.
- The present value of the minimum lease payments (£126,800) is substantially (99%) all of the fair value of the lease (£127,000).

Therefore Turnmill Ltd recognises:

- An asset (the machine); and
- A liability (the outstanding lease payments).

These are measured at the lower of the present value of the minimum lease payments and the fair value of the machine: £126,800.

The double entry is:

DEBIT	Property, plant and equipment at cost	£126,800	
CREDIT	Lease liability		£126,800

Over the term of the lease: the asset

The asset is depreciated over the lease term of four years, in exactly the same way as any other item of property, plant and equipment.

The double entry is:

DEBIT	Depreciation expense (£126,800 ÷ 4)	£31,700	
CREDIT	Property, plant and equipment: accumulated depreciation		£31,700

Over the term of the lease: the liability

The lease liability is similar to a loan. Interest is charged on the loan over the term of the lease and Turnmill Ltd repays the loan in equal instalments at the end of each year.

IAS 17 states that each lease instalment must be split between capital and interest. Interest must be allocated to each period so as to produce a 'constant periodic rate of interest on the remaining balance of the liability'. (IAS 17: Para. 25)

This is normally done by using the **actuarial method** (sometimes called the **effective interest rate method**).

Interest is charged at 10% on the outstanding liability at the beginning of each year and is recognised as an expense in profit or loss. The double entry for 20X1 is:

| DEBIT | Finance cost (£126,800 × 10%) (profit or loss) | £12,680 | |
| CREDIT | Lease liability (statement of financial position) | | £12,680 |

The double entry for the repayment on 31 December is:

| DEBIT | Lease liability | £40,000 | |
| CREDIT | Cash | | £40,000 |

Each year, the lease liability is increased by the interest on the outstanding amount and then reduced by the repayment. At the end of the first year, the outstanding liability is £99,480 (£126,800 + £12,680 – £40,000).

What happens over the whole term of the lease is shown below:

	Liability at 1 January £	Interest at 10% £	Repayment £	Liability at 31 December £
20X1	126,800	12,680	(40,000)	99,480
20X2	99,480	9,948	(40,000)	69,428
20X3	69,428	6,942	(40,000)	36,370
20X4	36,370	3,630*	(40,000)	–

* There is a rounding difference of £7 and this has been deducted from the interest charge for 20X4.

At the end of each year, the lease liability is shown in the statement of financial position. The total amount of £99,480 must be split between current liabilities and non-current liabilities. As the repayment is made at the end of the year, the current liability is the £40,000 instalment payable on 31 December 20X2 (ie within 12 months) less the interest charge for the year on the liability at 1 January 20X2:

	£
Repayment on 31 December 20X2	40,000
Less interest for 20X2 (£99,480 × 10%)	(9,948)
Current liabilities	30,052
Non-current liabilities (balancing figure)	69,428
	99,480

Alternatively, calculate the total liability at 31 December 20X2 and deduct it from the total liability at 31 December 20X1: £99,480 – £69,428 = £30,052.

The next Activity also looks at the calculations required where interest is charged using the actuarial method and lease payments are made in arrears.

Activity 3: Actuarial method – payments in arrears

A company leases an item of plant on 1 January 20X0. The fair value of the plant is £20,609 and the company leases it for 5 years, paying 5 annual instalments of £4,500, beginning on 31 December 20X0.

The company uses the actuarial method to allocate interest. The interest rate implicit in the lease is 3%. Plant is depreciated on a straight line basis.

Required

Complete the financial statement extracts below for the year ended 31 December 20X0.

Statement of financial position (extract) as at 31 December 20X0

	£
Non-current assets	
Non-current liabilities	
Current liabilities	

Statement of profit or loss and other comprehensive income (extract) for the year ended 31 December 20X0

	£

Workings (will not be provided in the assessment)

Property, plant and equipment	£

Lease liability	£

This worked example looks at the calculations required where interest is charged using the actuarial method and lease payments are made in **advance**.

Activity 4: Actuarial method – payments in advance

A company leases a car on 1 January 20X0. The fair value of the car is £5,000 and the company leases it for 4 years, paying 4 annual instalments of £1,500, beginning on 1 January 20X0.

The interest rate implicit in the lease is 3%. The car is depreciated on a straight line basis.

Required

Complete the financial statement extracts below for the year ended 31 December 20X0.

Statement of financial position (extract) as at 31 December 20X0

	£
Non-current assets	
Non-current liabilities	
Current liabilities	

Statement of profit or loss and other comprehensive income (extract) for the year ended 31 December 20X0

	£

Workings (will not be provided in the assessment)

Property, plant and equipment	£

Lease liability	£

2.5 Finance leases – sum-of-digits method

IAS 17 states that interest must be allocated to each period so as to produce a constant periodic rate of interest on the remaining balance of the liability (IAS 17: para. 25). The actuarial method is generally considered to be the most accurate.

However, IAS 17 explains that a lessee can use an approximate calculation. The sum-of-digits method is sometimes used as a reasonable alternative.

If the assessment scenario does not give an interest rate, you will need to use this method.

To calculate the finance charge in a particular year:

Step 1   Count how many interest-bearing periods there are in the contract (this will be 'n' in the formula used in Step 3).

Step 2   Assign a digit to each instalment. The digit 1 should be assigned to the final instalment, 2 to the penultimate instalment and so on.

Step 3   Add the digits. A quick method of adding the digits is to use the formula

$$\frac{n(n+1)}{2}$$

where n is the number of interest-bearing instalments.

Step 4   Calculate the total amount of interest payable over the lease term by comparing:

Total payments	X
Fair value of the asset	(X)
Total interest payable	X

Step 5 Calculate the amount of interest to be paid in the year specified by the requirement. Eg for Year 1, with 5 interest-bearing instalments and a sum of digits of 15, it would be: total interest payable × 5/15.

Activity 5: Sum-of-digits method

A company leases an item of plant on 1 January 20X0. The fair value of the plant is £20,609 and the company leases it for 5 years, paying 5 annual instalments of £4,500, beginning on 31 December 20X0.

The company uses the sum-of-digits method to allocate interest.

Required

Complete the financial statement extracts below for the year ended 31 December 20X0.

Statement of financial position (extract) as at 31 December 20X0

	£
Non-current assets	
Non-current liabilities	
Current liabilities	

Statement of profit or loss and other comprehensive income (extract) for the year ended 31 December 20X0

	£

Workings (will not be provided in the assessment)

Property, plant and equipment	£

Sum-of-digits calculations

Step 1 **Count how many interest-bearing periods there are in the contract (this will be 'n' in the formula used in Step 3).**

Steps 2 and 3 Add the digits using the formula: n(n + 1)/2.

Step 4 **Calculate the total amount of interest that will be payable over the lease term by comparing the total amount paid to the value of the asset.**

	£

Step 5 **Calculate the amount of interest to be paid in the year specified by the requirement.**

Note. For teaching purposes, all years are included in this solution.

	£

Lease liability	£

2.6 Operating leases

An operating lease is a lease other than a finance lease (IAS 17: para. 4).

With an operating lease, lease payments are recognised as an expense in the statement of profit or loss and other comprehensive income on a straight line basis over the lease term.

Activity 6: Operating or finance lease?

Witney Ltd leases an item of plant. Under the terms of the lease, Witney Ltd makes payments of £20,000 each year for 5 years. The present value of the minimum lease payments is £95,500. The plant has a useful life of 5 years and would cost £98,000 to purchase outright.

This lease is an operating lease.

Required

Is this statement true or false?

True	
False	

Illustration 4 – Operating lease

Faringdon Ltd leases a machine under an operating lease.

- The lease runs for 4 years from 1 January 20X1.
- The company pays £20,000 on 31 December each year.
- The useful life of the machine is 15 years.

Faringdon Ltd recognises an expense of £20,000 in profit or loss for each of the 4 years of the lease term.

Statement of profit or loss and other comprehensive income (extract)				
	20X1	**20X2**	**20X3**	**20X4**
	£	**£**	**£**	**£**
Lease rental	20,000	20,000	20,000	20,000

Activity 7: Leases – further issues

Mary Ltd rents a car under an operating lease agreement for three years. Mary Ltd had to put down an initial non-refundable deposit of £500 and must pay £700 per annum for each year of the lease.

Required

(a) How much must Mary Ltd record in the financial statements as the rental expense in Year 2?

£700	
£867	
£500	
£733	

Working

	£

A building has a useful life of 50 years. Jack Ltd rents it for a lease term of 5 years.

(b) Is this likely to be an operating lease or a finance lease?

Operating lease	
Finance lease	

3 Provisions, contingent liabilities and contingent assets (IAS 37)

The three items covered by IAS 37 represent uncertainties that may have an effect on future financial statements. They need to be accounted for consistently so that users have a fuller understanding of their effect on the financial statements.

A liability is a **present obligation** of the entity arising from **past events**, the settlement of which is expected to result in an **outflow** from the entity of resources embodying economic benefits (IAS 37: para. 10).

3.1 Provisions

A provision is a liability of uncertain timing or amount (IAS 37: para. 10).

A provision is to be recognised as a liability in the financial statements when:

- A company has a **present obligation** as a result of a past event
- It is **probable** that an **outflow** of economic benefits will be required to settle the obligation, although not certain
- A **reliable estimate** can be made of the amount of the obligation

Unless all of these conditions are met, no provision should be recognised.

A present obligation arises once an obligating event has occurred. An obligating event is an event that creates a **legal or constructive obligation** resulting in a company having no realistic alternative to settling the obligation.

A **legal obligation** derives from a contract, legislation or other operation of law.

A constructive obligation derives from a company's actions, such as an established pattern of past practice, or where the company has created a valid expectation.

The value of a provision should be assessed each year end. The amount of the change in the provision is recognised as an expense in the statement of profit or loss and other comprehensive income, and the total amount of the provision is shown as a liability on the statement of financial position.

If the provision is no longer required then the entry should be reversed. A provision can only be used in relation to the expenses for which it was originally created.

A note to the accounts should include a reconciliation of the provision balance from the previous year to the current balance, as well as a short description of the provision and any uncertainties related thereto.

3.2 Contingent liability

A contingent liability (IAS 37: para. 10) is either:

(a) A possible obligation arising from past events whose existence will be confirmed only by the occurrence or non-occurrence of one or more uncertain future events not wholly within the company's control; or

(b) A present obligation that arises from past events but not recognised because:

- It is not probable that an outflow of economic benefits will be required to settle the obligation; or
- The obligation cannot be measured with sufficient reliability.

A contingent liability is not recognised in the financial statements (IAS 37: para. 86); however, it should be disclosed as a note to the statements which largely includes:

- A brief description of the nature of the contingent liability
- An estimate of its financial effect

Where a contingent liability is considered to be a **remote** possibility then no disclosure is required in the notes to the financial statements.

3.3 Contingent asset

A contingent asset is a possible asset that arises from past events whose existence will be confirmed only by the occurrence or non-occurrence of one or more uncertain future events not wholly within the company's control (IAS 37: para. 10).

A company should not recognise a contingent asset in its financial statements. However, when the realisation of profit is virtually certain, then the asset is no longer contingent and its recognition in the statements is appropriate.

A contingent asset is disclosed only where an inflow of economic benefits is probable. Disclosure in the notes to the financial statements should include:

- A brief description of the nature of the contingent asset
- An estimate of its financial effect

Where a contingent asset is considered to be possible or remote then no disclosure is required in the notes to the financial statements (IAS 37: para. 31–35).

Summary table

	Liabilities	Assets
Virtually certain	Recognise a liability or provision	Recognise an asset
Probable	Recognise a provision	Contingent asset – note to the financial statements
Possible	Contingent liability – note to the financial statements	–

Activity 8: Provisions, contingent liabilities and contingent assets

Ivor Ltd has a possible obligation as a result of a claim against it by a customer. The company's solicitors have advised the directors that there is a 25% chance that the claim will be successful.

Required

(a) In the financial statements for the period, Ivor Ltd should:

Disclose a contingent liability	
Recognise a provision	

At the end of an accounting period, a company has a contingent asset where an inflow of economic benefits is probable and a contingent liability where the likelihood of an outflow of resources is possible.

(b) Which of the following would be the correct accounting treatment for each of these items?

Contingent asset	Contingent liability	
No disclosure is required	No disclosure is required	
Disclosure is required	No disclosure is required	
No disclosure is required	Disclosure is required	
Disclosure is required	Disclosure is required	

Activity 9: Recognise a provision?

A company guarantees to repair or replace items that become defective within three years of the date of sale. The chance of an individual item needing to be repaired or replaced is small. However, past experience suggests that it is probable that there will be some claims under the guarantee.

The company should recognise a provision for the costs of repairing and replacing items under the guarantee.

Required

Is this statement true or false?

True	
False	

3.4 Summary: Provisions and contingent liabilities

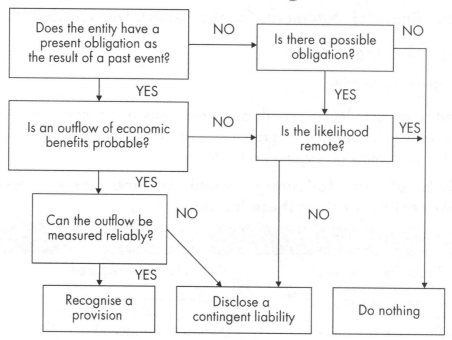

3.5 Summary: Contingent assets

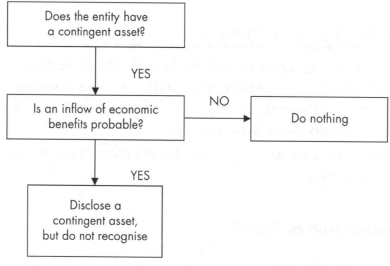

(IAS 37: illustrative example B)

4 Events after the reporting period (IAS 10)

This refers to any events (favourable or unfavourable) that occur between the year-end date and the date when the financial statements are authorised for issue (IAS 10: para. 3). Once the financial statements have been authorised for issue, they generally cannot be altered.

This standard recognises that there may be events which occur, or items of information that become available after the end of the financial year, that need to be reflected in the financial statements.

For example, if a customer becomes insolvent after the year end and the amount of the receivable is material, it may be necessary to make changes in the financial statements for the year to reflect this.

IAS 10 distinguishes between:

- **Adjusting events**
- **Non-adjusting events**

4.1 Adjusting events

Adjusting events provide evidence of conditions that existed at the year-end date. If material, changes should be made to the amounts included in the financial statements (IAS 10: para. 3).

Examples of adjusting events include:

- The settlement after the year-end date of a court case which confirms that a present obligation existed at the year-end date

- Assets, where a valuation shows impairment

- Inventories, where net realisable value falls below cost

- Trade receivables, where a customer has become insolvent

4.2 Non-adjusting events

Non-adjusting events are indicative of conditions that arose after the year-end date (IAS 10: para. 3).

No adjustment is made to the financial statements; instead, if material they are disclosed by way of notes which explain the nature of the event and, where possible, give an estimation of its financial effect.

Examples include:

- Business combinations
- Major purchase of assets
- Losses of production capacity, eg caused by fire, flood or strikes

Dividends declared after the reporting period but before the financial statements are authorised for issue are not recognised as a liability at the end of the reporting period because no obligation exists at that time.

Such dividends are disclosed in the notes to the financial statements in accordance with IAS 1 *Presentation of Financial Statements*.

4.3 Going concern

An entity cannot prepare its financial statements on a going concern basis if, after the year-end date, management determines either that it intends to liquidate the company or to cease trading, or that there is no realistic alternative to these courses of action.

Therefore, if an event occurs after the reporting date that affects going concern, the financial statements must be adjusted (IAS 10: para. 14).

4.4 Disclosure

Entities must disclose the date when the financial statements were authorised for issue and who gave that authorisation. This is usually done by way of a signature and date on the statement of financial position and directors' report (IAS 10: para. 17).

Activity 10: Events after the reporting period

The following issues have been raised by the directors of Sunny Ltd concerning the financial statements for the year ended 30 September 20X6.

Some items of inventory are valued at their cost of £156,590 in the financial statements. They were sold for £101,640 after the year end.

This is an adjusting event and the company should reduce the value of the inventory.

Required

(a) Is this statement true or false?

True	
False	

In October the directors announced their proposal to pay a final dividend of £75,000 for the year. This has not been recognised in the financial statements.

(b) Indicate whether this is an adjusting event or a non-adjusting event.

Adjusting event	
Non-adjusting event	

An employee was dismissed in August. The former employee started legal proceedings for unfair dismissal in October 20X6. The lawyers advise that Sunny Ltd will probably lose the case and think that a reliable estimate of damages that will be awarded against the company is £20,000.

(c) Indicate which statement is correct.

This is an adjusting event and a provision should be recognised at the year end.	
This is a non-adjusting event, therefore a provision should not be recognised.	

Activity 11: Non-adjusting event?

Lessing Ltd has prepared financial statements for the year ended 31 December 20X4. The financial statements are due to be approved on 31 March 20X5.

(1) On 20 January 20X5 Lessing Ltd sold land and buildings for £250,000. At 31 December 20X4 they had had a carrying amount of £100,000.

(2) On 15 February 20X5 a major customer went into liquidation. The directors of Lessing Ltd were advised that they were unlikely to receive any amounts owing to them. At 15 February 20X5 the customer owed £20,000, of which £15,000 related to sales made before the year end.

Required

Which of the above events should be treated as a non-adjusting event after the reporting period?

(1) only	
(2) only	
Neither (1) nor (2)	
Both (1) and (2)	

Assessment focus point

As well as short-form objective questions like the ones we have just done, IAS 10 and 37 may be tested by a written question. For example, part of Task 4 in one of the AAT's sample assessments asked candidates to 'explain, **with reasons**' how a legal claim should be treated in the financial statements. This meant that they had not only to state how the claim would be accounted for, but also to justify this treatment by applying each part of the IAS 37 definition of a provision.

You should refer to the Skills Bank at the beginning of this Course Book for advice on tackling written questions.

5 Revenue (IAS 18)

5.1 What is revenue?

Revenue is an entity's income from its main operating activities.

IAS 18 defines it as being:

'The gross inflow of economic benefits during the period arising in the course of the ordinary activities of the entity, when those inflows result in increase in equity, other than increases relating to contributions from equity shareholders' (IAS 18: para. 7).

In other words, it is the gross inflow of economic benefits (cash, receivables or other assets) arising from the ordinary activities of a company.

When an entity generates revenue:

	Debit £	Credit £
Cash or trade receivable (SOFP)	X	
Revenue (SPL)		X

Receipts in respect of the issues of shares are **not** income as they are transactions with shareholders. The definition of income in the *Conceptual Framework* excludes contributions from shareholders.

IAS 18 (para. 9) states that revenue is to be measured at the fair value of the consideration received or receivable. Fair value is the amount for which an asset could be exchanged, or a liability settled, between knowledgeable, willing parties in an arm's-length transaction.

The standard then sets out the rules for the recognition of the three types of revenue:

- Sale of goods
- Rendering of services
- Dividends

5.2 Sale of goods

Revenue from the sale of goods is to be recognised when all of the following criteria have been met (IAS 18: para. 14):

- The seller has transferred to the buyer the significant risks and rewards of ownership of the goods.

- The seller retains no continuing managerial involvement in the goods and no effective control over the goods.

- The amount of revenue can be measured reliably.

- It is probable that the economic benefits will flow to the seller.

- The costs incurred, or to be incurred, in respect of the transaction can be measured reliably.

5.3 Rendering of services

For the sale of services, revenue is to be recognised by reference to the stage of completion of the transaction at the year-end date. All of the following criteria must be met (IAS 18: para. 20):

- The amount of revenue can be measured reliably.

- It is probable that the economic benefits will flow to the seller of the service.

- At the year-end date, the stage of completion can be measured reliably.

- The costs incurred, and the costs to complete, in respect of the transaction can be measured reliably.

5.4 Dividends

Revenue from dividends is recognised when:

- It is probable that the economic benefits will flow to the company

- The amount of revenue can be measured reliably

- The shareholder's right to receive payment is established (usually when the dividends are declared)

Activity 12: Revenue

Olive Ltd has an investment in Bee Ltd. At 31 December 20X3 the directors of Bee Ltd have informally announced their intention to pay a dividend. Olive Ltd may receive £20,000 in dividend income; however, this has not yet been confirmed.

Required

According to IAS 18 *Revenue*, how should Olive Ltd report this transaction in its financial statements for the year ended 31 December 20X3?

Recognise dividend income of £20,000 from Bee Ltd	
Do not recognise dividend income from Bee Ltd	

Chapter summary

- The tax charge is included in profit or loss and described as 'tax expense'.

- The liability for tax is included in current liabilities.

- IAS 17 requires entities to account for the substance of a lease contract rather than its legal form.

- A lease is either an operating lease or a finance lease. The classification of a lease determines the accounting treatment.

- If the lease is a finance lease, the lease is treated as if the lessee has purchased an asset and financed the purchase by taking out a loan. The leased asset and the liability for the loan are recognised in the lessee's statement of financial position. The statement of profit or loss includes depreciation and interest on the loan.

- If the lease is an operating lease, the lease payments are charged to the lessee's profit or loss as rental and the leased asset is not recognised in the statement of financial position.

- A provision should only be recognised when:

    - An entity has a present obligation as a result of a past event

    - It is probable that a transfer of economic benefits will be required to settle the obligation

    - A reliable estimate can be made of the amount of the obligation

- The amount recognised should be the best estimate of the expenditure required to settle the present obligation at the year end.

- Contingent liabilities should not be recognised. They should be disclosed in the financial statements unless the possibility of a transfer of economic benefits is remote.

- Contingent assets should not be recognised. Probable contingent assets should be disclosed.

- Financial statements should be prepared on the basis of conditions existing at the year end.

- An adjusting event after the year end requires changes in the amounts to be included in the financial statements.

- A material non-adjusting event after the year end should be disclosed.

- Revenue is the income from an entity's main operating activities.

- Revenue is measured at the fair value of the consideration received or receivable.

- Revenue from the sale of goods is recognised when:
  - The entity has transferred the significant risks and rewards of ownership of the goods
  - The entity no longer has effective control over the goods sold
  - The amount of revenue and the related costs of the transaction can be measured reliably
  - It is probable that the economic benefits associated with the transaction will flow to the entity
- When the outcome of a transaction involving the rendering of services can be estimated reliably, revenue associated with the transaction is recognised by reference to the stage of completion of the transaction at the year end.

- **Adjusting events:** Events after the reporting period which provide evidence of conditions existing at the end of the reporting period

- **Constructive obligation:** An obligation which occurs where an entity indicates that it will accept certain responsibilities and, as a result, the entity has created a valid expectation that it will discharge those responsibilities

- **Contingent asset:** A possible asset that arises from past events and whose existence will be confirmed only by the occurrence of one or more uncertain future events not wholly within the entity's control

- **Contingent liability:** A possible obligation that arises from past events and whose existence will be confirmed only by the occurrence of one or more uncertain future events not wholly within the entity's control; or a present obligation that arises from past events but is not recognised because it is not probable that a transfer of economic benefits will be required to settle the obligation; or the amount of the obligation cannot be measured with sufficient reliability

- **Events after the reporting period:** Those events, both favourable and unfavourable, which occur between the end of the reporting period and the date on which the financial statements are authorised for issue

- **Finance lease:** A lease that transfers substantially all the risks and rewards of ownership of an asset to the lessee

- **Interest rate implicit in the lease:** The discount rate that, at the inception of the lease, causes the total present value of the minimum lease payments to be equal to the fair value of the leased asset

- **Lease:** A contract for the hire of a specific asset. The lessor retains ownership of the asset, but the lessee has the right to use the asset for an agreed period of time in return for the payment of specified rentals

- **Legal obligation:** An obligation which arises as the result of a contract, legislation or other operation of law

- **Liability:** A present obligation arising from past events, the settlement of which is expected to result in an outflow of resources embodying economic benefits

- **Minimum lease payments:** The total payments that the lessee is required to make over the lease term

- **Non-adjusting events:** Events after the reporting period which are indicative of conditions which arose after the end of the reporting period

- **Operating lease:** A lease other than a finance lease; similar to a rental agreement

- **Provision:** A liability of uncertain timing or amount
- **Revenue:** The gross inflow of economic benefits during the period arising in the course of the ordinary activities of the entity, when those inflows result in increases in equity, other than increases relating to contributions from equity shareholders

1 For the year ended 30 June 20X3, Angle Ltd estimated that the charge to tax was £85,500. The estimated charge for tax recognised in the financial statements for the year ended 30 June 20X2 was £11,000 higher than the actual amount paid to HMRC during 20X2/20X3.

What amounts should be recognised in the financial statements for the year ended 30 June 20X3?

Expense of £74,500; liability of £74,500	
Expense of £74,500; liability of £85,500	
Expense of £85,500; liability of £74,500	
Expense of £96,500; liability of £85,500	

2 A company's financial statements include the following note:

Profit from operations:

Profit from operations is stated after charging the following:

Depreciation:	owned assets	X
	leased assets	X

Assuming that the company has followed the correct accounting treatment set out in IAS 17 *Leases*, which type of lease agreement has it entered into?

A finance lease	
An operating lease	

3 Clanfield Ltd leases a machine under a finance lease.

- The lease runs for 4 years from 1 January 20X1.
- The company pays £20,000 on 31 December each year.
- The present value of the minimum lease payments is £76,000.

Calculate the total lease liability at 31 December 20X1, using the sum-of-digits method.

£	

4 Proper Ltd operates a chain of restaurants. The directors of Proper have drawn your attention to two events that have occurred during the year ended 31 December 20X5:

- After a private function in one of the restaurants, several people became ill, possibly as a result of food poisoning. Legal proceedings were started, seeking damages from the company. At 31 December, the case had not yet been settled, but the directors were advised that the company would probably not be found liable.

- As a result of this incident, the directors have decided to retrain most of the catering staff to make sure that they are aware of health and hygiene issues. The staff training means that the restaurants will have to close temporarily and the resulting loss of income is expected to be material. At 31 December 20X5 no staff training had taken place and the directors had not announced their decision to anybody likely to be affected.

Explain how each of the events should be treated in the financial statements for the year ended 31 December 20X5.

5 The events listed below all took place between the end of a company's reporting period and the date on which the financial statements were authorised for issue.

Which ONE of these events is likely to be an adjusting event after the reporting period?

Damage to inventory as a result of a flood	
Discovery of a fraud committed by one of the accounts staff	
Issue of new share capital	
Sale of a freehold property	

6 **Prepare brief notes to answer the following questions:**

(a) What is revenue, according to IAS 18 *Revenue*?

(b) When should an entity recognise revenue from the sale of goods?

Group accounts: the consolidated statement of financial position

Learning outcomes

1.1	**Explain the regulatory framework that underpins financial reporting**
	• The purpose of financial statements
	• Forms of equity, reserves and loan capital
	• Sources of regulation: international accounting standards and company law (Companies Act 2006)
2.1	**Examine the effect of international accounting standards on the preparation of financial statements**
	• Explain the effect of international accounting standards on the presentation, valuation and disclosure of items within the financial statements
	• Make any supporting calculations
3.2	**Draft a statement of financial position**
	• Make appropriate entries in the statement in respect of information extracted from a trial balance and additional information
4.2	**Draft a consolidated statement of financial position for a parent company with one partly-owned subsidiary**
	• Consolidate each line item in the statement of financial position
	• Calculate and treat goodwill, non-controlling interest, pre- and post-acquisition profits, equity and unrealised profit on inventories
	• Treat adjustment to fair value, impairment of goodwill and intercompany balances

Assessment context

You will be required to prepare a consolidated statement of financial position or a consolidated statement of profit or loss. On-screen workings will be provided for some of the calculations.

Qualification context

Consolidated financial statements are only tested in this course.

Business context

Many larger businesses are part of a group of companies (ie there is a parent company and at least one subsidiary). They are required to prepare financial statements for the shareholders of the group.

Chapter overview

Group accounts: the consolidated statement of financial position

Parent's separate financial statements

- Record the investment in the other company
- Both the investor and acquired company continue to exist as separate legal entities

Group financial statements

- Presents the results and financial position of the group as if they were a single economic entity
- Shows the assets and liabilities controlled by the parent
- Share capital is that of the parent only
- Parent's reserves plus the subsidiary's post-acquisition reserves

Definition of a subsidiary

A subsidiary is an entity controlled by another entity

- Power over the investee
- Exposure or rights to variable returns
- Ability to use its power to affect returns

Goodwill arises when the cost of the business combination is greater than the net assets acquired.

Consideration	X
Less fair value of net assets	(X)
Goodwill	X

To eliminate intra-group trade receivables and trade payables:

DEBIT   Intra-group trade payables
CREDIT Intra-group trade receivables

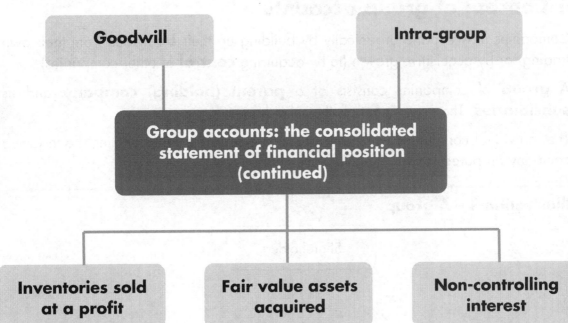

Goodwill

Intra-group

Group accounts: the consolidated statement of financial position (continued)

Inventories sold at a profit

Fair value assets acquired

Non-controlling interest

- Calculate the unrealised profit included in inventories
- Eliminate the unrealised profit from retained earnings and inventory in the books of the company making the sale

Sale by P to S:
Adjust in P's books

DEBIT   Retained earnings of P
CREDIT Consolidated inventories

Sale by S to P:
Adjust in S's books

DEBIT   Retained earnings of S
CREDIT Consolidated inventories

- The subsidiary's assets and liabilities must be brought into the consolidated financial statement at fair value rather than book value
- Any difference between fair value and book value is included in the group account as a consolidation adjustment

Non-controlling interest in a subsidiary can be measured at acquisition date in one of two ways:

- Partial goodwill method – measure NCI at acquisition date at the proportionate share of the fair value of the net assets
- Full goodwill method – measure NCI at acquisition date at fair value

Introduction

The next two chapters explain how to prepare simple accounts for a group of companies.

A **group** consists of a **parent** company and one or more **subsidiary** companies controlled by the parent. As well as its own financial statements, the parent prepares financial statements for the group as a single entity. These are known as **consolidated financial statements**.

This chapter concentrates on the consolidated statement of financial position.

1 Concept of group accounts

Companies may expand organically by building up their **business** from their own trading, or by acquisitive growth (ie by acquiring **control** of other companies).

A **group** of companies consists of a **parent (holding) company** and its **subsidiaries**. The parent controls the subsidiaries.

The individual companies within the group are separate legal entities. Each group company prepares its own financial statements.

Illustration 1 – A group

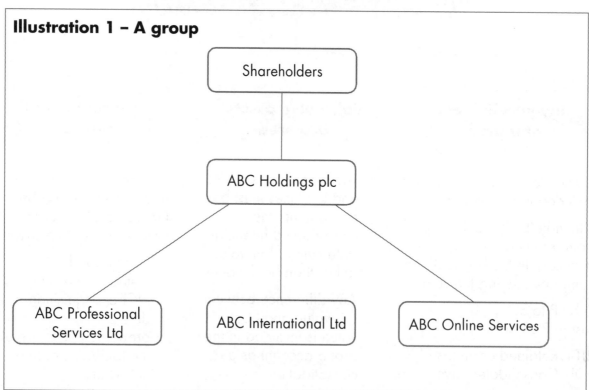

2 Parent's separate financial statements

2.1 Types of acquisition

When we acquire a sole trader or partnership we acquire individual assets and liabilities which are added to our statement of financial position, since we now own them.

All profits and losses, which the sole trader's assets would generate, are now under our control and reported in our statement of profit or loss and other comprehensive income.

When we acquire control of a company it is done by acquiring **shares** rather than individual assets and liabilities. The investment in the acquiring company's books (the parent) represents ownership of shares, which in turn represents ownership of the net assets of the acquired company (the subsidiary).

After the transaction the acquired company will continue to exist as a separate legal entity with its continuing national legislative reporting responsibilities.

In the financial statements of the parent:

- Investments in subsidiaries are included in the statement of financial position at cost (or **fair value**), under non-current assets

- Dividends receivable from subsidiaries are included in the statement of profit or loss

Illustration 2 – Parent's separate financial statements

The statements of financial position of Pegasus plc and Sylvester Ltd at 1 January 20X1 are as follows:

	Pegasus plc	Sylvester Ltd
	£000	£000
ASSETS		
Non-current assets		
Property, plant and equipment	20,000	900
Current assets		
Inventories	3,200	400
Trade receivables	2,500	175
Cash	1,800	125
	7,500	700
	27,500	1,600

	Pegasus plc £000	Sylvester Ltd £000
EQUITY AND LIABILITIES		
Equity		
Share capital	5,000	100
Retained earnings	19,450	1,200
	24,450	1,300
Current liabilities		
Trade payables	2,500	260
Tax liability	550	40
	3,050	300
Total equity and liabilities	27,500	1,600

Pegasus plc then acquires 100% of the share capital of Sylvester Ltd on 1 January 20X1 for £1,300,000 in cash.

This will be recorded at cost in the parent's separate financial statements (ie the parent's statement of financial position).

Activity 1: Pegasus plc – single entity financial statements

Using the information from Illustration 2:

Required

Show how Pegasus plc will record the investment in Sylvester Ltd and complete the statement of financial position of Pegasus plc at 1 January 20X1.

The investment in Sylvester Ltd will be recorded as follows:

	Debit £000	Credit £000

Pegasus plc
Statement of financial position as at 1 January 20X1

	£000
ASSETS	
Non-current assets	
Current assets	
Total assets	
EQUITY AND LIABILITIES	
Equity	
Current liabilities	
Total equity and liabilities	

2.2 Features of the parent's statement of financial position

(a) It shows the investment as an interest in shares at cost; this will remain unchanged from year to year.

(b) Other net assets remain unchanged, reflecting only those assets and liabilities held by Pegasus plc directly.

3 Group financial statements

3.1 The main concept

The individual financial statements of a parent do not reflect the commercial reality of the situation.

(a) Because the parent can control the subsidiary, it has the benefits and risks attaching to the subsidiary's assets and liabilities, even though it may not directly own them.

(b) The parent is directly affected by the subsidiary's results, because it can appropriate the subsidiary's profits as dividends.

In practice, the parent and the subsidiary operate as a single economic entity: the group.

Key term

A **subsidiary** is an entity that is **controlled** by another entity **(IFRS 10 *Consolidated Financial Statements*)**.

An investor **controls** an investee if and only if the investor has **all** the following (IFRS 10: para. 5, 6, 8):

(a) **Power** over the investee

(b) **Exposure, or rights, to variable returns** from its involvement with the investee

(c) The **ability to use its power** over the investee to **affect** the amount of the investor's **returns**

SUBSIDIARY = CONTROL NOT OWNERSHIP

Illustration 3 – Subsidiary?

Moat Ltd owns 6,000 'A' £1 ordinary shares in Grange Ltd. The share capital of Grange Ltd consists of:

Ordinary voting 'A' shares   10,000
Ordinary non-voting 'B' shares   20,000

Grange Ltd is a subsidiary of Moat Ltd.

Is this statement true or false?

True	
False	

Solution

True	✓
False	

Although Moat Ltd only holds 20% of the total share capital, it holds 60% of the voting rights. Therefore it has the majority of the voting rights and Grange Ltd is a subsidiary.

Provided Pegasus plc has control of the subsidiary, it is required to produce an additional set of financial statements which aim to record the **substance** of its relationship with Sylvester Ltd rather than its strict **legal form**.

This additional set of accounts is referred to as group, or consolidated, financial statements which:

(a) Present the results and financial position of a group of companies as if it was a **single business entity**

(b) Are issued to the shareholders of the parent

(c) Are issued in **addition** to and not **instead** of the parent's own financial statements

(d) Provide information on all companies controlled by the parent

As the consolidated financial statements present the parent and subsidiary as if they were a single business entity, the investment the parent makes in the subsidiary (ie the cash payment) needs to be cancelled out.

Illustration 4 – How to prepare a consolidated statement of financial position

To prepare a consolidated statement of financial position:

*   Add together the individual assets and liabilities of the parent and the subsidiary

*   Make adjustments to cancel out intra-group items

On 1 January 20X0 P Ltd acquired 100% of the issued ordinary share capital of S Ltd. S Ltd was incorporated on that date. At 31 December 20X0, the individual company statements of financial position were as follows:

	P Ltd £000	S Ltd £000
Property, plant and equipment	25,000	4,000
Investment in S Ltd	5,000	–
Current assets	30,000	16,000
	60,000	20,000
Share capital	20,000	5,000
Retained earnings	30,000	5,000
	50,000	10,000
Current liabilities	10,000	10,000
	60,000	20,000

Step 1 Cancel P Ltd's investment in S Ltd against the share capital of S Ltd.

Consolidation has the effect of replacing the cost of the investment with the net assets that it represents.

P Ltd bought the whole of the share capital of S Ltd for £5,000,000, its nominal value. The two items cancel exactly.

Step 2 Add the individual assets and liabilities of P Ltd and S Ltd together.

The share capital of the subsidiary never appears in the consolidated statement of financial position.

Consolidated statement of financial position as at 31 December 20X0

	£000
Property, plant and equipment (25,000 + 4,000)	29,000
Current assets (30,000 + 16,000)	46,000
	75,000
Share capital (P Ltd only)	20,000
Retained earnings (30,000 + 5,000)	35,000
	55,000
Current liabilities (10,000 + 10,000)	20,000
	75,000

Assessment focus point

While most consolidation questions will be computational, you may get a written question asking for an explanation of how an investment should be treated. So it is important to understand why you are consolidating as well as how to do it.

You should refer to the Skills Bank at the beginning of the Course Book for advice on how to tackle written questions.

In the next example, Pegasus plc's investment in Sylvester Ltd will be cancelled out using a 'cancellation' working.

Later in the chapter, the 'cancellation' working becomes the **'goodwill'** calculation (which is an important calculation in consolidation tasks).

An example of the cancellation working is as follows:

Cancellation	£000
Price paid	X
Less fair value of net assets at acquisition	
Share capital **(attributable to parent)**	(X)
Retained earnings **(attributable to parent)**	(X)
	X

Activity 2: Pegasus plc and Sylvester Ltd at 1 January 20X1

Here is a reminder of what the two statements of financial position look like after recording the investment in Sylvester Ltd.

	Pegasus plc £000	Sylvester Ltd £000
ASSETS		
Non-current assets		
Property, plant and equipment	20,000	900
Investment in Sylvester Ltd	1,300	
	21,300	900

	Pegasus plc £000	Sylvester Ltd £000
Current assets		
Inventories	3,200	400
Trade receivables	2,500	175
Cash	500	125
	6,200	700
Total assets	27,500	1,600
EQUITY AND LIABILITIES		
Equity		
Share capital	5,000	100
Retained earnings	19,450	1,200
	24,450	1,300
Current liabilities		
Trade payables	2,500	260
Tax liability	550	40
	3,050	300
Total equity and liabilities	27,500	1,600

Required

Draft the consolidated statement of financial position for Pegasus plc as at 1 January 20X1.

Pegasus plc
Consolidated statement of financial position as at 1 January 20X1

	£000
ASSETS	
Non-current assets	
Current assets	
Total assets	
EQUITY AND LIABILITIES	
Equity	
Current liabilities	
Total equity and liabilities	

Workings (not provided in the assessment)

Group structure

Cancellation	£000

3.2 Features of the consolidated statement of financial position

(a) The investment the parent has made in the subsidiary is not shown (as it has been cancelled in the goodwill working).

(b) The assets and liabilities are now those within the **control** of Pegasus plc, ie the resources available to the group.

(c) Share capital is that of the parent only because these accounts are prepared for the shareholders of Pegasus plc only.

4 Pre- and post-acquisition reserves

4.1 Why distinguish pre- and post-acquisition reserves?

In the previous example, Sylvester Ltd's net assets were represented not just by share capital but also by reserves. We call those reserves **'pre-acquisition reserves'** since they were controlled by someone else prior to Pegasus plc's investment in Sylvester Ltd on 1 January 20X1. They are not consolidated as they are cancelled with the cost of the investment.

Any profits made after acquisition – **post-acquisition reserves** – must be consolidated in the group financial statements.

In the *Financial Statements of Limited Companies* assessment you will be given an on-screen working to complete, so you can calculate the retained earnings to include in the consolidated statement of financial position.

An example of the retained earnings working is as follows:

Retained earnings	£000
Parent	X
Subsidiary – attributable to parent	X
Less intra-group adjustment	(X)
Less impairment	(X)
	X

The **intra-group** and **impairment** lines are included for completeness. These terms will be discussed later in the chapter.

Activity 3: Pegasus plc and Sylvester Ltd as at 31 December 20X3

Three years later, on 31 December 20X3, the summarised statements of financial position of Pegasus plc and Sylvester Ltd are as follows. (Sylvester's retained earnings were £1,200,000 on 1 January 20X1.)

	Pegasus plc £000	Sylvester Ltd £000
ASSETS		
Non-current assets		
Property, plant and equipment	24,000	4,200
Investment in Sylvester Ltd	1,300	
	25,300	4,200
Current assets	8,500	2,100
Total assets	33,800	6,300
EQUITY AND LIABILITIES		
Equity		
Share capital	5,000	100
Retained earnings	26,800	5,200
	31,800	5,300
Current liabilities	2,000	1,000
Total equity and liabilities	33,800	6,300

Required

Draft the consolidated statement of financial position for Pegasus plc and its subsidiary undertaking as at 31 December 20X3.

Pegasus plc

Consolidated statement of financial position as at 31 December 20X3

	£000
ASSETS	
Non-current assets	
Current assets	
Total assets	
EQUITY AND LIABILITIES	
Equity	
Current liabilities	
Total equity and liabilities	

Workings (not provided in the assessment)

Group structure

Cancellation	£000

Workings (will be provided in the assessment)

Retained earnings	£000

4.2 Points to note

(a) The group controls net assets of £35,800k (assets of £38,800k and liabilities of £3,000k).

(b) Since Sylvester Ltd is a 100% subsidiary, Pegasus plc also owns Sylvester Ltd's net assets of £5,300k (assets of £6,300k and liabilities of £1,000k).

(c) Share capital is only ever that of Pegasus plc, the parent.

(d) Included in the consolidated statement of financial position are the profits less losses made by Sylvester since acquisition. So, retained earnings are:

   (i) Pegasus plc (£26,800k); plus

   (ii) The post-acquisition retained earnings of Sylvester Ltd (£5,200k – £1,200k = £4,000k).

4.3 Other reserves

A company may have other reserves (such as a revaluation reserve) as well as retained earnings. These reserves should be treated in exactly the same way as retained earnings, which we have already seen.

If the reserve is pre-acquisition it forms part of the calculation of net assets at the date of acquisition and is therefore used in the cancellation (goodwill) calculation.

If the reserve is post-acquisition or there has been some movement on a reserve existing at acquisition, the consolidated statement of financial position will show the parent's reserve plus its share of the movement on the subsidiary's reserve.

5 Goodwill

5.1 Position to date

So far in this chapter the cost of the investment equalled the value of the **identifiable** net assets acquired and, accordingly, no surplus or deficit remained on cancellation.

In practice, where a parent acquires a subsidiary the cost of the investment is almost always more than the total fair value of the subsidiary's individual assets and liabilities. The difference represents goodwill.

5.2 Goodwill

Where the cost of the **business combination** is greater than the net assets acquired, the investor has paid for something more than the net assets of the acquired business.

The difference is called 'goodwill' and is measured as:

	£
Consideration transferred	X
Less fair value of identifiable assets and liabilities at acquisition	(X)
	X

Note. 'Consideration' is the price paid. In the assessment, the net assets are represented by share capital and reserves. (Fair value adjustments are considered in a later section.)

5.3 Accounting treatment

Goodwill is capitalised as an asset on the statement of financial position.

An example of the goodwill working is as follows:

Goodwill	£000
Consideration	X
Non-controlling interests at acquisition*	X
Net assets acquired	(X)
Impairment of goodwill	(X)
	X

*Non-controlling interest is discussed in the next section.

Note that the goodwill working has replaced the 'cancellation' working seen previously.

As goodwill is an intangible non-current asset with an indefinite useful life, an impairment test is conducted at least annually. Any resulting impairment loss is recognised against consolidated goodwill.

The double entry to record an impairment of goodwill is:

	Debit £	Credit £
Retained earnings (reduce reserves)	X	
Goodwill (reduce asset)		X

Activity 4: Thatch plc

Thatch plc acquired 100% of the issued share capital and voting rights of Straw Ltd on 1 January 20X6 for £8,000,000. At that date Straw Ltd had issued share capital of £3,000,000 and retained earnings of £2,000,000.

Extracts of the statements of financial position for the two companies at 31 December 20X6, as well as further information, are shown below.

	Thatch plc £000	Straw Ltd £000
ASSETS		
Property, plant and equipment	10,000	5,000
Investment in Straw Ltd	8,000	–
	18,000	5,000
Current assets	4,000	5,000
Total assets	22,000	10,000
EQUITY AND LIABILITIES		
Equity		
Share capital (£1 ordinary shares)	9,000	3,000
Retained earnings	6,000	5,000
	15,000	8,000
Liabilities		
Non-current liabilities	2,000	–
Current liabilities	5,000	2,000
	7,000	2,000
Total equity and liabilities	22,000	10,000

Further information:

In the current year, the directors of Thatch plc have concluded that goodwill is impaired by £1,000,000.

Required

Draft the consolidated statement of financial position for Thatch plc and its subsidiary undertaking as at 31 December 20X6.

Thatch plc
Consolidated statement of financial position as at 31 December 20X6

	£000
ASSETS	
Non-current assets	
Total assets	
EQUITY AND LIABILITIES	
Equity	
Liabilities	
Total equity and liabilities	

Workings (not provided in the assessment)
Group structure

Workings (on-screen proforma provided in the assessment)

Goodwill	£000

Retained earnings	£000

6 Non-controlling interests in the group statement of financial position

6.1 What are non-controlling interests?

The parent controls a subsidiary because it has >50% of the voting power

P
|
80%
|
S

The parent does not own all of the subsidiary

The **non-controlling interest** (NCI) is the 'equity in a subsidiary not attributable, directly or indirectly, to a parent' (IFRS 10: para. 22), ie the non-group shareholders' interest in the net assets of the subsidiary.

6.2 Points to note

(a) You do not have to own 100% of a company to control it.

(b) The group accounts will need to show the extent to which the assets and liabilities are controlled by the parent so we still add across, line by line, the parent and 100% of the subsidiary.

(c) The group accounts will also need to show the extent that the subsidiary's net assets are owned by other parties, namely the non-controlling interest. This results in a new working for the non-controlling interest (NCI).

For background information it is useful to be aware that there are two methods of valuing the non-controlling interest at acquisition (IFRS 3: para. 19):

- Fair value method
- Proportionate share method

In the *Financial Statements of Limited Companies* assessment the proportionate share method will be used. Therefore, task data will state that:

'Parent plc has decided that non-controlling interest will be valued at their proportionate share of net assets.'

An example of the NCI working is as follows:

NCI	£000
Share capital – attributable to NCI	X
Share premium – attributable to NCI	X
Retained earnings – attributable to NCI	X
Revaluation reserve – attributable to NCI	X
	X

Activity 5: Apple Ltd

Apple Ltd acquired 600,000 £1 ordinary shares in Orange Ltd for £4,000,000 on 1 January 20X2. At that date, the capital and reserves of Orange Ltd were:

	£000
Share capital (£1 ordinary shares)	1,000
Retained earnings	5,000
	6,000

Required

Calculate the amount of goodwill arising on the acquisition.

£ _____

Illustration 5 – Consolidated statement of financial position

On 1 January 20X4 A Ltd acquired 8,000,000 ordinary shares in B Ltd. On that date, the retained earnings reserve of B Ltd was £10,000,000. At 31 December 20X4, the statements of financial position of A Ltd and B Ltd were as follows:

	A Ltd £000	B Ltd £000
Property, plant and equipment	50,000	10,000
Investment in B Ltd	25,000	–
Current assets	40,000	25,000
	115,000	35,000
Share capital (£1 ordinary shares)	25,000	10,000
Retained earnings	75,000	15,000
	100,000	25,000
Current liabilities	15,000	10,000
	115,000	35,000

Step 1 Establish the group structure

A Ltd owns 80% (8,000/10,000) of the equity share capital of B Ltd.

Step 2 Calculate goodwill

Because there is a non-controlling interest, goodwill is calculated as the cost of the investment plus the non-controlling interest, **less the net assets acquired**.

The non-controlling interest (NCI) is measured as the non-controlling interest's share of B Ltd's net assets at the date of acquisition.

	£000	£000
Consideration transferred (price paid)		25,000
Plus non-controlling interest at acquisition (W)		4,000
Less fair value of net assets acquired		(20,000)
Goodwill		9,000
Working: NCI at acquisition		
Fair value of net assets acquired:		
Share capital	10,000	
Retained earnings	10,000	
	20,000	
NCI share (20%)	4,000	

Step 3 Calculate the consolidated retained earnings reserve

The consolidated retained earnings reserve only includes the group share **of post-acquisition profits**.

	£000	£000
A Ltd		75,000
B Ltd: at 31 December 20X4	15,000	
Less at acquisition	(10,000)	
	5,000	
Group share (80%)		4,000
		79,000

Step 4 Calculate the non-controlling interest

This is the non-controlling interest's share of the net assets of B Ltd at the reporting date.

	£000
Share capital attributable to NCI (20% × 10,000)	2,000
Retained earnings attributable to NCI (20% × 15,000)	3,000
	5,000

Step 5 Prepare the consolidated statement of financial position

Consolidated statement of financial position as at 31 December 20X4

	£000
Intangible assets: Goodwill (Step 2)	9,000
Property, plant and equipment	60,000
Current assets	65,000
	134,000

	£000
Share capital	25,000
Retained earnings (Step 3)	79,000
	104,000
Non-controlling interest (Step 4)	5,000
	109,000
Current liabilities	25,000
	134,000

Activity 6: Church plc

Church plc acquired 75% of the issued share capital and voting rights of Steeple Ltd at the date of the latter's incorporation on 1 January 20X5. The consideration was £5,000,000.

Extracts of the statements of financial position for the two companies at 31 December 20X6 are shown below.

	Church plc £000	Steeple Ltd £000
ASSETS		
Non-current assets		
Property, plant and equipment	10,000	7,000
Investment in Steeple Ltd	5,000	–
	15,000	7,000
Current assets	8,500	5,000
Total assets	23,500	12,000
EQUITY AND LIABILITIES		
Equity		
Share capital (£1 ordinary shares)	12,000	4,000
Retained earnings	1,500	1,000
	13,500	5,000
Liabilities		
Non-current liabilities	4,000	2,000
Current liabilities	6,000	5,000
	10,000	7,000
Total equity and liabilities	23,500	12,000

Further information:

• Church plc has decided that non-controlling interest will be valued at its proportionate share of net assets.

Required

Draft the consolidated statement of financial position for Church plc and its subsidiary undertaking as at 31 December 20X6.

Church plc
Consolidated statement of financial position as at 31 December 20X6

	£000
ASSETS	
Non-current assets	
Total assets	
EQUITY AND LIABILITIES	
Equity	
Total equity	
Liabilities	
Total equity and liabilities	

Workings (not provided in the assessment)

Group structure

Non-controlling interest at acquisition	£000

Non-controlling interest at year end	£000

Workings (on-screen proforma provided in the assessment)

Goodwill	£000

Retained earnings	£000

7 Intra-group adjustments

7.1 Issue

Group companies are likely to enter into transactions with each other. These may include:

- Sales by one group company to another
- Intra-group sales and purchases leading to outstanding receivables and payables
- Loans by one group company to another
- Receipts and payments of dividends

The purpose of **consolidation** is to present the parent and its subsidiaries as if they are trading as one entity.

Therefore, accounting standards state that in the group financial statements 'intra-group balances, transactions, income and expenses shall be eliminated in full'. (IFRS 10: para. B86)

7.2 Intra-group receivables and payables

Trading transactions will normally be recorded via a **current account** between the trading companies, which would also keep a track of amounts received and/or paid.

The current account receivable in one company's books should equal the current account payable in the other. These two balances are cancelled on consolidation so that the group is represented as a single economic entity. Therefore, intra-group receivables and payables are eliminated in the group financial statements.

7.3 Reconciliation of intra-group balances

Where current accounts do not agree at the year end this will be due to in-transit items such as inventories and cash.

Prior to consolidation, adjustments will need to be made for the cash or goods in transit. This is usually done by following through the transaction to its ultimate destination (accounting standards are not specific).

7.4 Method

Make the adjustments for in-transit items on your proforma answer after consolidating the assets and liabilities.

Adjustment for cash in transit

Adjustment for cash in transit	Debit £	Credit £
Cash	X	
Trade receivables		X

Goods in transit

Goods in transit	Debit £	Credit £
Inventories	X	
Trade payables		X

Intra-group cancellation

Eliminate intra-group payables and receivables	Debit £	Credit £
Intra-group trade payables	X	
Intra-group trade receivables		X

BPP
LEARNING MEDIA

Activity 7: Intra-group balances

X Ltd owns 80% of the equity share capital of Y Ltd. At the year end, X Ltd has trade receivables of £20,000 and Y Ltd has trade receivables of £15,000. The trade receivables of Y Ltd include an amount of £1,500 which is due from X Ltd.

Required

Calculate the amount for trade receivables included in the consolidated statement of financial position.

£ [   ]

7.5 Inventory sold at a profit within the group

Inventory should be stated at the lower of cost and net realisable value (IAS 2: para. 2.9).

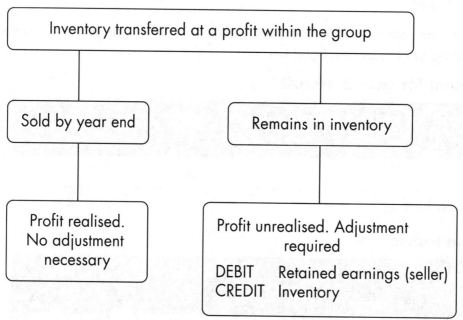

If inventory has been transferred within the group at a profit, and remains in inventory at the year end, it will be overstated as:

(a)   The inventory will be in the books at the marked-up price (and so needs to be written down to its original cost to the group)

(b)   The company which made the sale will have recorded a profit on the transaction as well (which must be eliminated in the group accounts)

If the parent makes the sale, adjustments must be made to:

- The parent's retained earnings working
- The inventory on the face of the statement of financial position

If the subsidiary makes the sale, adjustments must be made to:

(a)   The **subsidiary's retained earnings working** (before taking the parent's percentage);

(b)   The **non-controlling interest working** (the subsidiary's net assets will be reduced); and

(c)   The inventory on the face of the statement of financial position.

These adjustments take place as consolidation adjustments and do not affect the parent or subsidiary's individual financial statements.

Illustration 6 – Intra-group sales

Kilvert Ltd owns 60% of the issued share capital of Woodford Ltd. At the year end, their statements of financial position showed inventories of £100,000 and £50,000 respectively. Kilvert Ltd sells goods to Woodford Ltd at a mark-up of 25% on cost. At the year end, goods which had been purchased from Kilvert Ltd for £30,000 remained in the inventories of Woodford Ltd.

Calculate the amount of inventories that should be recognised in the consolidated statement of financial position of the group at the year end.

£	

Solution

£	144,000

Inventories:

	£
Kilvert Ltd	100,000
Woodford Ltd	50,000
Less provision for unrealised profit (30,000 × 25/125)	(6,000)
	144,000

Activity 8: Door plc

Door plc acquired 60% of the issued share capital and voting rights of Window Ltd on 31 December 20X0 for £27,000,000. At that date, Window Ltd had issued share capital of £10,000,000 and retained earnings of £32,000,000.

Below are the statements of financial position for both companies at 31 December 20X1.

	Door plc £000	Window Ltd £000
ASSETS		
Non-current assets		
Property, plant and equipment	200,000	40,000
Investment in Window Ltd	27,000	–
	227,000	40,000
Current assets		
Inventories	22,000	18,000
Trade and other receivables	75,000	49,000
Cash and cash equivalents	4,000	15,000
	101,000	82,000
Total assets	328,000	122,000
EQUITY AND LIABILITIES		
Equity		
Share capital	100,000	10,000
Retained earnings	147,000	42,000
	247,000	52,000
Non-current liabilities		
Bank loan	–	20,000
Current liabilities		
Trade and other payables	81,000	50,000
Total liabilities	81,000	70,000
Total equity and liabilities	328,000	122,000

Further information:

(a) There was cash in transit of £4,000,000 from Door plc to Window Ltd at year end.

(b) Included in Window Ltd's trade and other receivables is £40,000,000 owed from Door plc. Included in Door plc's trade and other payables is £36,000,000 due to Window Ltd.

(c) During the year, Window Ltd sold some inventory to Door plc for £40,000,000. These goods had cost Window Ltd £30,000,000. Half of these goods still remain in inventories at the year end. There were no intra-group balances outstanding at the end of the year in respect of this transaction in trade receivables or trade payables.

(d) Door plc has decided that non-controlling interest will be valued at its proportionate share of net assets.

Required

Draft the consolidated statement of financial position for Door plc and its subsidiary undertaking as at 31 December 20X1.

Door plc
Consolidated statement of financial position

	£000
ASSETS	
Non-current assets	
Current assets	
Total assets	

	£000
EQUITY AND LIABILITIES	
Total equity	
Non-current liabilities	
Current liabilities	
Total liabilities	
Total equity and liabilities	

Workings (not provided in the assessment)

Group structure

Non-controlling interest at acquisition	£000

Non-controlling interest at year end	£000

Adjustment for cash in transit

Adjustment for cash in transit	Debit £000	Credit £000

Intra-group cancellation

Eliminate intra-group payables and receivables	Debit £000	Credit £000

Trade receivables	£000

Workings (on-screen proforma provided in the assessment)

Goodwill	£000

Inventories	£000
Consolidated inventories (prior to any company adjustment)	
Inter-company adjustment	

Retained earnings	£000

7.6 Intra-group loans

A company may make a loan to another member of the group. Where this arises it must be eliminated in the consolidated financial statements.

For example, if a parent has made a loan of £10,000 to a subsidiary, and this is outstanding at the year end, the journal to eliminate it in the group statement of financial position (SOFP) is:

Intra-group cancellation

Eliminate intra-group loan and loan receivable	Debit £	Credit £
Intra-group loan payable (subsidiary – SOFP)	10,000	
Intra-group loan receivable (parent – SOFP)		10,000

8 Fair value adjustments

Let us remind ourselves that goodwill is defined as:

	£
Consideration transferred	X
Less fair value of identifiable assets and liabilities at acquisition	(X)
	X

Assets and liabilities in an entity's own financial statements are often not stated at their fair value.

The identifiable assets and liabilities of subsidiaries are, therefore, required to be brought into the consolidated financial statements at their fair value rather than their book value.

The difference between fair values and book values is a consolidation adjustment. In the group financial statements adjustments need to be made to:

- Non-current assets (which reflects control of assets on the SOFP)

- Goodwill (amount attributable to the parent in respect of the fair value adjustment)

- NCI (amount attributable to NCI in respect of the fair value adjustment)

Illustration 7 – Fair value adjustments

Hardy plc acquired 80% of the issued share capital and voting rights of Woolf Ltd on 31 December 20X1 for £3,000,000.

Statement of financial position (extract) as at 31 December 20X1

	Hardy plc £000	Woolf Ltd £000
Non-current assets		
Property, plant and equipment	5,000	2,200
Investment in Woolf Ltd	3,000	
	8,000	2,200
Equity		
Share capital	5,000	2,000
Retained earnings	900	500
	5,900	2,500

Further information:

- At 31 December 20X1 the fair value of the non-current assets of Woolf Ltd was £300,000 more than carrying value. This valuation has not been recorded in the books of Woolf Ltd (ignore any effect of depreciation for the year).

- Hardy plc has decided that non-controlling interest will be valued at their proportionate share of net assets.

Complete the extracts to the consolidated statement of financial position for Hardy plc and its subsidiary undertaking for the year ended 31 December 20X1.

Hardy plc
Consolidated statement of financial position (extract) as at 31 December 20X1

	Hardy plc £000
Non-current assets	
Goodwill	760
Property, plant and equipment (5,000 + 2,200 + 300)	7,500
	8,260
Equity	
Share capital – £1 ordinary shares	5,000
Retained earnings	900
Non-controlling interest	560
	6,460

Workings (not provided in the assessment)

Group structure

Hardy plc

80%

Woolf Ltd

Workings (on-screen proforma provided in the assessment)

Goodwill	£000
Consideration	3,000
Non-controlling interest at acquisition	560
Net assets acquired	(2,800)
	760

Non-controlling interest (NCI) at acquisition/year end	£000
Share capital – attributable to NCI (2,000 × 20%)	400
Retained earnings – attributable to NCI (500 × 20%)	100
Revaluation reserve – attributable to NCI (300 × 20%)	60
	560

9 Assessment-standard question

Now that we have considered a range of consolidation adjustments we will work through an assessment-standard question.

The next example provides the necessary practice in preparing a consolidated statement of financial position.

In group accounts questions you will be required to process a number of adjustments in one question.

To be successful in these tasks, a solid method is vital. The steps you should follow are to:

(1) Read the requirement(s) and scan the task.

(2) Review the 'further information' carefully and identify which on-screen workings are available.

(3) Work methodically down the statements of financial position for the parent and the subsidiary. Enter the figures:

- In a financial statement proforma (if they require no further adjustment)

- In an on-screen working (if they require adjustment and an on-screen working is provided)

- On scrap paper (if they require adjustment and an on-screen working is not provided)

(4) Complete the workings and include your totals in the proforma.

(5) Then, total your consolidated statement of financial position.

(6) Review your answer carefully, checking you have dealt with all the items. Does it make sense?

Note. In the assessment you will need to click on a pop-up box for the 'further information'.

Activity 9: Morse plc

Morse plc acquired 60% of the issued share capital and voting rights of Lewis Ltd on 1 January 20X0 for £24,000,000. At that date, Lewis Ltd had issued share capital of £10,000,000, share premium of £5,000,000 and retained earnings of £11,263,000.

Extracts of the statements of financial position for the two companies at 31 December 20X0 are shown below.

Statements of financial position as at 31 December 20X0

	Morse plc £000	Lewis Ltd £000
ASSETS		
Non-current assets		
Property, plant and equipment	63,781	27,184
Investment in Lewis Ltd	24,000	–
	87,781	27,184
Current assets		
Inventories	18,283	14,684
Trade and other receivables	29,474	14,023
Cash and cash equivalents	2,872	88
	50,629	28,795
Total assets	138,410	55,979
EQUITY AND LIABILITIES		
Equity		
Share capital	45,000	10,000
Share premium	13,000	5,000
Retained earnings	33,416	17,763
Total equity	91,416	32,763
Non-current liabilities		
Long-term loans	25,000	8,000

	Morse plc £000	Lewis Ltd £000
Current liabilities		
Trade and other payables	16,231	15,042
Tax liability	5,763	174
	21,994	15,216
Total liabilities	46,994	23,216
Total equity and liabilities	138,410	55,979

Further information:

(a) At 1 January 20X0 the fair value of the non-current assets of Lewis Ltd was £2,500,000 more than carrying amount. This valuation has not been recorded in the books of Lewis Ltd (ignore any effect of depreciation for the year).

(b) Included in Morse plc's trade and other receivables is £13,000,000 owed from Lewis Ltd. Included in Lewis Ltd's trade and other payables is £13,000,000 due to Morse plc.

(c) During the year Morse plc sold some inventory to Lewis Ltd for £50,000,000. These goods had cost Morse plc £30,000,000. A quarter of these goods still remain in inventories at the year end. There were no intra-group balances outstanding at the end of the year in respect of this transaction in trade receivables or trade payables.

(d) The directors of Morse plc have concluded that goodwill has been impaired by £674,000 during the year.

(e) Morse plc has decided that non-controlling interest will be valued at its proportionate share of net assets.

Required

Draft the consolidated statement of financial position for Morse plc and its subsidiary undertaking as at 31 December 20X0.

Morse plc
Consolidated statement of financial position as at 31 December 20X0

		£000
ASSETS		
Non-current assets		
	▼	
	▼	
Current assets		
	▼	
	▼	
	▼	
Total assets		
EQUITY AND LIABILITIES		
	▼	
	▼	
	▼	
	▼	
Total equity		
Non-current liabilities		
	▼	
Current liabilities		
	▼	
	▼	
Total liabilities		
Total equity and liabilities		

Picklist:

Cash and cash equivalents
Goodwill
Inventories
Long-term loans
Property, plant and equipment
Non-controlling interest
Retained earnings
Share capital
Share premium
Tax liability
Trade and other payables
Trade and other receivables
Non-controlling interest at acquisition
Non-controlling interest at year end
Net assets acquired

Workings (not provided in the assessment)

Group structure

Non-controlling interest at acquisition	£000

Non-controlling interest at year end	£000

Eliminate intra-group receivable and payable	Debit £000	Credit £000

Workings (on-screen proforma provided in the assessment)

Goodwill	£000

Inventories	£000
Consolidated inventories (prior to any company adjustment)	
Inter-company adjustment	

Retained earnings	£000

Note. In the assessment picklists for the narrative entries are provided for the on-screen workings.

Chapter summary

- A group of companies consists of a parent (holding) company and one or more subsidiaries under the control of the parent.
- A parent must prepare consolidated financial statements for its group.
- An entity is a subsidiary of another (the parent) if that other entity can control it.
- An investor controls an investee if, and only if, the investor has all the following:
  - Power over the investee
  - Exposure, or rights, to variable returns from its involvement with the investee
  - The ability to use its power over the investee to affect the amount of the investor's returns
- To prepare a consolidated statement of financial position:
  (1) Calculate the proportion of the subsidiary's shares owned by the parent
  (2) Calculate goodwill: consideration transferred (cost of investment) plus non-controlling interest less net assets acquired
  (3) Calculate consolidated retained earnings reserve: parent plus group share of post-acquisition reserves of subsidiary
  (4) Calculate non-controlling interest: non-controlling interest's share of net assets of subsidiary at year end
  (5) Complete the consolidated statement of financial position by adding the parent's assets and liabilities and the subsidiary's assets and liabilities together, line by line
- Goodwill is recognised as an asset and carried at cost. It must be reviewed for impairment at least annually.
- Non-controlling interest at acquisition is normally measured at the proportionate share of the fair value of the subsidiary's net assets.
- The identifiable assets and liabilities of a subsidiary are included in the consolidated financial statements at their fair values at the date of the acquisition.
- Adjustment to eliminate unrealised profit on intra-group sales:

  Sale from parent to subsidiary

  DEBIT   Consolidated retained earnings

  CREDIT   Inventories

  Sale from subsidiary to parent

  DEBIT   Consolidated retained earnings (group share)

  DEBIT   Non-controlling interest (non-controlling interest's share)

  CREDIT   Inventories

- **Business:** An integrated set of activities and assets that is capable of being conducted and managed for the purpose of providing a return in the form of dividends, lower costs or other economic benefits directly to investors or other owners

- **Business combination:** A transaction or other event in which an acquirer obtains control of one or more businesses

- **Consolidated financial statements:** The financial statements of a group presented as those of a single economic entity

- **Consolidation:** The process of adjusting and combining financial information from the individual financial statements of a parent and its subsidiary to prepare consolidated financial statements

- **Control:** An investor controls an investee when the investor is exposed, or has rights, to variable returns from its involvement with the investee and has the ability to affect those returns through its power over the investee

- **Fair value:** The price that would be received to sell an asset or paid to transfer a liability in an orderly transaction between market participants at the measurement date

- **Goodwill:** An asset representing the future economic benefits arising from other assets acquired in a business combination that are not individually identified and separately recognised

- **Group:** A parent (holding) company and its subsidiaries

- **Identifiable:** Either separable or arising from contractual or other legal rights

- **Non-controlling interest:** The equity in a subsidiary not attributable to the parent

- **Parent:** An entity that controls one or more subsidiaries

- **Power:** An investor has power over an investee when it has existing rights that give it the current ability to direct its relevant activities

- **Subsidiary:** An entity that is controlled by another entity (the parent)

Test your learning

1 A plc owns the following investments in other companies:

- B Ltd: 15% of the ordinary shares and 80% of the preference shares
- C Ltd: 80% of the ordinary shares
- D Ltd: 45% of the ordinary shares
- E Ltd: 25% of the ordinary shares and 60% of the loan stock

A plc has the right to appoint three of the four directors of D Ltd.

Which of the four companies are subsidiaries of A plc?

C Ltd only	
B Ltd and C Ltd	
C Ltd and D Ltd	
All four companies	

2 The directors of Sella Ltd are considering acquiring a significant investment of equity shares in another company.

Prepare brief notes for the directors of Sella Ltd to answer the following questions:

(a) What is a subsidiary, according to IFRS 10 Consolidated Financial Statements?

(b) Under what circumstances does one company control another?

3 The summarised statements of financial position of Left plc and Right Ltd as at 31 December 20X9 were as follows:

	Left plc £000	Right Ltd £000
Investment in Right Ltd	9,000	–
Other assets	45,000	15,000
	54,000	15,000
Share capital	10,000	5,000
Retained earnings	28,000	3,000
	38,000	8,000
Liabilities	16,000	7,000
	54,000	15,000

On 1 January 20X9 Left plc acquired 95% of the share capital of Right Ltd for £9,000,000 in cash. At that date the retained earnings of Right Ltd were £2,000,000. There is no impairment of goodwill.

(a) How much goodwill arose on the combination?

£1,000,000	
£1,400,000	
£2,000,000	
£2,350,000	

(b) What amount should be recognised as consolidated retained earnings at 31 December 20X9?

£28,950,000	
£29,000,000	
£30,850,000	
£31,000,000	

(c) What amount should be recognised as non-controlling interest at 31 December 20X9?

£250,000	
£300,000	
£350,000	
£400,000	

4   **Explain why the assets and liabilities of an acquired subsidiary should be adjusted to fair value before they are included in the consolidated statement of financial position.**

5   Grand plc sells goods which cost £15,000 to its 100% subsidiary, Small Ltd, for £20,000. None of these goods remain in the inventories of Small Ltd at the year end.

No adjustment for unrealised profit is required in the consolidated financial statement of financial position.

Is this statement true or false?

True	
False	

6   The following statements of financial position relate to Salt plc and its subsidiary, Pepper Ltd, at 31 March 20X7:

	Salt plc £000	Pepper Ltd £000
Assets		
Non-current assets:		
Property, plant and equipment	8,000	6,000
Investment in Pepper Ltd	4,000	–
	12,000	6,000
Current assets:		
Inventories	2,400	1,440
Trade and other receivables	2,640	2,400
Cash and cash equivalents	480	360
	5,520	4,200
Total assets	17,520	10,200
Equity and liabilities		
Equity:		
Share capital (£1 ordinary shares)	5,000	1,000
Retained earnings	7,960	6,200
Total equity	12,960	7,200
Non-current liabilities	1,200	1,080
Current liabilities:		
Trade payables	2,500	1,700
Tax payable	860	220
	3,360	1,920
Total liabilities	4,560	3,000
Total equity and liabilities	17,520	10,200

Additional data:

(1)   Salt plc purchased 800,000 ordinary shares in Pepper Ltd on 1 April 20X5 when the retained earnings reserve of Pepper Ltd was £2,500,000.

(2)   At 31 March 20X7, the trade payables of Salt plc included £960,000 which was owed to Pepper Ltd.

Prepare the consolidated statement of financial position of Salt plc and its subsidiary as at 31 March 20X7.

Consolidated statement of financial position as at 31 March 20X7

	£000
ASSETS	
Non-current assets:	
Intangible assets: Goodwill	
Property, plant and equipment	
Current assets:	
Inventories	
Trade and other receivables	
Cash and cash equivalents	
Total assets	
EQUITY AND LIABILITIES	
Equity attributable to owners of the parent:	
Share capital	
Retained earnings	
Non-controlling interest	
Total equity	
Non-current liabilities	
Current liabilities:	
Trade payables	
Tax payable	
Total liabilities	
Total equity and liabilities	

Workings

(Complete the left-hand column by writing in the correct narrative from the list provided.)

Goodwill		£000
	▼	
	▼	
	▼	

Picklist:

Net assets acquired
Non-controlling interests at acquisition
Price paid
Retained earnings attributable to Salt plc
Share capital attributable to Salt plc

Retained earnings		£000
	▼	
	▼	

Picklist:

Pepper Ltd attributable to Salt plc
Salt plc

Non-controlling interest at acquisition		£000
	▼	
	▼	

Picklist:

Current assets attributable to NCI
Non-current assets attributable to NCI
Price paid
Retained earnings attributable to NCI
Share capital attributable to NCI

Non-controlling interest at year end	£000
▼	
▼	

Picklist:

Current assets attributable to NCI
Non-current assets attributable to NCI
Price paid
Retained earnings attributable to NCI
Share capital attributable to NCI

Group accounts: further aspects

10

Learning outcomes

1.1	**Explain the regulatory framework that underpins financial reporting**
	• The purpose of financial statements
2.1	**Examine the effect of international accounting standards on the preparation of financial statements**
	• Explain the effect of international accounting standards on the presentation, valuation and disclosure of items within the financial statements
	• Make any supporting calculations
3.1	**Draft a statement of profit or loss and other comprehensive income**
	• Make appropriate entries in the statement in respect of information extracted from a trial balance and additional information
4.1	**Draft a consolidated statement of profit or loss for a parent company with one partly-owned subsidiary**
	• Consolidate each line item in the statement of profit or loss
	• Treat inter-company sales and other intercompany items, impairment losses on goodwill and dividends paid by a subsidiary company to its parent company
	• Calculate and treat unrealised profit on inventories and non-controlling interest

Assessment context

You will be required to prepare a consolidated statement of financial position and/or a consolidated statement of profit or loss. On-screen workings will be provided for some of the calculations.

Qualification context

Consolidated financial statements are only tested in this course.

Business context

Many larger businesses are part of a group of companies (ie there is a parent company and at least one subsidiary). The shareholders of the parent company use consolidated financial statements to assess the financial position and performance of the group.

Chapter overview

Group accounts: further aspects

Consolidated statement of profit or loss

Shows the results of the group for an accounting period as if it were a single business entity

Eliminate intra-group transactions

Eliminate intra-group transactions from the revenue and cost of sales figures:

DEBIT Group revenue
CREDIT Group cost of sales

with the total amount of the intra-group sales between the companies.

This adjustment is needed regardless of whether any of the goods are still in inventories at the year end.

Eliminate unrealised profit

Eliminate unrealised profit on goods still in inventories at the year end:

DEBIT Cost of sales (SPL) × (PUP)
CREDIT Inventories (SOFP) × (PUP)

in the books of the company making the sale.

This is only needed if there are any goods still in inventories at the year end.

Introduction

This chapter explains how to prepare a consolidated statement of profit or loss and looks at a number of further aspects of group accounts: intra-group transactions and unrealised profit.

Assessment focus point

Another category of investment, associates, were assessable under the previous standards, AQ2013. BPP has had confirmation from AAT that **associates** are not assessable under AQ2016 and so **will not be tested in the assessment**.

1 Consolidated statement of profit or loss

The consolidated statement of profit or loss shows the results of the group for an accounting period as if it were a single entity.

1.1 The basic idea

As with the consolidated statement of financial position, there are basically two steps:

- Add together the statements of the parent and the subsidiary
- Make adjustments to cancel out intra-group items

Exactly the same philosophy is adopted as for the statement of financial position, ie control in the first instance.

1.2 Recognising control

To recognise control, the parent and subsidiary's income and expenses must be added on a line by line basis.

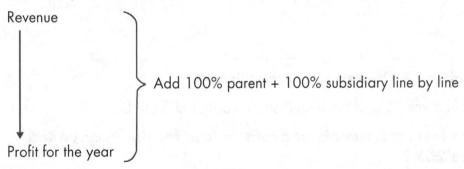

Revenue

Profit for the year

Add 100% parent + 100% subsidiary line by line

Note. Exclude dividend income from the subsidiary.

The parent controls the assets and liabilities which generate the income and expenses. Therefore, the consolidated statement of profit or loss shows profits resulting from the **control** exercised by the parent.

1.3 Recognising ownership

The consolidated statement of profit or loss also needs to show ownership of the profit or loss for the period.

This is reflected in a new reconciliation presented at the foot of the consolidated statement of profit or loss.

Recognising control and ownership

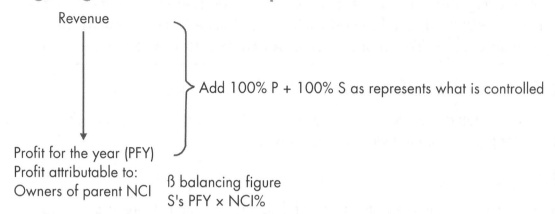

Revenue

Add 100% P + 100% S as represents what is controlled

Profit for the year (PFY)
Profit attributable to:
Owners of parent NCI   ß balancing figure
S's PFY × NCI%

To complete the ownership reconciliation:

(1)   Copy down total profit for the year, per the consolidated financial statements
(2)   Calculate the amount due to non-controlling interest shareholders (W)
(3)   Make the amount attributable to owners of the parent a balancing figure

The amount due to the non-controlling interest (NCI) shareholders is calculated as:

Workings (not provided in the assessment)

Non-controlling interest	£
NCI% × subsidiary's profit for the year per their individual statement of profit or loss	X

Illustration 1 – Ownership reconciliation

Thatch plc owns 75% of the issued share capital of Slate Ltd.

Extracts from statements of profit or loss for the year ended 30 June 20X9

	Thatch plc	Slate Ltd
	£000	£000
Profit from operations	685	90
Dividends received from Slate Ltd	15	–
Profit before tax	700	90
Tax	(150)	(30)
Profit for the year	550	60

Prepare the consolidated statement of profit or loss for Thatch plc and its subsidiary, for the year ended 30 June 20X9.

Solution

Consolidated statement of profit or loss for the year ended 30 June 20X9 (extract)

	£000
Profit before tax	775
Tax	(180)
Profit for the year from continuing operations	595
Attributable to:	
Equity holders of the parent	580
Non-controlling interests (25% × 60)	15
	595

Activity 1: Baker plc

Baker plc acquired 80% of the issued share capital of Bun Ltd on 1 January 20X5.

Extracts of the statements of profit or loss for the two companies for the year ended 31 December 20X9, as well as further information, are shown below.

Baker plc

Statement of profit or loss for the year ended 31 December 20X9

	Baker plc £000	Bun Ltd £000
Revenue	115	60
Cost of sales	(65)	(28)
Gross profit	50	32
Distribution costs	(5)	(8)
Administrative expenses	(14)	(11)
Profit from operations	31	13
Finance costs	(1)	(1)
Profit before tax	30	12
Tax	(8)	(2)
Profit for the year	22	10

Further information:

There were no impairment losses on goodwill during the year.

Required

Draft the consolidated statement of profit or loss for Baker plc and its subsidiary undertaking for the year ended 31 December 20X9.

Baker plc
Statement of profit or loss for the year ended 31 December 20X9

	£000
Revenue	
Profit from operations	
Profit before tax	
Profit for the year	

Workings (not provided in the assessment)

Group structure

Non-controlling interest	£000

2 Approach to the consolidated statement of profit or loss

As we saw in the previous chapter, consolidation questions can include a range of adjustments. A methodical approach will enable you to maximise your mark!

The recommended approach to preparing the consolidated statement of profit or loss is similar to the approach to preparing a consolidated statement of financial position.

The steps you should follow are to:

Step 1 Read the requirement(s) and scan the task.

Step 2 Review the 'further information' carefully and identify which on-screen workings are available.

Step 3 Work methodically down the statements of profit or loss for the parent and subsidiary. Enter the figures:

- In a financial statement proforma (if they require no further adjustment)

- In an on-screen working (if they require adjustment and an on-screen working is provided)

- On scrap paper (if they require adjustment and an on-screen working is not provided)

Step 4 Complete the workings and include your totals in the proforma.

Step 5 Total your consolidated statement of profit or loss down to 'profit for the year'.

Step 6 Complete the profit reconciliation, remembering to calculate non-controlling interests and make profit attributable to equity holders of the parent a balancing figure.

Step 7 Review your answer carefully, checking you have dealt with all the items. Does it make sense?

3 Intra-group trading in the group statement of profit or loss

3.1 Issue

It is common for companies within a group to trade with each other. In the single entity financial statements, these sales and purchases represent valid transactions.

However, when considering the group as if it were a single entity, intra-group trading represents transactions which the group undertakes with itself. They have to be eliminated on consolidation as, otherwise, revenue and cost of sales will be overstated.

Also, the value of inventories in the consolidated statement of profit or loss may need to be adjusted to ensure it represents the cost to the group.

3.2 Method

There are two potential adjustments needed when group companies trade with each other:

(a)   Eliminate intra-group transactions from the revenue and cost of sales figures with the **total** amount of the intra-group sales between the companies:

Eliminate intra-group sale	Debit £	Credit £
Group revenue	X	
Group cost of sales		X

This adjustment is needed regardless of whether any of the goods are still in inventories at the year end.

(b)   Eliminate unrealised profit on goods still in inventories at the year end in the books of the company making the sale:

Eliminate unrealised profit	Debit £	Credit £
Cost of sales (SPL)	X	
Inventories (SOFP)		X

As with the statement of financial position, this is only needed if there are any goods still in inventories at the year end.

If the subsidiary makes the sale and the goods are still in inventories at the year end, adjustments must be made to non-controlling interests. In the ownership reconciliation, the amount attributable to non-controlling interests will be reduced by their share of the unrealised profit.

Activity 2: Intra-group sale

Timber Ltd is a 100%-owned subsidiary of Wood Ltd. During the year, Timber Ltd sold goods that originally cost £30,000 to Wood Ltd for £40,000. At the year end, half those goods remained in inventory.

Required

What adjustment should be made to the cost of sales figure in the consolidated statement of profit or loss to reflect this transaction?

Reduce by £25,000	
Reduce by £30,000	
Reduce by £35,000	
Reduce by £40,000	

3.3 Dividends

Any dividends the parent receives from the subsidiary must also be removed from the parent's statement of profit or loss, as these represent intra-group receipts. Therefore, it will not be included in the consolidated statement of profit or loss, as the group company cannot pay a dividend to itself.

(The other side of the intra-group transaction will be addressed in the statement of changes in equity. However, this is not examinable.)

Activity 3: Pike plc

Pike plc acquired 70% of the issued share capital and voting rights of Shrimp Ltd on 1 January 20X1.

Extracts of the statements of profit or loss for the two companies for the year ended 31 December 20X1, as well as further information, are shown below.

Pike plc
Statement of profit or loss for the year ended 31 December 20X1

	Pike plc £000	Shrimp Ltd £000
Revenue	321	104
Cost of sales	(184)	(32)
Gross profit	137	72
Other income – dividend received from Shrimp Ltd	10	
Distribution costs	(18)	(9)
Administrative expenses	(20)	(18)
Profit from operations	109	45
Finance costs	(5)	(3)
Profit before tax	104	42
Tax	(30)	(12)
Profit for the year	74	30

Further information:

During 20X1, Pike plc sold goods to Shrimp Ltd for £14,000. These goods were not in the inventory of Shrimp Ltd at 31 December 20X1.

Required

Draft the consolidated statement of profit or loss for Pike plc and its subsidiary undertaking for the year ended 31 December 20X1.

Pike plc
Statement of profit or loss for the year ended 31 December 20X1

	£000
Revenue	
▼	
▼	
▼	
▼	
Profit from operations	
▼	
Profit before tax	
▼	
Profit for the year	

Picklist:

Administrative expenses
Cost of sales
Distribution costs
Finance costs
Gross profit
Revenue
Tax

Note. In the assessment, picklists will also be provided for the workings.

Workings (not provided in the assessment)

Group structure

Non-controlling interest	£000

Total inter-company adjustment	Debit £000	Credit £000

Workings (on-screen proforma provided in the assessment)

Revenue	£000

Cost of sales	£000

The next example looks at the sale of goods in the year with the goods still on hand at the year end. The parent sold the goods to the subsidiary.

Activity 4: Platini plc

Platini plc bought 90% of the ordinary shares of Maldini Ltd two years ago on 1 January 20W9.

Extracts of the statements of profit or loss for the two companies for the year ended 31 December 20X1, as well as further information, are shown below.

Platini plc
Statement of profit or loss for the year ended 31 December 20X1

	Platini plc £000	Maldini Ltd £000
Revenue	565	140
Cost of sales	(235)	(58)
Gross profit	330	82
Other income – dividend received from Maldini Ltd	20	
Distribution costs	(65)	(18)
Administrative expenses	(90)	(10)
Profit from operations	195	54
Finance costs	(5)	(2)
Profit before tax	190	52
Tax	(50)	(12)
Profit for the year	140	40

Further information:

During the year Platini plc sold some inventory to Maldini Ltd for £21,000. These goods had cost Platini plc £18,000. These goods were still in the inventories of Maldini Ltd at 31 December 20X1.

Required

Draft the consolidated statement of profit or loss for Platini plc and its subsidiary undertaking for the year ended 31 December 20X1.

Platini plc

Statement of profit or loss for the year ended 31 December 20X1

	£000
Revenue	
Profit from operations	
Profit before tax	
Profit for the year	

Workings (not provided in the assessment)

Group structure

Non-controlling interest	£000

Total inter-company adjustment	Debit £000	Credit £000

Eliminate unrealised profit	Debit £000	Credit £000

Workings (on-screen proforma provided in the assessment)

Revenue	£000

Cost of sales	£000

In the next example there has been another intra-group sale. Some of the goods are on hand at year end and, this time, the subsidiary is the seller.

Activity 5: Platypus plc

Platypus plc bought 75% of the ordinary shares of Serpent Ltd on 1 January 20X0.

Extracts of the statements of profit or loss for the two companies for the year ended 31 December 20X5, as well as further information, are shown below.

Platypus plc
Statement of profit or loss for the year ended 31 December 20X5

	Platypus plc £000	Serpent Ltd £000
Revenue	213	126
Cost of sales	(87)	(38)
Gross profit	126	88
Other income – dividend received from Serpent Ltd	10	
Distribution costs	(35)	(18)
Administrative expenses	(36)	(14)
Profit from operations	65	56
Finance costs	(6)	(3)
Profit before tax	59	53
Tax	(15)	(18)
Profit for the year	44	35

Further information:

- During the year Serpent Ltd sold goods, which had cost £19,000, to Platypus plc for £25,000. Half these goods still remain in inventories at the year end.

- The directors of Platypus plc have concluded that goodwill has not been impaired.

- Platypus plc has decided that non-controlling interest will be valued at its proportionate share of net assets.

Required

Prepare the consolidated statement of profit or loss for Platypus plc and its subsidiary undertaking for the year ended 31 December 20X5.

Platypus plc
Statement of profit or loss for the year ended 31 December 20X5

	£000
Revenue	
▽	
▽	
▽	
▽	
Profit from operations	
▽	
Profit before tax	
▽	
Profit for the year	

Picklist:

Administrative expenses
Cost of sales
Distribution costs
Finance costs
Gross profit
Revenue
Tax

Note. In the assessment, picklists will also be provided for the workings.

Workings (not provided in the assessment)

Group structure

Non-controlling interest	£000

Total inter-company adjustment	Debit £000	Credit £000

Eliminate unrealised profit	Debit £000	Credit £000

Provision for unrealised profit calculation	£000

Workings (on-screen proforma provided in the assessment)

Revenue	£000

Cost of sales	£000

Assessment focus point

A consolidated statement of profit or loss could appear as Task 6 of your assessment **instead of a consolidated statement of financial position**. It could also appear **in addition to a consolidated statement of financial position**, as it did in one of the AAT's sample assessments, but if this is the case, you will usually only need to produce the statement **up to and including profit before tax**.

Chapter summary

- To prepare a consolidated statement of profit or loss:

  - Add together the statements of the parent and the subsidiary, line by line
  - Split the profit for the year between the parent and the non-controlling interest

- Where one company sells goods to another, two adjustments must be made to the consolidated statement of profit or loss:

  (1) To eliminate the sale:

  DEBIT   Revenue
  CREDIT   Cost of sales

  (2) To eliminate unrealised profit:

  - Increase cost of sales by amount of unrealised profit

  - If the sale is from subsidiary to parent, deduct NCI's share of unrealised profit from profit or loss attributable to NCI

- Consolidated financial statements must include all subsidiaries of the parent.

- Uniform accounting policies must be used.

- All business combinations must be accounted for by applying the acquisition method.

Keywords

- **Acquisition:** A business combination in which one company (the parent) acquires and controls the other (the subsidiary)

1 **Explain why adjustments are made in consolidated financial statements when one group company sells goods to another.**

2 Stansfield Ltd is a 75% subsidiary of Purton Ltd. An extract from its statement of profit or loss is shown below:

	£000
Profit before tax	7,500
Tax	(2,000)
Profit for the year	5,500

During the year, Purton Ltd sold goods to Stansfield Ltd. As a result, inventories in the consolidated statement of financial position have been reduced to reflect unrealised profit of £12,000.

The profit for the year attributable to non-controlling interests is £1,375,000.

Is this statement true or false?

True	
False	

3 Denston Ltd has owned 60% of the share capital of Hawkedon Ltd and 30% of the share capital of Clare Ltd for many years. Revenue for the year ended 30 September 20X9 for each of the three companies was as follows:

	£
Denston Ltd	950,000
Hawkedon Ltd	500,000
Clare Ltd	300,000

What figure for revenue will be reported in the consolidated statement of profit or loss for the year ended 30 September 20X9?

£1,250,000	
£1,340,000	
£1,450,000	
£1,540,000	

4 Aldeburgh plc has owned 100% of the share capital of Southwold Ltd for many years. Cost of sales for the year ended 31 December 20X9 for each of the two companies was as follows:

	£
Aldeburgh plc	800,000
Southwold Ltd	600,000

During the year Aldeburgh plc sold goods that had originally cost £100,000 to Southwold Ltd for £125,000. All of these goods remained in the inventories of Southwold Ltd at 31 December 20X9.

What figure for cost of sales will be reported in the consolidated statement of profit or loss for the year ended 30 September 20X9?

£1,250,000	
£1,275,000	
£1,300,000	
£1,400,000	

5   Below are the statements of profit or loss for Thames plc and Stour Ltd:

	Thames plc £000	Stour Ltd £000
Revenue	2,280	1,200
Cost of sales	(1,320)	(660)
Gross profit	960	540
Other income (dividend from Stour Ltd)	85	–
Operating expenses	(360)	(180)
Profit before tax	685	360
Tax	(240)	(120)
Profit for the year	445	240

Further information:

(1)   The issued share capital of Stour Ltd consists of 100,000 ordinary shares of £1 each.

(2)   Thames plc acquired 85,000 of the ordinary shares of Stour Ltd on 1 January 20X0.

(3)   During the year, Stour Ltd made sales totalling £600,000 to Thames plc. All these goods had been sold by 31 December 20X3.

(4)   There is no impairment of goodwill.

(5)   During the year Stour Ltd paid a dividend of £100,000.

Prepare the consolidated statement of profit or loss of Thames plc and its subsidiary for the year ended 31 December 20X3.

Consolidated statement of profit or loss for the year ended 31 December 20X3

	£000
Revenue	
Cost of sales	
Gross profit	
Other income	
Operating expenses	
Profit before tax	
Tax	
Profit for the year	
Attributable to:	
Equity holders of the parent	
Non-controlling interest	

Workings

Revenue	£000
Thames plc	
Stour Ltd	
Total inter-company adjustment	

Cost of sales	£000
Thames plc	
Stour Ltd	
Total inter-company adjustment	

Interpreting financial statements

Learning outcomes

5.1	Calculate ratios with regard to profitability, liquidity, efficient use of resources and financial position
	• Calculate the following ratios:
	Profitability
	– return on capital employed
	– return on equity
	– return on assets
	– gross profit percentage
	– expense/revenue percentage
	– operating profit percentage
	Liquidity
	– current ratio
	– the quick ratio or 'acid test' ratio
	Use of resources
	– inventory turnover
	– inventory holding period (days)
	– trade receivables collection period
	– trade payables payment period
	– working capital cycle
	– asset turnover (net assets)
	– asset turnover (total assets)
	Financial position
	– interest cover
	– gearing
5.2	Appraise the relationship between elements of the financial statements with regard to profitability, liquidity, efficient use of resources and financial position, by means of ratio analysis
	• Identify, with reasons, whether a ratio is better or worse as compared to a comparative ratio
	• Suggest the factors that influence ratios and how they interrelate
5.3	Effectively present an analysis with recommendations
	• Present the key findings of their analysis to meet user requirements
	• Suggest how ratios could be improved and the potential consequences of doing so

Assessment context

Each exam paper will include a question on the analysis of a set of financial statements, using ratios.

Qualification context

Interpreting financial statements using ratio analysis is only tested in this course.

Business context

Both external users wishing to invest in a company, provide finance or make some other decision with regard to the company and internal users such as management make extensive use of analysis tools to understand and interpret financial information. This chapter is key to anyone wanting to make use of financial information for decision making.

Chapter overview

Current ratio $\dfrac{\text{Current assets}}{\text{Current liabilities}} = X : 1$

Interest cover $\dfrac{\text{Profit from operations}}{\text{Finance costs}} = X \text{ times}$

The quick ratio or 'acid test' ratio $\dfrac{\text{Current assets} - \text{Inventories}}{\text{Current liabilities}} = X : 1$

Gearing $\dfrac{\text{Non-current liabilities}}{\text{Total equity} + \text{Non-current liabilities}} = X \text{ times}$

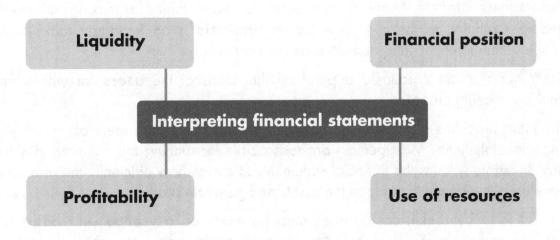

Liquidity

Financial position

Interpreting financial statements

Profitability

Use of resources

Return on capital employed $\dfrac{\text{Profit from operations}}{\text{Total equity} + \text{Non-current liabilities}} \times 100\%$

Inventory turnover $\dfrac{\text{Cost of sales}}{\text{Inventories}} = X \text{ times}$

Return on equity $\dfrac{\text{Profit after tax}}{\text{Total equity}} \times 100\%$

Trade receivables collection period $\dfrac{\text{Trade receivables}}{\text{Revenue}} \times 365 \text{ days}$

Gross profit percentage $\dfrac{\text{Gross profit}}{\text{Revenue}} \times 100\%$

Trade payables payment period $\dfrac{\text{Trade payables}}{\text{Cost of sales}} \times 365 \text{ days}$

Exp/revenue percentage $\dfrac{\text{Specified expense}}{\text{Revenue}} \times 100\%$

Working capital cycle Inventory days + Receivables days – Payable days

Operating profit percentage $\dfrac{\text{Profit from operations}}{\text{Revenue}} \times 100\%$

Asset turnover (total assets) $\dfrac{\text{Revenue}}{\text{Total assets}} = X \text{ times}$

Asset turnover (net assets) $\dfrac{\text{Revenue}}{\text{Total assets} - \text{Current liabilities}} = X \text{ times}$

Introduction

The objective of financial statements is to enable users to make economic decisions. This chapter concentrates on the start of the decision-making process: analysing and interpreting the information in financial statements.

1 Purpose of interpreting ratios in a business environment

Stakeholders use the financial statements to assist them in making informed decisions relating to the company. **Ratio analysis** is an important tool which enables them to understand and interpret the accounts.

The ratios that are calculated depend on the needs of the **users** for whom the analysis is being prepared.

The main providers of finance are normally the most important users of an entity's financial statements. Management are responsible for running the company day to day. Investors will use the financial statements to assess how efficiently the directors have used investment to manage the assets and generate profit.

For ratios to be useful, comparisons must be made on a year to year basis, or between companies. On their own they do not provide a basis for sensible decision making.

Activity 1: Stakeholders

Required

List TWO reasons the following stakeholders may be interested in the information provided by financial statements.

Managers	
Owners/shareholders	
Providers of finance	
Tax authorities	
Suppliers	

Financial analysts	
Government	

2 Ratio analysis

There are certain ratios which can be calculated from a set of accounts which will give an indication of the company's performance. The ratios can be split into the following categories:

(a) Profitability – measures the relationship between income and expenses; also the profits or losses measured against equity

(b) **Liquidity** – focuses on the relationship between assets and liabilities and the ability of the company to pay its payables as they become due

(c) Use of resources – analyses the profits or losses in relation to the assets and liabilities of the company

(d) Financial position – compares the relationship between the equity and the liabilities of the company

Ratio analysis is a technique used to interpret financial information. It involves calculating ratios by comparing one figure in the financial statements with another.

For example, revenue is £100,000 and gross profit is £25,000. The gross profit margin is 25%.

However, this tells us very little on its own. Is a gross profit margin of 25% good or bad? The ratios must be compared with other information:

(a) The previous year's financial statements (is the gross profit margin better or worse than last year?)

(b) Budgeted financial statements (is gross profit more or less than forecast?)

(c) The financial statements of another company (is the gross profit margin better or worse than that of a competitor?)

(d) Average figures for the industry (how profitable is the company in relation to the industry as a whole?)

3 Profitability ratios

3.1 Gross profit percentage

Formula to learn

Gross profit percentage = $\dfrac{\text{Gross profit}}{\text{Revenue}} \times 100 = X\%$

The **gross profit percentage** should be similar from year to year for the same company. A significant change (especially a fall) requires further investigation into buying and selling prices. Inventory cut-off procedures should also be considered, as incorrect inventory valuations will affect gross profit twice: this year's closing inventory becomes next year's opening inventory.

3.2 Operating profit percentage

Formula to learn

Operating profit percentage = $\dfrac{\text{Profit from operations}}{\text{Revenue}} \times 100 = X\%$

Profit from operations is profit before finance costs and tax. This avoids distortion when comparisons are made between two different companies where one is heavily financed by means of loans, and the other is financed entirely by ordinary share capital.

3.3 Expense/revenue percentage

Formula to learn

Expense/revenue percentage = $\dfrac{\text{Specified expense}}{\text{Revenue}} \times 100 = X\%$

The expense/revenue ratio is very useful when exploring how an expense has been affected by growth in sales from one year to the next, or for comparing the cost control of two different companies.

3.4 Return on capital employed

Formula to learn

Return on capital employed = $\dfrac{\text{Profit from operations}}{\text{Total equity} + \text{Non-current liabilities}} \times 100 = X\%$

Return on capital employed expresses the profit of a company in relation to the **capital employed** to generate it. The percentage return is best thought of in relation to other investments, eg a bank interest rate. If you want to use this to compare different companies, be careful if they are not in the same industry. For example, a recruitment consultancy will not have much capital compared to a construction company, therefore comparisons are difficult.

3.5 Return on equity

Formula to learn

Return on shareholders' funds = $\dfrac{\text{Profit after tax}}{\text{Total equity}} \times 100 = X\%$

Whilst the return on capital employed looks at the overall return on the long-term sources of finance, **return on equity** focuses on the return for the ordinary shareholders. Assuming that there are no preference shares or minority interests, the profit available to the ordinary shareholders is profit after tax, therefore we compare this to equity interests. If minority interest and/or preference share dividends exist, these should be deducted from profit after tax as they reduce the amounts available for the ordinary shareholders. Equity can be taken to be the total in the equity section of the statement of financial position.

4 Liquidity ratios

4.1 Current ratio (working capital ratio)

Formula to learn

Current ratio (working capital ratio) = $\dfrac{\text{Current assets}}{\text{Current liabilities}} = X : 1$

Working capital is needed by all companies in order to finance day to day trading activities. Sufficient working capital enables a company to hold adequate inventories, to allow a measure of credit to its customers and to pay its suppliers on the due date.

This ratio measures the relationship between the current assets and current liabilities on the statement of financial position. A company should not operate at a level that is too low, as it will not have sufficient assets to cover its debts as they fall due. However, a company shouldn't operate at a level that is too high, as this may suggest that the company has too much inventory, receivables or cash.

4.2 Acid test (quick) ratio

Formula to learn

Acid test (quick) ratio = $\dfrac{\text{Current assets} - \text{Inventories}}{\text{Current liabilities}} = X : 1$

This is similar to the current ratio except that it omits the inventories figure from current assets. This is because inventories are the least liquid current asset that a company has, as it has to be sold, turned into receivables and then the cash has to be collected. A ratio of less than 1:1 could indicate that the company would have difficulty paying its debts as they fall due.

Activity 2: Current and quick ratio

The following information has been extracted from the statement of financial position of Gloryline Ltd:

	£000
Inventories	4,750
Receivables	11,350
Cash	2,900
Trade payables	7,400
Other current liabilities	2,100

Required

Calculate the current ratio and the quick ratio.

Current ratio

Quick ratio

5 Ratios showing the use of resources

5.1 Inventory holding period

Formula to learn

$$\text{Inventory holding period (days)} = \frac{\text{Inventories}}{\text{Cost of sales}} \times 365 = X \text{ days}$$

Inventory holding period is the number of days' inventory held by a company on average. This figure will depend on the type of goods sold by the company. A company selling fresh fruit and vegetables should have a low inventory holding period, as these goods will quickly become inedible. A manufacturer of aged wine will, by default, have very long inventory holding periods. It is important for a company to keep its inventory days as low as possible, subject of course to being able to meet its customers' demands.

5.2 Inventory turnover (times per year)

Formula to learn

Inventory turnover = $\dfrac{\text{Cost of sales}}{\text{Inventories}}$ = X times

This will show on average how many times a company is able to sell its total inventory in a year. Just as a company will strive to keep inventory days low, it should strive to keep inventory turnover high.

5.3 Trade receivables collection period (days)

Formula to learn

Trade receivables collection period (days) =

$\dfrac{\text{Trade receivables}}{\text{Revenue}} \times 365$ = X days

This ratio shows, on average, how long it takes for trade debtors to settle their account with the company. The collection period should be compared with that of the previous year, or with a similar company. Over time we are looking to reduce the overall average collection time.

5.4 Trade payables payment period (days)

Formula to learn

Trade payables payment period (days) = $\dfrac{\text{Trade payables}}{\text{Cost of sales}} \times 365$ = X days

This ratio is measuring the time it takes for us to settle our trade payable balances. Trade payables provide the company with a valuable source of short-term finance, but delaying payment for too long a period of time can cause operational problems: suppliers may stop providing goods and services until payment is received.

5.5 Working capital cycle

Inventory days + receivable days – payable days

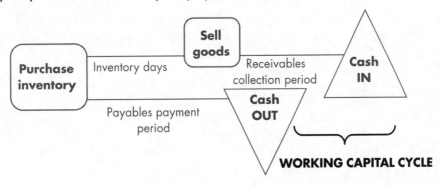

The **working capital cycle** has to be financed, as cash has not yet been received from the sale of goods before the supplier has to be paid. The longer the cycle, the more financing is required and the higher the risk of bankruptcy. This is why it is good to have short inventory days and receivables collection periods, and longer payables payment periods.

However, this must be weighed against the fact that a company must not run a risk of stock-outs (if inventory days are too small) or customer and supplier dissatisfaction by insisting on short and long payment periods respectively.

5.6 Asset turnover (net assets) ratio

Formula to learn

Asset turnover (net assets) ratio = $\dfrac{\text{Revenue}}{\text{Total assets} - \text{current liabilities}}$ = X times

This ratio measures the efficiency of the use of net assets in generating revenue. It is a measure of the number of pounds of revenue generated per pound of net assets invested in the company.

Ideally the ratio should be increasing, but we need to be careful when making assessments based on this ratio: we could have bought lots of assets late in the year and they simply have not had much time to start generating revenue. If this is the case, the ratio will almost certainly fall, but this is not a reflection on the ability of the assets to generate revenue; it is simply a timing issue.

5.7 Asset turnover (total assets) ratio

Formula to learn

Asset turnover (total assets) ratio = $\dfrac{\text{Revenue}}{\text{Total assets}}$ = X times

This ratio gives us similar information to the asset turnover (net assets).

Activity 3: Brookstream

The summarised statement of financial position of Brookstream Ltd is shown below:

	£000	£000
Assets		–
Non-current assets		1,400
Current assets		400
Total assets		1,800
Equity:		
Share capital		200
Share premium		100
Retained earnings		600
		900
Non-current liabilities	600	
Current liabilities	300	
Total liabilities		900
Total equity and liabilities		1,800

Sales revenue for the year was £2 million and profit from operations was £300,000.

Required

Calculate the following ratios:

(a) Return on capital employed (ROCE)

[ ]

(b) Operating profit percentage

[ ]

(c) Asset turnover (based on net assets)

[ ]

Activity 4: Inventory turnover

Draft statement of profit or loss for the year ended 30 June 20X5 (extract)

	£000	£000
Sales		6,900
Opening inventories	900	
Purchases	4,500	
Closing inventories	(1,200)	
Cost of sales		(4,200)
Gross profit		2,700

Required

Calculate inventory turnover (using cost of sales).

---

6 Financial position

6.1 Interest cover

Formula to learn

$$\text{Interest cover} = \frac{\text{Profit from operations}}{\text{Finance costs}} = X \text{ times}$$

The **interest cover** ratio considers the number of times a company could pay its interest payments using its profit from operations. The main concern is that a company does not have so much debt finance that it risks not being able to settle the debt as it falls due.

6.2 Gearing

Formula to learn

$$\text{Gearing} = \frac{\text{Non-current liabilities}}{\text{Total equity} + \text{Non-current liabilities}} \times 100 = X\%$$

Gearing is concerned with the long-term financial stability of the company. It is looking at how much the company is financed by debt. The higher the gearing ratio, the less secure will be the financing of the company and possibly the company's future.

Illustration 1: Gearing

A highly geared company is perceived as a risky investment. Consider the three companies below:

	A plc £000	B plc £000	C plc £000
10% loan stock	Nil	1,000	2,000
Equity share capital	1,000	1,000	1,000
Reserves	1,000	1,000	1,000
	2,000	2,000	2,000
Gearing	0%	33%	50%

	A plc £000	B plc £000	C plc £000
Profit from operations	1,000	1,000	1,000
Interest payable	–	(100)	(200)
Profit before tax	1,000	900	800
Tax at 30%	(300)	(270)	(240)
Profit available for shareholders	700	630	560

Suppose that profit from operations falls by 50%. This is the effect on equity shareholders:

	A plc £000	B plc £000	C plc £000
Profit from operations	500	500	500
Interest payable	–	(100)	(200)
Profit before tax	500	400	300
Tax at 30%	(150)	(120)	(90)
Profit available for shareholders	350	280	210
Decrease in profits available to shareholders	50%	55%	62.5%

Suppose that profit from operations increases by 50%.

	A plc £000	B plc £000	C plc £000
Profit from operations	1,500	1,500	1,500
Interest payable	–	(100)	(200)
Profit before tax	1,500	1,400	1,300
Tax at 30%	(450)	(420)	(390)
Profit available for shareholders	1,050	980	910
Increase in profits available to shareholders	50%	55%	62.5%

Risk is uncertainty as to the amount of benefits. If a company is highly geared, profits available for shareholders (and therefore dividends) may fluctuate considerably as the result of a relatively small change in the level of profit from operations.

Activity 5: Financial position

The following information has been extracted from the statement of financial position of Trap Ltd:

	£000
Share capital	15,000
Retained earnings	4,900
Total equity	19,900
Non-current liabilities	
Bank loan	9,000

Profit from operations for the year was £2,800,000 and finance costs for the year were £540,000.

Required

Calculate the gearing ratio and interest cover.

Gearing ratio

Interest cover

7 Assessment tasks

Now that we have considered a range of ratios we will work through assessment-standard questions.

In the assessment, the topic will be tested in two tasks:

First task, part (a)	Identify the formulae that are used to calculate specified ratios. You will enter your answer by means of a picklist or drag and drop options.
First task, part (b)	Calculating ratios. Here, you will complete the requirement by typing in numbers.
Second task	A written requirement in which you will be provided with ratios and asked to perform an analysis of them. You may also need to provide a recommendation or suggestions to a third party.

7.1 Identify ratio formulae/calculate ratios

Ratio analysis – written requirements

Whilst the first task is knowledge based, to succeed in the written requirement you will need to consider how to set out your response.

When analysing **each** ratio, the logical approach is to:

(1) Comment on the performance of the company in relation to the comparative ratio

(2) Explain the implications of this

(3) Suggest a reason for the difference

(4) Consider the implications of the difference

Activity 6: New Ltd

You have been asked to calculate ratios for New Ltd in respect of its financial statements for the year ending 31 December 20X1, to assist your manager in his analysis of the company.

New Ltd's statement of profit or loss and statement of financial position are set out below.

BPP
LEARNING MEDIA

New Ltd
Statement of profit or loss for the year ended 31 December 20X1

	£000
Revenue	1,430
Cost of sales	(960)
Gross profit	470
Distribution costs	(150)
Administrative expenses	(140)
Profit from operations	180
Finance costs	(10)
Profit before tax	170
Tax	(50)
Profit for the year from continuing operations	120

Statement of financial position at 31 December 20X1

	£000
Assets	
Non-current assets	
Property, plant and equipment	1,280
Current assets	
Inventories	240
Trade receivables	150
Cash and cash equivalents	135
	525
Total assets	1,805

	£000
Equity and liabilities	
Equity	
Share capital	1,250
Retained earnings	200
Total equity	1,450
Non-current liabilities	
10% debentures	100
Current liabilities	
Trade payables	205
Tax liabilities	50
	255
Total liabilities	355
Total equity and liabilities	1,805

Required

(a) Identify the formulas that are used to calculate each of the following ratios:

Gross profit percentage		▼
Operating profit percentage		▼
Return on capital employed		▼
Current ratio		▼
Inventory holding period		▼
Trade payables payment period		▼
Interest cover		▼
Gearing ratio		▼

Picklist:

Cost of sales/Inventories
Current assets/Current liabilities
(Current assets – Inventories)/Current liabilities
Gross profit/Revenue × 100
Inventories/Cost of sales × 365
Non-current liabilities/(Total equity + Non-current liabilities) × 100
Profit from operations/Finance costs
Profit from operations/Revenue × 100
Profit from operations/(Total equity + Non-current liabilities) × 100
Revenue/Total assets
Trade payables/Cost of sales × 365
Trade receivables/Revenue × 365

(b) Calculate the above ratios to one decimal place.

Gross profit percentage	
Operating profit percentage	
Return on capital employed	
Current ratio	
Inventory holding period	
Trade payables payment period	
Interest cover	
Gearing ratio	

7.2 Interpreting ratios

Ratio calculations are the first step in interpreting financial statements. The calculations themselves do not provide firm answers. Rather, they focus attention on significant aspects of an entity's performance and position.

There is no such thing as an 'ideal' ratio. Whether a particular ratio is a sign of strength or weakness may depend on a number of factors, including:

- Whether the ratio is improving or deteriorating
- Any other information that is available (including possible reasons for a result)
- The nature of the business

For example, it is often said that the **quick ratio** should be greater than 1:1. A company has a quick ratio of 0.5:1. Does this mean that the company has severe liquidity problems?

Not necessarily; either of the following could apply:

(a) The company is a retailer. All sales are for cash; there are no trade receivables. The average quick ratio in the industry is 0.4:1.

(b) The quick ratio for the previous year was 0.2:1. Other information suggests that the company has had severe liquidity problems, but it is recovering.

In the assessment, you will be asked to comment on specific ratios. As well as making observations ('gross profit percentage has increased during the year') it is important that you attempt to **interpret** the ratios; for example, by suggesting reasons **why** gross profit percentage might have increased, based on any other relevant information you are given.

This means that, as well as knowing how to calculate each ratio, you need to understand:

- What each ratio means
- Whether increases/decreases are good or bad

7.3 Limitations of ratio analysis

Ratios should always be interpreted in the context of the financial statements as a whole and of any other information that is available.

Ratio analysis also has some serious limitations.

(a) Financial statements are based on historical information. They may be several months out of date by the time that they are published. Very recent or forecast information is more useful for decision making.

(b) Most ratios are calculated on closing figures taken from the statement of financial position. This means that ROCE, asset turnover and the working capital ratios may not compare like with like (because the figures taken from the statement of profit or loss and other comprehensive income are for the whole period).

(c) Businesses can use 'window dressing' to improve the appearance of the statement of financial position. For example, they can order goods to be delivered just after the year end, so that inventories and payables are lower than usual; or they can collect debts just before the year end so that cash is higher than usual and receivables are lower than usual.

(d) Some businesses are seasonal. This means that the choice of reporting date (year end) can be crucial, as the financial position varies according to the time of year.

(e) Financial statements only include information which can be measured in money terms. For example, they do not normally contain information about:

- An entity's effect on the natural environment
- Its effect on the community
- The human resources available to it (its management and employees)
- Some internally generated intangible assets, such as brand names

These factors can have an important effect on an entity's performance. For example, consumers may choose to buy goods from entities that have been seen to adopt 'green' policies.

(f) Ratios are normally based on historical cost accounts. This means that they ignore the effect of inflation and trends can be distorted. If inflation is high, an entity may appear to be more profitable than is actually the case.

(g) Ratios for an individual business are often compared with ratios for a similar business, or with industry averages. These comparisons may be misleading.

(h) Businesses may use different accounting policies. For example, some businesses revalue non-current assets, while others carry them at historical cost. This can have a significant effect on key ratios.

(i) Businesses within the same industry can operate in completely different markets. They may also adopt different strategies. For example, some food stores may specialise in quality (relatively few sales at high margins), while other stores may concentrate on high-volume, low-margin sales.

(j) Size differences may affect the way in which a business operates. A large company can often achieve economies of scale that are not available to a smaller business. For example, it may make use of trade discounts for bulk buying. Large companies are likely to have a different approach to managing working capital. They may be able to take advantage of extended credit terms and they may only hold fast-moving inventory lines. They may also adopt a more aggressive policy towards customers with outstanding debts than would be the case in a small family business.

(k) Ratios may not always be calculated according to the same formula. For example, there are several possible variations on the calculation of gearing.

Illustration 2: Interpretation

The following information relates to two companies. The ratios have been calculated for the year ended 31 December 20X8. The two companies operate in the same line of business.

	Smith Ltd	Jones Ltd
ROCE	23.4%	42.2%
Gross profit percentage	65%	30%
Operating profit percentage	5%	10%
Expenses/revenue percentage	60%	20%
Asset turnover (based on net assets)	4.7 times	4.2 times
Current ratio	1.1:1	1.3:1
Quick ratio	0.6:1	0.7:1
Inventory turnover	4.5 times	19.1 times
Trade receivables collection period	36 days	12 days
Trade payables payment period	104 days	16 days
Gearing	30%	24%
Interest cover	11 times	20 times

Profitability

- Smith Ltd has the higher gross profit percentage, 65% compared with Jones Ltd's 30%.

- However, overall Jones Ltd is performing much better than Smith Ltd, with ROCE of 42.2% compared with 23.4%.

- Asset turnover for the two companies is roughly comparable, so the difference in ROCE is largely a reflection of operating profit percentage. Smith Ltd has an operating profit percentage of 5%, only half that of Jones Ltd.

- The difference in gross profit percentage may indicate that the two companies have different strategies. Smith Ltd may be concentrating on low-volume, high-margin sales, while Jones Ltd may be selling its products very cheaply in order to generate more revenue.

- Smith Ltd incurs much higher operating expenses (relative to its sales revenue) than Jones Ltd, as shown by the expenses/revenue percentage, which is three times that of Jones Ltd. This may be because it is less efficient at controlling administrative costs. Alternatively, it may have incurred high 'one-off' costs, such as legal fees, during the year.

Liquidity and use of resources (working capital management)

- The current ratios are 1.1:1 and 1.3:1 respectively. Both companies are likely to be able to meet their current liabilities in the near future.

- However, Smith Ltd has an acid test ratio of 0.6:1 and Jones Ltd's position is only slightly better. This suggests potential liquidity problems for both companies, or a type of business which tends to have a low quick ratio (see above).

- Jones Ltd appears to be much better at managing its working capital than Smith Ltd.

    - Smith Ltd's inventory turnover is 4.5 times compared with 19 times for Jones Ltd. Given the healthy gross profit ratio, this difference seems to suggest poor management by Smith Ltd, rather than a decline in the company's business.

    - Smith Ltd takes over three months, on average, to pay its suppliers. In contrast, Jones Ltd's average supplier payment period is less than one month. Jones Ltd evidently has sufficient cash to pay its suppliers promptly. It is possible that Smith Ltd does not.

    - Smith Ltd takes just over one month, on average, to collect receivables. Most companies allow roughly 30 days' credit, but this compares badly with the performance of Jones Ltd (which has an average collection period of just under two weeks). This suggests either poor management by Smith Ltd or (more probably) that the management of Jones Ltd is extremely efficient. Alternatively, the two companies may have different types of customer. Smith Ltd's customers may be mainly large companies; Jones Ltd may deal mainly with individuals from whom it can demand payment almost immediately.

- All the above information seems to indicate that Smith Ltd may be suffering liquidity problems.

Gearing

- Although Smith Ltd is more **highly geared** than Jones Ltd, neither company's gearing ratio seems to be unduly high.

- Neither company appears to be having difficulty in generating enough profit to cover interest charges on their loans (interest cover is 11 times and 20 times respectively). Smith Ltd's lower interest cover reflects this company's much lower operating profit percentage, as well as its higher gearing.

Conclusion

On the basis of the information provided, Jones Ltd appears to be more profitable (in relative terms) and in a stronger financial position than Smith Ltd. Jones Ltd has a low acid test ratio, but there are no other signs of trading problems.

In contrast, Smith Ltd's financial position gives cause for concern. There are several signs that it may be experiencing liquidity problems. In addition, there are indications that working capital could be better managed.

Assessment focus point

When writing your answer to an analysis and interpretation question, you need to say **why** changes have happened as well as point out that they have. Sometimes there can be more than one reason.

You should refer to the Skills Bank at the beginning of this Course Book for advice on tackling written questions. There is specific, detailed advice relating to analysis and interpretation questions.

Activity 7: Interpreting ratios

A business normally allows customers 30 days' credit. However, the information in the latest financial statements suggests that the average collection period is actually 45 days.

A major customer went into liquidation during the year and the debt was written off. This could be a reason for the difference.

Required

Is this statement true or false?

True	
False	

Suggest ONE other possible reason to explain the difference.

Activity 8: Effect of revaluation

Harkeats Ltd revalues some of its properties upwards. This affects its key ratios.

Required

Indicate whether the following statements are true or false for the period immediately after the revaluation:

	True	False
Asset turnover is higher.		
Gearing is higher.		
Operating profit percentage is lower.		
Return on capital employed is lower.		

Activity 9: Benjamin Lens

Benjamin Lens is a potential investor in Glass Ltd and has asked you to assist him in his risk assessment of the company. He has asked you to comment on the performance of the company in relation to that industry and to advise on whether he should invest in the company.

You have calculated the following ratios in respect of Glass Ltd's latest financial statements and also have each of their industry averages for comparative purposes.

Ratio	Glass Ltd	Industry average
Gross profit percentage	33%	34%
Operating profit percentage	12.5%	17%
Return on capital employed	11.72%	15.3%
Current ratio	2.5 times	1.5 times
Inventory holding period	87 days	31 days
Receivables collection period	31 days	30.79 days
Interest cover	9 times	3.82 times
Gearing ratio	22%	83%

Required

Prepare a reply to Benjamin that includes:

(a) **Comments on whether Glass Ltd has performed better or worse in respect of the calculated ratios, giving possible reasons, as compared to the industry average**

(b) **Advice on whether to invest in the company**

329

- Different types of limited company have different objectives.

- The most important users of an entity's financial statements are usually the persons to whom management has stewardship responsibilities and/or the main providers of finance.

- Ratio analysis is used to interpret financial information. Ratios are normally compared with other information (eg the previous years' financial statements, industry averages).

- Return on capital employed (ROCE) measures the profit that a business generates from the resources available to it.

- Operating profit percentage measures the overall profitability of a business.

- Gross profit percentage measures gross profit as a percentage of sales.

- The expenses/revenue percentage measures operating expenses (or a specific expense) as a percentage of sales.

- Asset turnover measures the efficiency with which a business uses its resources to generate sales.

- The current ratio shows the extent to which a business's current liabilities are covered by current assets.

- The quick ratio (acid test ratio) measures the immediate solvency of a business by showing the extent to which its current liabilities are covered by cash and receivables.

- Inventory turnover shows how rapidly a business's inventory is sold, on average, during the year.

- The trade receivables collection period is the average period taken to collect receivables.

- The trade payables payment period is the average period taken to pay suppliers.

- The working capital cycle is the period of time from the point at which cash goes out of a business to pay for inventories and the point at which cash comes back into the business as sales revenue.

- The gearing ratio measures the extent to which a company is financed by debt rather than by owners' equity.

- Interest cover shows the extent to which interest payments are 'covered' by profit from operations.

- There is no such thing as an 'ideal' ratio. Whether a particular ratio is a sign of strength or weakness may depend on a number of factors.

- Ratios should always be interpreted in the context of the accounts as a whole and of any other information that is available.

- Ratio analysis has some serious limitations. Comparisons with ratios for a similar business or with industry averages may be misleading.

Keywords

- **Asset turnover** (total assets) = $\dfrac{\text{Revenue}}{\text{Total assets}}$

- **Asset turnover** (net assets) = $\dfrac{\text{Revenue}}{\text{Total assets} - \text{Current liabilities}}$

- **Capital employed** = Capital and reserves (equity) + Non-current liabilities

- **Current ratio** = $\dfrac{\text{Current assets}}{\text{Current liabilities}}$

- **Expense/revenue percentage** = $\dfrac{\text{Operating expenses}}{\text{Revenue}} \times 100\%$

- **Gearing** = $\dfrac{\text{Non-current liabilities}}{\text{Total equity} + \text{Non-current liabilities}} \times 100\%$

- **Gross profit percentage** = $\dfrac{\text{Gross profit}}{\text{Revenue}} \times 100 = X\%$

- **Highly geared:** Having a high proportion of debt compared with equity

- **Interest cover** = $\dfrac{\text{Profit from operations}}{\text{Finance costs}}$

- **Inventory holding period** = $\dfrac{\text{Inventories}}{\text{Cost of sales}} \times 365 \text{ days}$

- **Inventory turnover** = $\dfrac{\text{Cost of sales}}{\text{Inventories}}$

- **Liquidity:** The ability of an entity to meet its debts as they fall due

- **Operating profit percentage** = $\dfrac{\text{Profit from operations}}{\text{Total assets}} \times 100 = X\%$

- **Quick ratio** = $\dfrac{\text{Current assets} - \text{Inventories}}{\text{Current liabilities}}$

- **Ratio analysis:** A technique used to interpret financial information. It involves calculating ratios by comparing one figure in the financial statements with another

- **Return on capital employed (ROCE)** = $\dfrac{\text{Profit from operations}}{\text{Total equity} + \text{Non-current liabilities}} \times 100 = X\%$

- **Return on equity** = $\dfrac{\text{Profit after tax}}{\text{Total equity}} \times 100 = X\%$

- **Trade payables payment period** = $\dfrac{\text{Trade payables}}{\text{Cost of sales}} \times 365 \text{ days}$

- **Trade receivables collection period** = $\dfrac{\text{Trade receivables}}{\text{Revenue}} \times 365 \text{ days}$

- **Working capital:** Resources that are available for use in day to day trading operations (normally current assets less current liabilities)

- **Working capital cycle** = Inventory days + Receivable days – Payable days

$$\text{Or } \frac{\text{Specified expense}}{\text{Revenue}} \times 100\%$$

Test your learning

1   Gross profit is £20,000 and operating expenses are £12,000. The gross profit percentage is 25%.

   What is the operating profit percentage?

8%	
10%	
15%	
40%	

2   If return on capital employed is 20% and the operating profit percentage is 10%, asset turnover is 0.5 times.

   Is this statement true or false?

True	
False	

3   **State the formulas that are used to calculate each of the following ratios:**

   (a)   Return on capital employed

   (b)   Acid test ratio

   (c)   Inventory holding period (days)

   (d)   Interest cover

4   The summarised statement of financial position of Bellbrock Ltd is shown below:

	£000	£000
Non-current assets		57,000
Current assets		22,800
		79,800
Equity:		
Ordinary shares		10,000
Revaluation reserve		4,600
Retained earnings		11,400
		26,000
Non-current liabilities	39,000	
Current liabilities	14,800	
		53,800
		79,800

What is the gearing ratio?

40%	
60%	
80%	
150%	

5   The formula for calculating the operating profit percentage is:

$$\frac{\text{Profit from operations}}{\text{Total assets}} \times 100$$

Is this statement true or false?

True	
False	

6   You have been asked to calculate ratios for Jackson Ltd in respect of its financial statements for the year ended 30 April 20X2.

Summarised statement of profit or loss for the year ended 30 April 20X2 (extract)

	£000
Revenue	4,100
Cost of sales	(2,625)
Gross profit	1,475

Additional information:

At 30 April 20X2, inventories were £480,000, trade receivables were £956,000 and trade payables were £267,000.

(a) **State the formula that is used to calculate each of the following ratios.**

(Complete the middle column by writing in the correct formula from the list provided.)

(b) **Calculate the ratios.**

	Formula	Calculation
Gross profit percentage	▼	

Picklist:

Gross profit/Revenue × 100
Gross profit/Total assets × 100
Gross profit/Total assets – Current liabilities × 100
Gross profit/Total equity × 100

	Formula	Calculation
Inventory turnover	▼	

Picklist:

Cost of sales/Inventories
Inventories/Cost of sales
Inventories/Revenue
Revenue/Inventories

	Formula	Calculation
Trade receivables collection period	▼	

Picklist:

Cost of sales/Trade receivables × 365
Revenue/Trade receivables × 365
Trade receivables/Cost of sales × 365
Trade receivables/Revenue × 365

	Formula	Calculation
Trade payables payment period	▼	

Picklist:

Cost of sales/Trade payables × 365
Revenue/Trade payables × 365
Trade payables/Cost of sales × 365
Trade payables/Revenue × 365

7   The operating profit percentage can be improved by reducing administrative expenses.

Is this statement true or false?

True	
False	

8   A friend is considering investing in a company, Elder Ltd. She has obtained the latest financial statements of Elder Ltd and has asked you to calculate and interpret key ratios based on these. She has also asked you to compare the ratios that you have calculated with those of another company in the same industry and of a similar size.

Explain the reasons why your analysis, although useful, may have serious limitations.

9   Michael Beacham has been asked to lend money to Goodall Ltd for a period of three years. He employed a financial adviser to advise him whether to make a loan to the company. The financial adviser has obtained the financial statements of the company for the past two years, calculated some ratios and found the industry averages. However, she was unable to complete her report. Michael has asked you to analyse the ratios and to advise him on whether he should make a loan to Goodall Ltd or not. The ratios are set out below.

	20X3	20X2	Industry average
Gearing ratio	67%	58%	41%
Interest cover	1.2	2.3	4.6
Quick ratio/acid test ratio	0.5	0.8	1.1
Return on equity	9%	13%	19%

Write a report for Michael Beacham that includes the following:

(a)   Comments on Goodall Ltd's financial position and the performance of the company as shown by the ratios.

(b)   A conclusion on whether Michael should lend money to Goodall Ltd. Base your conclusion only on the ratios calculated and the analysis performed.

Activity answers

CHAPTER 1 Introduction to limited companies

Activity 1: Limited companies

(a)

With 'limited liability':

A company may only have a certain prescribed maximum liability on its statement of financial position.	
The shareholders of a company are protected in that they can only lose their investment in the company, should the company fail.	✓
A company can only enter into transactions involving debt up to a certain limit before gaining express approval from the shareholders in general meeting.	
The shareholders may only invest in a company up to a prescribed limit per shareholder.	

(b) A complete set of financial statements includes which of the following?

All of the above	
(i), (ii), (iii), (iv) and (v)	
(i), (ii), (iv), (v) and (vi)	✓
(i), (ii), (iv) and (v)	

Activity 2: Issue of shares at a premium

Orion Ltd
Statement of financial position (extract) at 1 July 20X4

	£
Assets	
Cash and cash equivalents (50,000 + 160,000)	210,000
Equity	
Share capital (50,000 + 100,000)	150,000
Share premium	60,000

Working

The double entry to record the issue is:

	Debit £	Credit £
Cash (200,000 × 80p)	160,000	
Share capital (200,000 × 50p)		100,000
Share premium (200,000 × 30p)		60,000

Activity 3: Bonus issue

Dark Ltd
Statement of financial position (extract)

	£
Equity	
Share capital (£1 ordinary shares) (100,000 + 20,000)	120,000
Share premium (40,000 – 20,000)	20,000
Retained earnings	200,000
	340,000

Working

The double entry to record the bonus issue is:

	Debit £	Credit £
Share premium (100,000/5)	20,000	
Share capital		20,000

Activity 4: Rights issue

Light Ltd
Statement of financial position (extract)

	£
Equity	
Share capital (£1 ordinary shares) (200,000 + 50,000)	250,000
Share premium (50,000 + 10,000)	60,000
Retained earnings	300,000
	610,000

Working

The double entry to record the rights issue is:

	Debit £	Credit £
Bank (200,000/4 × 1.20)	60,000	
Share capital (200,000/4 × 1.00)		50,000
Share premium (balancing figure)		10,000

Activity 5: Retained earnings

Orion Ltd
Statement of financial position (extract) as at 31 December 20X5

	£
Equity	
Retained earnings (W)	65,000

Working

Retained earnings	£
Retained earnings at 1 January 20X5	50,000
Total profit for the year	20,000
Dividends paid	(5,000)
	65,000

BPP
LEARNING MEDIA

339

Activity 6: Bank loan

Orion Ltd
Statement of financial position (extract) as at 31 December 20X6

	£
Non-current liabilities	
Bank loan (W)	200,000
Current liabilities	
Trade and other payables (W)	8,000

Orion Ltd
Statement of profit or loss (extract) for the year ended 31 December 20X6

	£
Finance charges (W)	16,000

Working

The double entry to record the finance charge is:

	Debit £	Credit £
Finance charge (SPL)	16,000	
Cash		8,000
Trade and other payables		8,000

CHAPTER 2 The frameworks and ethical principles

Activity 1: Duties and responsibilities of the directors

(ii), (iii) and (iv)	✓
(i), (ii), (iii) and (iv)	
(i), (iii) and (iv)	
(i), (ii) and (iii)	

Activity 2: Users of the financial statements

Investors	Lenders
• To assess the performance of management • To see how much money can be expected to be paid in dividends (return on their investment) • To see if the company will continue in the foreseeable future • To see if the company is expanding or declining This enables investors to determine if they should buy new shares (become an investor or expand their holding), sell their shares, or keep their current shareholding unchanged.	• To check if the company will be able to pay finance costs (return on their investment) • To see if the company will be able to meet its loan repayment commitments • To assess the value of security available to the lender This enables lenders to decide if they should grant a new loan (or extend an existing one), call in a loan, or continue to offer the same loan facility.

Activity 3: Materiality

BigCo?	
SmallCo?	✓

With regard to BigCo, the materiality concept states that this loss is immaterial because the average financial statement user would not be concerned with something that is only 0.1% of net income.

For SmallCo, the loss is 20% of net income. This is a substantial loss for the company. Investors and creditors would be concerned about a loss this big. To the smaller company, this £100,000 would be considered material.

Activity 4: Elements of the financial statements

(a)

an asset	✓
a liability	
equity	
income	
expenses	

(b)

an asset	
a liability	
equity	✓
income	
expenses	

(c)

True	
False	✓

Activity 5: Measurement bases

(a)

A company can sell machine A for £9,000.	Realisable value
If a company had to buy machine B now, it would pay £20,000.	Current cost
Machine C will be used by a company to generate sales. It is expected to generate discounted net cash flows of £20,000 over the next 5 years.	Present value
Three years ago, machine D cost the company £15,000.	Historical cost

(b) Measuring the asset under the historical cost basis, the asset will be recorded at:

£20,000	✓
£22,000	
£25,000	
£30,000	

Activity 6: Fundamental principles

Illustration	Fundamental principle
Professional judgements should be made fairly so they are free from all forms of prejudice and bias.	Objectivity
A member must not bring the profession into disrepute by making disparaging references to the work of others.	Professional behaviour
Members shall not agree to carry out a task if they lack the competence to carry it out to a satisfactory standard.	Professional competence and due care
A member shall not be associated with reports, communications or other information where they believe that the information contains a false or misleading statement.	Integrity
The need to comply with the principle of confidentiality continues even after the end of the relationship between a member and a client or employer.	Confidentiality

Activity 7: Which threat?

	✓
Self-interest	
Advocacy	
Intimidation	✓

'Significant pressure' indicates intimidation threat.

Activity 8: Objectivity

	✓
Failure to keep up to date on CPD	
A personal financial interest in the client's affairs	✓
Being negligent or reckless with the accuracy of the information provided to the client	

A personal financial interest in the client's affairs will affect objectivity. Failure to keep up to date on CPD is an issue of professional competence, while providing inaccurate information reflects upon professional integrity.

Activity 9: Problem solving

Apply safeguards to eliminate or reduce the threat to an acceptable level	3
Evaluate the seriousness of the threat	2
Discontinue the action or relationship giving rise to the threat	4
Identify a potential threat to a fundamental ethical principle	1

CHAPTER 3 The statement of financial position

Activity 1: Accruals

1	Purchases are adjusted for opening and closing inventories to arrive at the cost of sales (to match the cost of sales to the sales made during the period).
2	Non-current assets are depreciated (to match the cost of an asset to the accounting periods expected to benefit from its use).

You may have thought of others.

Activity 2: Dalmatian Ltd

Dalmatian Ltd
Statement of financial position (extract) as at 31 March 20X1

	£000
ASSETS	
Non-current assets	
Property, plant and equipment (W)	26,408
Current assets	
Inventories (W)	625
Trade and other receivables (W)	650
Cash and cash equivalents	1,250
	2,525
Total assets	28,933
EQUITY AND LIABILITIES	
Equity	
Share capital	10,000
Retained earnings (W)	11,883
	21,883
Non-current liabilities	
Bank loan	5,000

	£000
Current liabilities	
Trade and other payables (2,000 + 50)	2,050
Total liabilities	7,050
Total equity and liabilities	28,933

Workings (will not be provided in the assessment)

Property, plant and equipment	Property £000	Plant and equipment £000	Total £000
Cost	32,000	9,500	41,500
Accumulated depreciation b/fwd	(6,400)	(4,156)	(10,556)
Carrying amount b/fwd	25,600	5,344	30,944
Current year depreciation (10% × 32,000; 25% × 5,344)	(3,200)	(1,336)	(4,536)*
	22,400	4,008	26,408

* Retained earnings must be reduced by depreciation of £4,536,000.

Inventories	£000
Furs	500
Products	75
Toys	50
	625

Retained earnings must be reduced by the inventory write-down of (£650,000 – £625,000) £25,000.

Prepayments	£000
$^9/_{12}$ × 12,000	9

Retained earnings must increase by the prepaid expense of £9,000.

Workings (will be provided in the assessment)

Property, plant and equipment	£000
Property – cost	32,000
Plant and equipment – cost	9,500
Property – accumulated depreciation (6,400 + 3,200)	(9,600)
Plant and equipment – accumulated depreciation (4,156 + 1,336)	(5,492)
	26,408

Inventories	£000
Inventories at cost	650
Less adjustment	(25)
	625

Trade and other receivables	£000
Trade and other receivables	750
Irrecoverable debt	(75)*
Provision for doubtful receivables (750 – 75 = 675; 675 × 5% = 34)	(34)*
Prepayments	9
	650

* Retained earnings must be reduced by the irrecoverable debts expense of (£75,000 + £34,000) £109,000.

Retained earnings	£000
Per trial balance	16,544
Depreciation	(4,536)
Inventory write-down	(25)
Irrecoverable and doubtful debt expense (75 + 34)	(109)
Prepayments	9
	11,883

Activity 3: Depreciation

Silver Ltd
**Statement of profit or loss (extract) for the year ended
31 December 20X2**

	£000
Cost of sales (W)	65,700
Distribution expenses (W)	27,850
Administrative expenses (W)	36,950

Statement of financial position (extract) as at 31 December 20X2

	£000
ASSETS	
Non-current assets	
Property, plant and equipment (W)	84,500

Workings (will not be provided in the assessment)

Depreciation	£000
Buildings (5% × 70,000)	3,500
Plant and equipment (25% × (32,000 – 8,000)	6,000
	9,500

Workings (on-screen proforma provided in the assessment)

Cost of sales	£000
Cost of sales	60,000
Depreciation (60% × 9,500)	5,700
	65,700

Distribution expenses	£000
Distribution expenses	25,000
Depreciation (30% × 9,500)	2,850
	27,850

Administrative expenses	£000
Administrative expenses	36,000
Depreciation (10% × 9,500)	950
	36,950

Property, plant and equipment	£000
Land and buildings – cost	100,000
Plant and equipment – cost	32,000
Land and buildings – accumulated depreciation (30,000 + 3,500)	(33,500)
Plant and equipment – accumulated depreciation (8,000 + 6,000)	(14,000)
	84,500

Activity 4: Inventories

Hudson Ltd
Statement of financial position (extract) as at 31 December 20X2

	£000
ASSETS	
Current assets	
Inventories (W)	6,100

Workings (will not be provided in the assessment)

Closing inventories	£000
Per further information	6,600
Less write-down (800 – 300)	(500)
	6,100

Workings (on-screen proforma provided in the assessment)

Cost of sales	£000
Opening inventories	5,000
Purchases	6,000
Less inventories write-down	(6,100)
	4,900

Activity 5: Irrecoverable and doubtful debts

Jude Ltd
Statement of financial position (extract) as at 31 December 20X4

	£000
ASSETS	
Current assets	
Trade receivables (W)	14,250

Administrative expenses for the year ended 31 December 20X4

Administrative expenses	£000
Administrative expenses	12,000
Irrecoverable debt	1,000
Allowance for doubtful receivables (W)	250
	13,250

Workings (will not be provided in the assessment)

Movement in allowance for doubtful receivables	£000
Allowance for doubtful debts as at 31 December 20X4 (below)	750
Allowance for doubtful debts as at 1 January 20X4 (per TB)	(500)
	250

Workings (on-screen proforma provided in the assessment)

Trade receivables	£000
Trade receivables	16,000
Irrecoverable debt	(1,000)
Allowance for doubtful debts ((16,000 – 1,000) × 5%)	(750)
	14,250

Activity 6: Accruals and prepayments

Nate Ltd
Statement of financial position (extract) as at 31 December 20X2

	£000
ASSETS	
Current assets	
Trade and other receivables (6,000 + 300)	6,300
LIABILITIES	
Current liabilities	
Trade and other payables (1,000 + 800)	1,800

Administrative expenses for the year ended 31 December 20X2

Administrative expenses	£000
Administrative expenses	5,400
Accruals	800
Prepayments ($1,200 \times {}^{3}/_{12}$)	(300)
	5,900

CHAPTER 4 The statements of financial performance

Activity 1: Other comprehensive income

	True	False
The gain is part of the company's performance.	✓	
The gain should be recognised in profit or loss.		✓

The building is part of the resources of the company, which have increased in value. In theory, it could now be sold for more than its original cost, resulting in extra income and a cash inflow.

The gain is not yet realised (the cash has not yet been received). It is not certain that the gain will ever be realised. The company may not sell the building, or the market may collapse so that the building falls in value in the future.

Activity 2: Mayer Ltd SOCE

Mayer Ltd
Statement of changes in equity for the year ended 31 December 20X7

	Share capital £	Revaluation reserve £	Retained earnings £	Total equity £
Balance at 1 January 20X7	100,000	40,000	35,000	175,000
Changes in equity				
Total comprehensive income		5,000	20,000	25,000
Dividends			(10,000)	(10,000)
Issue of share capital	20,000			20,000
Balance at 31 December 20X7	120,000	45,000	45,000	210,000

Activity 3: Brindley Ltd SPLOCI and SOCE

Task 1:

(a) Brindley Ltd

Statement of profit or loss and other comprehensive income for the year ended 31 March 20X9

	£
Revenue	206,500
Cost of sales (W)	(134,050)
Gross profit	72,450
Distribution costs (W)	(10,500)
Administrative expenses (W)	(32,033)
Profit from operations	29,917
Finance costs	(162)
Profit before tax	29,755
Tax	(12,700)
Profit for the year from continuing operations	17,055
Other comprehensive income for the year	5,000
Total comprehensive income for the year	22,055

(b) Brindley Ltd

Statement of changes in equity for the year ended 31 March 20X9

	Share capital £	Revaluation reserve £	Retained earnings £	Total equity £
Balance at 1 April 20X8	42,000	0	17,852	59,852
Changes in equity				
Total comprehensive income		5,000	17,055	22,055
Dividends			(1,260)	(1,260)
Balance at 31 March 20X9	42,000	5,000	33,647	80,647

Task 2:

Brindley Ltd

Statement of financial position as at 31 March 20X9

	£
ASSETS	
Non-current assets	
Property, plant and equipment (W)	81,000
Current assets	
Inventories	16,700
Trade and other receivables (W)	31,738
	48,438
Total assets	129,438
EQUITY AND LIABILITIES	
Equity	
Share capital	42,000
Revaluation reserve	5,000
Retained earnings	33,647
	80,647
Current liabilities	
Trade and other payables (W)	23,121
Tax liability	12,700
Bank overdraft	12,970
Total liabilities	48,791
Total equity and liabilities	129,438

Workings (will not be provided in the assessment)

Motor vehicles – depreciation	£
Motor vehicles – depreciation per the trial balance	1,000
Depreciation charge (2,500 × 20%) (include in distribution costs)	500
Motor vehicles – accumulated depreciation at 31 March 20X9	1,500

Taxation	Debit £	Credit £
Tax	12,700	
Tax liability		12,700

Dividend

There is no provision for this dividend as it is only proposed. It would be disclosed in a note to the financial statements.

Workings (will be provided in the assessment)

Property, plant and equipment	£
Land and buildings – cost	80,000
Motor vehicles – cost	2,500
Land and buildings – accumulated depreciation	–
Motor vehicles – accumulated depreciation (1,000 + 500)	(1,500)
	81,000

Trade and other receivables	£
Trade and other receivables	31,000
Prepayments (984 × $^9/_{12}$)	738
	31,738

Trade and other payables	£
Trade and other payables	23,000
Accruals $(363 \times \frac{1}{3})$	121
	23,121

Cost of sales	£
Opening inventory	12,000
Purchases	138,750
Closing inventory	(16,700)
	134,050

Distribution costs	£
Distribution costs	10,000
Depreciation charge $(2,500 \times 20\%)$	500
	10,500

Administrative expenses	£
Administration expenses	7,650
Directors' remuneration	25,000
Accruals	121
Prepayments	(738)
	32,033

CHAPTER 5 The statement of cash flows

Activity 1: Silver Ltd – working capital movement

Reconciliation of profit before tax to net cash from operating activities (extract)

	£000
Profit before tax	X
Adjustments for:	
Adjustment in respect of inventories (150 – 102)	(48)
Adjustment in respect of trade receivables (390 – 315)	(75)
Adjustment in respect of trade payables (227 – 199)	28
Cash generated from operations	X

Activity 2: Silver Ltd – interest and tax paid

Reconciliation of profit before tax to net cash from operating activities (extract)

	£000
Cash generated from operations	X
Interest paid	(66)
Tax paid (W)	(110)
Net cash from operating activities	X

Workings (not provided in the assessment)

Tax paid	£000
Balance b/d	160
Statement of profit or loss and other comprehensive income charge	140
Balance c/d	(190)
Tax paid	110

357

Activity 3: Silver Ltd – PPE and dividend received

Reconciliation of profit before tax to net cash from operating activities (extract)

	£000
Profit before tax	284
Adjustments for:	
Depreciation	90
Loss on disposal of property, plant and equipment	13
Finance costs	66
Dividends received	(43)
Adjustment in respect of inventories (150 – 102)	(48)
Adjustment in respect of trade receivables (390 – 315)	(75)
Adjustment in respect of trade payables (227 – 199)	28
Cash generated from operations	315
Interest paid	(66)
Tax paid	(110)
Net cash from operating activities	139

Statement of cash flows (extract) for the year ended 31 December 20X2

	£000
Net cash from operating activities	139
Investing activities	
Proceeds on disposal of property, plant and equipment (W)	32
Purchases of property, plant and equipment (W)	(210)
Dividends received	43
Net cash used in investing activities	(135)

Workings

Proceeds on disposal of property, plant and equipment	£000
Carrying amount of property, plant and equipment sold (85 – 40)	45
Loss on disposal	(13)
	32

Purchases of property, plant and equipment	£000
Property, plant and equipment at start of year	305
Depreciation charge	(90)
Carrying amount of purchases of property, plant and equipment sold	(45)
Property, plant and equipment at end of year	(380)
Total purchases of property, plant and equipment additions	(210)

Activity 4: Silver Ltd – financing activities

Statement of cash flows (extract) for the year ended 31 December 20X2

	£000
Financing activities	
Proceeds of share issue (160 – 100)	60
Proceeds from bank loans (100 – 0)	100
Dividends paid	(100)
Net cash from financing activities	60

Activity 5: Silver Ltd – cash

Reconciliation of profit before tax to net cash from operating activities

	£000
Profit before tax	284
Adjustments for:	
Depreciation	90
Loss on sale of property, plant and equipment	13
Finance costs	66
Dividends received	(43)
Adjustment in respect of inventories (150 – 102)	(48)
Adjustment in respect of trade receivables (390 – 315)	(75)
Adjustment in respect of trade payables (227 – 199)	28
Cash generated from operations	315
Interest paid	(66)
Tax paid (W)	(110)
Net cash from operating activities	139

Statement of cash flows for the year ended 31 December 20X2

	£000
Net cash from operating activities	139
Investing activities	
Proceeds on disposal of property, plant and equipment (W)	32
Purchases of property, plant and equipment (W)	(210)
Dividends received	43
Net cash used in investing activities	(135)
Financing activities	
Proceeds of share issue (160 – 100)	60
Proceeds from bank loans (100 – 0)	100
Dividends paid	(100)

	£000
Net cash from financing activities	60
Net increase in cash and cash equivalents	64
Cash and cash equivalents at the beginning of the year (98 – 1)	(97)
Cash and cash equivalents at the end of the year (85 – 52)	(33)

Activity 6: Statement of cash flow – Emma Ltd

(a) Reconciliation of profit before tax to net cash from operating activities

	£000
Profit before tax	87
Adjustments for:	
Depreciation	42
Finance costs	8
Dividends received	(45)
Gain on disposal of property, plant and equipment	(15)
Adjustment in respect of trade receivables (168 – 147)	(21)
Adjustment in respect of inventories (214 – 210)	(4)
Adjustment in respect of trade payables (136 – 121)	15
Cash generated from operations	67
Interest paid	(8)
Tax paid (W)	(18)
	41

(b)   Statement of cash flows for the year ended 31 December 20X8

	£000
Net cash from operating activities	41
Investing activities	
Proceeds on disposal of property, plant and equipment (W)	35
Purchases of property, plant and equipment (W)	(176)
Dividends received	45
Net cash used in investing activities	(96)
Financing activities	
Proceeds from issue of share capital (250 + 180 – 200 – 160)	70
Proceeds from bank loans (80 – 50)	30
Dividends paid	(24)
Net cash from financing activities	76
Net increase in cash and cash equivalents	21
Cash and cash equivalents at the beginning of the year	(14)
Cash and cash equivalents at the end of the year	7

Workings (not provided in the assessment)

Tax paid	£000
Balance b/d (SOFP)	44
Tax charge (SPL)	31
Balance c/d (SOFP)	(57)
	18

Workings (on-screen proforma provided in the assessment)

Proceeds on disposal of property, plant and equipment	£000
Carrying amount of property, plant and equipment sold (33 – 13)	20
Gain on disposal	15
	35

Purchases of property, plant and equipment	£000
Property, plant and equipment at start of year	514
Depreciation charge	(42)
Carrying amount of property, plant and equipment sold	(20)
Property, plant and equipment at the end of year	(628)
	(176)

Activity 7: Interpreting the statement of cash flows

A bonus issue of shares	
An increase in inventories	
An increase in trade payables	✓
An increase in a long-term loan	

An increase in inventories reduces cash generated from operations. A bonus issue of shares does not affect cash. An increase in long-term loans increases the overall cash balance for the year, but as it is a financing cash flow it is not included in cash generated from operations.

Activity 1: Purchase of property, plant and equipment

£28,000	
£30,000	
£33,500	✓
£38,700	

Working

	£
Purchase price	28,000
Delivery costs	2,000
Installation costs	3,500
	33,500

Activity 2: Revaluation gain

Journal

Account name	Debit £	Credit £
Freehold property: cost/valuation	100,000	
Freehold property: accumulated depreciation	31,250	
Revaluation reserve		131,250

Working

Accumulated depreciation at 31 December 20X5:

£250,000 × 5/40 = £31,250

Activity 3: Pisces Ltd – year ended 31 December 20X3

(a) **Pisces Ltd**

Statement of profit or loss and other comprehensive income for the year ended 31 December 20X3

	£
Revenue	300,000
Cost of sales	(100,000)
Gross profit	200,000
Distribution costs	(40,000)
Administrative expenses	(60,000)
Profit from operations	100,000
Finance costs	(14,000)
Profit before tax	86,000
Tax	(10,000)
Profit for the year from continuing operations	76,000
Other comprehensive income for the year	224,000
Total comprehensive income for the year	300,000

(b) **Pisces Ltd**

Statement of changes in equity for the year ended 31 December 20X3

	Share capital £	Revaluation reserve £	Retained earnings £	Total equity £
Balance at 1 January 20X3	100,000	0	30,000	130,000
Changes in equity				
Total comprehensive income		224,000	76,000	300,000
Dividends			(10,000)	(10,000)
Balance at 31 December 20X3	100,000	224,000	96,000	420,000

(c) Pisces Ltd

Statement of financial position as at 31 December 20X3

	£
ASSETS	
Non-current assets	
Property, plant and equipment (376,000 + 224,000)	600,000
EQUITY AND LIABILITIES	
Equity	
Share capital	100,000
Retained earnings	96,000
Revaluation reserve	224,000
Total equity	420,000

Workings (not provided in the assessment)

Account name	Debit £	Credit £
Non-current asset cost account (to make cost equal to valuation)	200,000	
Accumulated depreciation (to cancel all the previous depreciation)	24,000	
Revaluation reserve (OCI)		224,000

Activity 4: Ray Ltd

Ray Ltd

Statement of financial position (extract) as at 31 December 20X7

	£
ASSETS	
Non-current assets	
Property, plant and equipment (200,000 − 8,000 + 8,000 − 20,000)	180,000

Administrative expenses for the year ended 31 December 20X7

	£
Administrative expenses	50,000
Depreciation charge	4,000
Revaluation loss	12,000
	66,000

Workings

Property, plant and equipment – carrying amount prior to revaluation	£
Cost at 1 January 20X6	200,000
Depreciation charge 31 December 20X6 (200,000/50)	(4,000)
Depreciation charge 31 December 20X7	(4,000)
Carrying amount at 31 December 20X7 prior to revaluation	192,000

Revaluation loss	£
Carrying amount at 31 December 20X7 prior to revaluation	192,000
Revalued amount at 31 December 20X7	(180,000)
Revaluation loss	12,000

Account name	Debit £	Credit £
Statement of profit or loss	12,000	
Accumulated depreciation (to cancel all the previous depreciation)	8,000	
Non-current asset cost account (to make cost equal to valuation)		20,000

Activity 5: Pisces Ltd – year ended 31 December 20X4

(a) Pisces Ltd

Statement of profit or loss and other comprehensive income for the year ended 31 December 20X4

	£
Revenue	400,000
Cost of sales	(200,000)
Gross profit	200,000
Distribution costs	(30,000)
Administrative expenses (50,000 + 13,234)	(63,234)
Profit from operations	106,766
Finance costs	(14,000)
Profit before tax	92,766
Tax	(10,000)
Profit for the year from continuing operations	82,766
Other comprehensive (loss)/income for the year	(224,000)
Total comprehensive (loss)/income for the year	(141,234)

(b) Pisces Ltd

Statement of changes in equity for the year ended 31 December 20X4

	Share capital £	Revaluation reserve £	Retained earnings £	Total equity £
Balance at 1 January 20X4	100,000	224,000	96,000	420,000
Changes in equity				
Total comprehensive (loss)/(income)		(224,000)	82,766	(141,234)
Dividends			(10,000)	(10,000)
Balance at 31 December 20X4	100,000	0	168,766	268,766

(c) **Pisces Ltd**

Statement of financial position (extract) as at 31 December 20X4

	£
ASSETS	
Non-current assets	
Property, plant and equipment (600,000 – 250,000)	350,000
EQUITY AND LIABILITIES	
Equity	
Share capital	100,000
Retained earnings	168,766
Revaluation reserve	0
Total equity	268,766

Workings (not provided in the assessment)

Account name	Debit £	Credit £
Accumulated depreciation (to cancel all the previous depreciation)	12,766	
Revaluation reserve	224,000	
Statement of profit and loss (600,000 – 350,000 – 224,000 – 12,766)	13,234	
Non-current asset cost account (to make cost equal to valuation) (600,000 – 350,000)		250,000

Activity 6: Changing the method of depreciation

£	4,000

Carrying amount at 1 January 20X3:

	£
Cost	20,000
Accumulated depreciation (£20,000 × 2/10)	(4,000)
	16,000

Depreciation charge for the year ended 31 December 20X3 is 25% × £16,000 = £4,000.

Activity 7: Disposals revision

£	240,000

Gain on disposal:

	£000	£000
Sales proceeds		700
Less carrying amount		
Valuation	500	
Accumulated depreciation (500 × 4/50):	(40)	
		(460)
		240

CHAPTER 7 Intangible assets and inventories

Activity 1: Staff

True	
False	✓

An asset is a resource controlled by the entity as a result of past events and from which future economic benefits are expected to flow to the entity (*Conceptual Framework*: Chapter 4, para. 8). Although the staff give the company access to future economic benefits (revenue from selling the products that they develop), the company almost certainly does not control this resource. Employees are normally free to leave the company and work elsewhere.

Therefore, neither the staff nor their skills can be recognised as assets in the company's statement of financial position and IAS 38 specifically states that a workforce cannot be treated as an intangible asset.

Activity 2: New process

Recognised as an intangible asset in the statement of financial position	
Recognised as an expense in profit or loss	✓

The expenditure does not meet the IAS 38 criteria for capitalisation, as the technical feasibility of the project and the entity's ability to use or sell it are uncertain. Therefore the expenditure must be recognised as an expense in profit or loss in the period in which it is incurred.

Activity 3: Brand

True	✓
False	

IAS 38 prohibits the recognition of internally generated brands as assets.

Activity 4: Intangible assets

(a)

True	
False	✓

(b)

Technical feasibility	✓
Expenditure reliably measured	✓
Initial investigation suggests the project may generate future economic benefits	
Intention to complete and use/sell asset	✓
Resources inadequate to complete project	

Activity 5: Impairment

(a)

£21,500	
£21,800	✓
£22,000	
£30,000	

(b)

£Nil	
£60,000	✓
£300,000	
£360,000	

(c)

(ii) only	✓
(iii) only	
(ii) and (iii)	
(i), (ii) and (iii)	

(d)

True	
False	✓

There is no indicator that the peppermint maker is impaired and therefore an impairment test does not need to be performed.

Activity 6: Inventories

£5,600	
£5,770	
£5,200	
£4,960	✓

Activity 1: Oscar Ltd – current year tax

Oscar Ltd
Statement of profit or loss and other comprehensive income (extract)
for the year to 31 December 20X0

	£000
Tax	208

Statement of financial position (extract) as at 31 December 20X0

	£000
Current liabilities	
Tax liability	208

Activity 2: Oscar Ltd – under- or overprovision

£208,000	
£220,000	
£234,000	
£246,000	✓

Activity 3: Actuarial method – payments in arrears

Complete the financial statement extracts below for the year ended 31 December 20X0.

Statement of financial position (extract) as at 31 December 20X0

	£
Non-current assets	
Property, plant and equipment (W)	16,487
Non-current liabilities	
Lease liability (W)	12,729
Current liabilities	
Lease liability (W)	3,998

Statement of profit or loss and other comprehensive income (extract) for the year ended 31 December 20X0

	£
Depreciation charge (W)	4,122
Finance charges (W)	618

Workings (will not be provided in the assessment)

Property, plant and equipment	£
Fair value of the plant on 1 January 20X0	20,609
Depreciation charge (20,609/5) (SPL)	(4,122)
Balance c/d 31 December 20X0	16,487

Lease liability	£
Fair value of the plant on 1 January 20X0	20,609
Interest (20,609 × 3%) (to SPL)	618
Payment on 31 December 20X0	(4,500)
Total lease liability c/d on 31 December 20X0	16,727
Total lease liability b/d on 1 January 20X1	16,727
Interest (16,727 × 3%)	502
Payment on 31 December 20X1	(4,500)
Total lease liability c/d on 31 December 20X1 (SOFP – NCL)	12,729
Therefore, current liabilities at 31 December 20X0 (16,727 – 12,729)	3,998

Activity 4: Actuarial method – payments in advance

Complete the financial statement extracts below for the year ended 31 December 20X0.

Statement of financial position (extract) as at 31 December 20X0

	£
Non-current assets	
Property, plant and equipment (W)	3,750
Non-current liabilities	
Lease liability (W)	2,105
Current liabilities	
Lease liability (W)	1,500

Statement of profit or loss and other comprehensive income (extract) for the year ended 31 December 20X0

	£
Depreciation charge (W)	1,250
Finance charges (W)	105

Workings (will not be provided in the assessment)

Property, plant and equipment	£
Fair value of the plant on 1 January 20X0	5,000
Depreciation charge (5,000/4) (SPL)	(1,250)
Balance c/d 31 December 20X0	3,750

Lease liability	£
Fair value of the plant on 1 January 20X0	5,000
Payment on 1 January 20X0	(1,500)
	3,500
Interest (3,500 × 3%) (SPL)	105
Total lease liability c/d on 31 December 20X0	3,605

Lease liability	£
Total lease liability b/d on 1 January 20X1	3,605
Payment on 1 January 20X1 (SOFP – CL)	(1,500)
Total lease liability c/d on 1 January 20X1 (SOFP – NCL)	2,105

Activity 5: Sum-of-digits method

Statement of financial position (extract) as at 31 December 20X0

	£
Non-current assets	
Property, plant and equipment (W)	16,487
Non-current liabilities	
Lease liability (W)	12,743
Current liabilities	
Lease liability (W)	3,996

Statement of profit or loss and other comprehensive income (extract) for the year ended 31 December 20X0

	£
Depreciation charge (W)	4,122
Finance charges (W)	630

Workings (will not be provided in the assessment)

Property, plant and equipment	£
Fair value of the plant on 1 January 20X0	20,609
Depreciation charge (20,609/5)	(4,122)
Balance c/d 31 December 20X0	16,487

Sum-of-digits calculations

Step 1

There are 5.

Step 2 and 3

$$\frac{5(6)}{2} = 15$$

Step 4

	£
Total payments (5 × £4,500)	22,500
Fair value of the asset	(20,609)
Total interest payable	1,891

Step 5 Note. For teaching purposes, all years are included in this solution.

	£
Year 1 interest: 5/15 × £1,891 =	630
Year 2 interest: 4/15 × £1,891 =	504
Year 3 interest: 3/15 × £1,891 =	378
Year 4 interest: 2/15 × £1,891 =	252
Year 5 interest: 1/15 × £1,891 =	126
(rounding difference)	1,890

Lease liability	£
Fair value of the plant on 1 January 20X0	20,609
Interest (sum-of-digits calculations)	630
Payment on 31 December 20X0	(4,500)
Total lease liability c/d on 31 December 20X0	16,739
Total lease liability b/d on 1 January 20X1	16,739
Interest (sum-of-digits calculations)	504
Payment on 31 December 20X1	(4,500)
Total lease liability c/d on 31 December 20X1	12,743
Therefore, current liabilities at 31 December 20X0 (16,739 – 12,743)	3,996

Activity 6: Operating or finance lease?

True	
False	✓

This is a finance lease.

The following factors suggest that the risks and rewards of ownership have been transferred:

- The lease term is for the whole of the asset's useful life (five years).

- The present value of the minimum lease payments (£95,500) amounts to substantially all the fair value of the leased asset (£98,000).

Activity 7: Leases – further issues

(a) How much must Mary Ltd record in the financial statements as the rental expense in Year 2?

£700	
£867	✓
£500	
£733	

Working

	£
Total payable 500 + (700 × 3)	2,600
Period of lease agreement	3
Annual rental expense (2,600/3)	867

(b)

Operating lease	✓
Finance lease	

Activity 8: Provisions, contingent liabilities and contingent assets

(a)

Disclose a contingent liability	✓
Recognise a provision	

(b)

Contingent asset	Contingent liability	
No disclosure is required	No disclosure is required	
Disclosure is required	No disclosure is required	
No disclosure is required	Disclosure is required	
Disclosure is required	Disclosure is required	✓

Activity 9: Recognise a provision?

True	✓
False	

Is there a present obligation as the result of a past event? Yes. The company has a legal obligation under the guarantee.

Is the transfer of economic benefits in settlement probable? Yes. IAS 37 (para. 14) states that in this, and similar, situations the individual obligations should be considered as a whole.

Can a reliable estimate be made of the amount of the obligation? Yes. The company should be able to use its past experience to predict the percentage of items that will need to be repaired or replaced.

Conclusion: recognise a provision for the best estimate of the costs of repairing or replacing items sold before the year end under the guarantee.

Activity 10: Events after the reporting period

(a)

True	✓
False	

This is an adjusting event as the sale of inventory provides evidence as to the net realisable value of the inventory reported in the financial statements for the year. IAS 2 (para. 2.9) states that inventory should be valued at the lower of cost and net realisable value.

(b)

Adjusting event	
Non-adjusting event	✓

(c)

This is an adjusting event and a provision should be recognised at the year end.	✓
This is a non-adjusting event, therefore a provision should not be recognised.	

This is an adjusting event as the employee was alleging unfair dismissal during the financial year. A provision of £20,000 should be raised in the 20X6 accounts.

Activity 11: Non-adjusting event?

(1) only	✓
(2) only	
Neither (1) nor (2)	
Both (1) and (2)	

Sale of land and buildings: this is a non-adjusting event because it does not concern conditions that existed at the year end.

Liquidation of a major customer: this is an adjusting event; it provides evidence of conditions that existed at the year end (a trade receivable is worthless).

Activity 12: Revenue

Recognise dividend income of £20,000 from Bee Ltd	
Do not recognise dividend income from Bee Ltd	✓

Activity 1: Pegasus plc – single entity financial statements

The investment in Sylvester Ltd will be recorded as follows:

	Debit £000	Credit £000
Investment in Sylvester Ltd	1,300	
Cash		1,300

Pegasus plc
Statement of financial position as at 1 January 20X1

	£000
ASSETS	
Non-current assets	
Property, plant and equipment	20,000
Investment in Sylvester Ltd	1,300
	21,300
Current assets	
Inventories	3,200
Trade receivables	2,500
Cash (1,800 – 1,300)	500
	6,200
Total assets	27,500
EQUITY AND LIABILITIES	
Equity	
Share capital	5,000
Retained earnings	19,450
	24,450

	£000
Current liabilities	
Trade payables	2,500
Tax liability	550
	3,050
Total equity and liabilities	27,500

Activity 2: Pegasus plc and Sylvester Ltd at 1 January 20X1

Pegasus plc
Consolidated statement of financial position as at 1 January 20X1

	£000
ASSETS	
Non-current assets	
Property, plant and equipment (20,000 + 900)	20,900
Current assets	
Inventories (3,200 + 400)	3,600
Trade receivables (2,500 + 175)	2,675
Cash (500 + 125)	625
	6,900
Total assets	27,800
EQUITY AND LIABILITIES	
Equity	
Share capital	5,000
Retained earnings	19,450
	24,450
Current liabilities	
Trade payables (2,500 + 260)	2,760
Tax liability (550 + 40)	590
	3,350
Total equity and liabilities	27,800

Workings (not provided in the assessment)

Group structure

Pegasus plc

↓ 100%

Sylvester Ltd

Cancellation	£000
Price paid	1,300
Less fair value of net assets at acquisition	
Share capital **(attributable to parent)**	(100)
Retained earnings **(attributable to parent)**	(1,200)
	0

Activity 3: Pegasus plc and Sylvester Ltd as at 31 December 20X3

Pegasus plc
Consolidated statement of financial position as at 31 December 20X3

	£000
ASSETS	
Non-current assets	
Property, plant and equipment (24,000 + 4,200)	28,200
	28,200
Current assets (8,500 + 2,100)	10,600
Total assets	38,800
EQUITY AND LIABILITIES	
Equity	
Share capital	5,000
Retained earnings (W)	30,800
	35,800
Current liabilities (2,000 + 1,000)	3,000
Total equity and liabilities	38,800

Workings (not provided in the assessment)

Group structure

Pegasus plc

↓ 100%

Sylvester Ltd

Cancellation	£000
Price paid	1,300
Share capital	(100)
Retained earnings	(1,200)
	0

Workings (will be provided in the assessment)

Retained earnings	£000
Parent	26,800
Subsidiary: attributable to parent (5,200 – 1,200 = 4,000; 4,000 × 100%)	4,000
	30,800

Activity 4: Thatch plc

Thatch plc
Consolidated statement of financial position as at 31 December 20X6

	£000
ASSETS	
Non-current assets	
Property, plant and equipment (10,000 + 5,000)	15,000
Goodwill (W)	2,000
	17,000
Current assets (4,000 + 5,000)	9,000
Total assets	26,000

	£000
EQUITY AND LIABILITIES	
Equity	
Share capital	9,000
Retained earnings (W)	8,000
	17,000
Liabilities	
Non-current liabilities	2,000
Current liabilities (5,000 + 2,000)	7,000
	9,000
Total equity and liabilities	26,000

Workings (not provided in the assessment)

Group structure

Thatch plc

↓ 100%

Straw Ltd

Workings (on-screen proforma provided in the assessment)

Goodwill	£000
Consideration	8,000
Net assets acquired: £3m + £2m	(5,000)
Impairment	(1,000)
	2,000

Retained earnings	£000
Parent	6,000
Subsidiary – attributable to Thatch plc (5,000 – 2,000) × 100%	3,000
Less impairment	(1,000)
	8,000

Activity 5: Apple Ltd

£	400,000

Goodwill:

	£000
Consideration (price paid)	4,000
Non-controlling interest at acquisition	2,400
Net assets acquired: £1m + £5m	(6,000)
	400

Working

Non-controlling interest at acquisition

	£000
Share capital attributable to NCI (40% × 1,000)	400
Retained earnings attributable to NCI (40% × 5,000)	2,000
	2,400

Activity 6: Church plc

Church plc
Consolidated statement of financial position as at 31 December 20X6

	£000
ASSETS	
Non-current assets	
Property, plant and equipment (10,000 + 7,000)	17,000
Goodwill (W)	2,000
	19,000
Current assets (8,500 + 5,000)	13,500
Total assets	32,500

	£000
EQUITY AND LIABILITIES	
Equity	
Share capital	12,000
Retained earnings (W)	2,250
Non-controlling interest (W)	1,250
Total equity	15,500
Liabilities	
Non-current liabilities (4,000 + 2,000)	6,000
Current liabilities (6,000 + 5,000)	11,000
	17,000
Total equity and liabilities	32,500

Workings (not provided in the assessment)

Group structure

Church plc

↓ 75%

Steeple Ltd

Non-controlling interest at acquisition	£000
Share capital – attributable to NCI (4,000 × 25%)	1,000
Retained earnings – attributable to NCI (acquired on incorporation)	0
	1,000

Non-controlling interest at year end	£000
Share capital – attributable to NCI (4,000 × 25%)	1,000
Retained earnings – attributable to NCI (1,000 × 25%)	250
	1,250

Workings (on-screen proforma provided in the assessment)

Goodwill	£000
Consideration	5,000
Non-controlling interest at acquisition	1,000
Net assets acquired (share capital only)	(4,000)
	2,000

Retained earnings	£000
Parent	1,500
Subsidiary – attributable to Church plc (1,000 × 75%)	750
	2,250

Activity 7: Intra-group balances

£	33,500

Trade receivables:

	£
X Ltd	20,000
Y Ltd	15,000
Less inter-company balance	(1,500)
	33,500

Note. Don't make the mistake of taking 80% of Y Ltd's receivables!

Activity 8: Door plc

Door plc
Consolidated statement of financial position

	£000
ASSETS	
Non-current assets	
Property, plant and equipment (200,000 + 40,000)	240,000
Goodwill (W)	1,800
	241,800

	£000
Current assets	
Inventories (W)	35,000
Trade receivables (W)	84,000
Cash and cash equivalents (4,000 + 15,000 + 4,000)	23,000
	142,000
Total assets	383,800
EQUITY AND LIABILITIES	
Share capital	100,000
Retained earnings (W)	150,000
Non-controlling interest (W)	18,800
Total equity	268,800
Non-current liabilities	
Bank loan	20,000
Current liabilities	
Trade payables (81,000 + 50,000 − 36,000)	95,000
Total liabilities	115,000
Total equity and liabilities	383,800

Workings (not provided in the assessment)

Group structure

Door plc

↓ 60%

Window Ltd

Non-controlling interest at acquisition	£000
Share capital – attributable to NCI (10,000 × 40%)	4,000
Retained earnings – attributable to NCI (32,000 × 40%)	12,800
	16,800

Non-controlling interest at year end	£000
Share capital – attributable to NCI (10,000 × 40%)	4,000
Retained earnings – attributable to NCI ((42,000 – 5,000) × 40%)	14,800
	18,800

Adjustment for cash in transit

Adjustment for cash in transit	Debit £000	Credit £000
Cash	4,000	
Trade receivables		4,000

Intra-group cancellation

Eliminate intra-group payables and receivables	Debit £000	Credit £000
Trade payables (Door plc)	36,000	
Trade receivables (Window Ltd)		36,000

Trade receivables	£000
Door plc	75,000
Window Ltd	49,000
Cash in transit from Door plc to Window Ltd	(4,000)
Intra-group receivables	(36,000)
	84,000

Workings (on-screen proforma provided in the assessment)

Goodwill	£000
Consideration	27,000
Non-controlling interests at acquisition	16,800
Net assets acquired: (£10m + £32m)	(42,000)
	1,800

Inventories	£000
Consolidated inventories (prior to any company adjustment)	40,000
Inter-company adjustment	(5,000)
	35,000

Retained earnings	£000
Parent	147,000
Subsidiary – attributable to Door plc ((42,000 – 32,000 – 5,000) × 60%)	3,000
	150,000

Activity 9: Morse plc

Morse plc
Consolidated statement of financial position as at 31 December 20X0

	£000
ASSETS	
Non-current assets	
Goodwill (W)	6,068
Property, plant and equipment (63,781 + 27,184 + 2,500)	93,465
	99,533
Current assets	
Inventories (W)	27,967
Trade and other receivables (29,474 + 14,023 – 13,000)	30,497
Cash and cash equivalents (2,872 + 88)	2,960
	61,424
Total assets	160,957
EQUITY AND LIABILITIES	
Share capital	45,000
Share premium	13,000
Retained earnings (W)	31,642
Non-controlling interest (W)	14,105
Total equity	103,747

	£000
Non-current liabilities	
Long-term loans (25,000 + 8,000)	33,000
Current liabilities	
Trade and other payables (16,231 + 15,042 – 13,000)	18,273
Tax liability (5,763 + 174)	5,937
	24,210
Total liabilities	57,210
Total equity and liabilities	160,957

Workings (not provided in the assessment)

Group structure

Morse plc

↓ 60%

Lewis Ltd

Non-controlling interest at acquisition	£000
Share capital – attributable to NCI (40% of 10,000)	4,000
Share premium – attributable to NCI (40% of 5,000)	2,000
Retained earnings – attributable to NCI (40% of 11,263)	4,505
Revaluation reserve – attributable to NCI (40% of 2,500)	1,000
	11,505

Non-controlling interest at year end	£000
Share capital – attributable to NCI (40% of 10,000)	4,000
Share premium – attributable to NCI (40% of 5,000)	2,000
Retained earnings – attributable to NCI (40% of 17,763)	7,105
Revaluation reserve – attributable to NCI (40% of 2,500)	1,000
	14,105

BPP
LEARNING MEDIA

Eliminate intra-group receivable and payable	Debit £000	Credit £000
Trade payable to Morse plc	13,000	
Trade receivable from Lewis Ltd		13,000

Workings (on-screen proforma provided in the assessment)

Goodwill	£000
Consideration	24,000
Non-controlling interest at acquisition	11,505
Net assets acquired (10,000 + 5,000 + 11,263 + 2,500)	(28,763)
Impairment	(674)
	6,068

Inventories	£000
Consolidated inventories (prior to any company adjustment)	32,967
Inter-company adjustment (1/4 × (50,000 – 30,000))	(5,000)
	27,967

Retained earnings	£000
Parent (33,416 – 5,000)	28,416
Subsidiary – attributable to parent (17,763 – 11,263) × 60%	3,900
Impairment	(674)
	31,642

CHAPTER 10 Group accounts: further aspects

Activity 1: Baker plc

Baker plc
Statement of profit or loss for the year ended 31 December 20X9

	£000
Revenue (115 + 60)	175
Cost of sales (65 + 28)	(93)
Gross profit	82
Distribution costs (5 + 8)	(13)
Administrative expenses (14 + 11)	(25)
Profit from operations	44
Finance costs (1 + 1)	(2)
Profit before tax	42
Tax (8 + 2)	(10)
Profit for the year	32
Equity holders of the parent	30
Non-controlling interest	2
	32

Workings (not provided in the assessment)
Group structure

Baker plc

↓ 80%

Bun Ltd

Non-controlling interest	£000
Bun Ltd's profit for the year attributable to NCI – 20% of £10	2

Activity 2: Intra-group sale

Reduce by £25,000	
Reduce by £30,000	
Reduce by £35,000	✓
Reduce by £40,000	

To cancel the sale: reduce both revenue and cost of sales by £40,000

To eliminate the unrealised profit: increase cost of sales by £5,000 (£10,000 ÷ 2)

Activity 3: Pike plc

Pike plc
Statement of profit or loss for the year ended 31 December 20X1

	£000
Revenue (W)	411
Cost of sales (W)	(202)
Gross profit	209
Distribution costs (18 + 9)	(27)
Administrative expenses (20 + 18)	(38)
Profit from operations	144
Finance costs (5 + 3)	(8)
Profit before tax	136
Tax (30 + 12)	(42)
Profit for the year	94
Equity holders of the parent	85
Non-controlling interest	9
	94

Workings (not provided in the assessment)

Group structure

Pike plc

70%

Shrimp Ltd

Non-controlling interest	£000
Shrimp Ltd's profit for the year attributable to NCI – 30% of £30	9

Total inter-company adjustment	Debit £000	Credit £000
Revenue	14	
Cost of sales		14

Workings (on-screen proforma provided in the assessment)

Revenue	£000
Pike plc	321
Shrimp Ltd	104
Total inter-company adjustment	–14
	411

Cost of sales	£000
Pike plc	184
Shrimp Ltd	32
Total inter-company adjustment	–14
	202

Activity 4: Platini plc

Platini plc
Statement of profit or loss for the year ended 31 December 20X1

	£000
Revenue (W)	684
Cost of sales (W)	(275)
Gross profit	409
Distribution costs (65 + 18)	(83)
Administrative expenses (90 + 10)	(100)
Profit from operations	226
Finance costs (5 + 2)	(7)
Profit before tax	219
Tax (50 + 12)	(62)
Profit for the year	157
Equity holders of the parent	153
Non-controlling interest	4
	157

Workings (not provided in the assessment)

Group structure

Platini plc

90%

Maldini Ltd

Non-controlling interest	£000
Maldini Ltd's profit for the year attributable to NCI – 10% of £40	4

Total inter-company adjustment	Debit £000	Credit £000
Revenue	21	
Cost of sales		21

Eliminate unrealised profit	Debit £000	Credit £000
Cost of sales	3	
Inventories		3

Workings (on-screen proforma provided in the assessment)

Revenue	£000
Platini plc	565
Maldini Ltd	140
Total inter-company adjustment	–21
	684

Cost of sales	£000
Platini plc	235
Maldini Ltd	58
Total inter-company adjustment (–21 + 3)	–18
	275

Activity 5: Platypus plc

Platypus plc
Statement of profit or loss for the year ended 31 December 20X5

	£000
Revenue	314
Cost of sales	(103)
Gross profit	211
Distribution costs (35 + 18)	(53)
Administrative expenses (36 + 14)	(50)
Profit from operations	108
Finance costs (6 + 3)	(9)
Profit before tax	99
Tax (15 + 18)	(33)
Profit for the year	66
Equity holders of the parent	58
Non-controlling interest	8
	66

Workings (not provided in the assessment)

Group structure

Platypus plc

75%

Serpent Ltd

Non-controlling interest	£000
Serpent Ltd's profit for the year attributable to NCI – 25% of (£35 – £3) = £32	8

Total inter-company adjustment	Debit £000	Credit £000
Revenue	25	
Cost of sales		25

Eliminate unrealised profit	Debit £000	Credit £000
Cost of sales (see PUP calculation)	3	
Inventories (see PUP calculation)		3

Provision for unrealised profit calculation	£000
Revenue	25
Cost of sales	(19)
Profit	6
PUP (½ goods in inventories at the year end (6,000 × ½))	3

Workings (on-screen proforma provided in the assessment)

Revenue	£000
Platypus plc	213
Serpent Ltd	126
Total inter-company adjustment	–25
	314

Cost of sales	£000
Platypus plc	87
Serpent Ltd	38
Total inter-company adjustment (–25 + 3)	–22
	103

CHAPTER 11 Interpreting financial statements

Activity 1: Stakeholders

Note. For each group of stakeholder, answers may include two of the following.

Managers	• Profitability • Long-term growth • Security of their job • Likelihood of bonus • Number of employees • Day to day running issues
Owners/shareholders	• Profitability • Likely return • Chance of capital growth • Whether business will continue to trade
Providers of finance	• Whether return on finance will continue to be met • Other providers and security of their debt • Likelihood of repayment of capital amount
Tax authorities	• Profits made • Breakdown of expenses • VAT liability recorded
Suppliers	• Likelihood of payment on time • Likelihood of payment at all • Whether they should continue to supply
Financial analysts	• Whether to recommend the shares as a buy or sell • Profitability • Future prospects
Government	• Statistics • Size of company • Growth rates • Average payment periods • Tax liabilities • Foreign trade

Activity 2: Current and quick ratio

Current ratio

2.0:1

Quick ratio

1.5:1

Current ratio $\quad \dfrac{\text{Current assets}}{\text{Current liabilities}} \quad \dfrac{4{,}750 + 11{,}350 + 2{,}900}{7{,}400 + 2{,}100} = 2$

Quick ratio $\quad \dfrac{\text{Current assets} - \text{Inventories}}{\text{Current liabilities}} \quad \dfrac{11{,}350 + 2{,}900}{7{,}400 + 2{,}100} = 1.5$

Activity 3: Brookstream

(a)

20%

$$\dfrac{\text{Profit from operations}}{\text{Total equity} + \text{Non-current liabilities}} \quad \dfrac{300}{1{,}500} \times 100\% = 20\%$$

(b)

15%

$$\dfrac{\text{Profit from operations}}{\text{Revenue}} \quad \dfrac{300}{2{,}000} \times 100\% = 15\%$$

(c)

1.33 times

$$\dfrac{\text{Revenue}}{\text{Total assets} - \text{Current liabilities}} \quad \dfrac{2{,}000}{1{,}500} = 1.33 \text{ times}$$

Activity 4: Inventory turnover

3.5 times

Inventory turnover $\quad \dfrac{\text{Cost of sales}}{\text{Inventories}} \quad \dfrac{4{,}200}{1{,}200} = 3.5$

Activity 5: Financial position

Gearing ratio

> 31.1%

Interest cover

> 5.2 times

Gearing ratio $\dfrac{\text{Non-current liabilities}}{\text{Total equity + Non-current liabilities}}$ $\dfrac{9,000}{19,900+9,000} = 31.1\%$

Interest cover $\dfrac{\text{Profit from operations}}{\text{Finance costs}}$ $\dfrac{2,800}{540} = 5.2$ times

Activity 6: New Ltd

(a)

Gross profit percentage	$\dfrac{\text{Gross profit}}{\text{Revenue}} \times 100$
Operating profit percentage	$\dfrac{\text{Profit from operations}}{\text{Revenue}} \times 100$
Return on capital employed	$\dfrac{\text{Profit from operations}}{\text{Total equity + Non-current liabilities}} \times 100$
Current ratio	$\dfrac{\text{Current assets}}{\text{Current liabilities}}$
Inventory holding period	$\dfrac{\text{Inventories}}{\text{Cost of sales}} \times 365 \text{ days}$
Payables payment period	$\dfrac{\text{Trade payables}}{\text{Cost of sales}} \times 365$
Interest cover	$\dfrac{\text{Profit from operations}}{\text{Finance costs}}$
Gearing ratio	$\dfrac{\text{Non-current liabilities}}{\text{Total equity + Non-current liabilities}} \times 100$

(b)

Gross profit percentage	$\frac{£470}{£1,430} \times 100 = 32.9\%$
Operating profit percentage	$\frac{£180}{£1,430} \times 100 = 12.6\%$
Return on capital employed	$\frac{£180}{£1,450 + £100} \times 100 = 11.6\%$
Current ratio	$\frac{£525}{£255} = 2.1{:}1$
Inventory holding period	$\frac{£240}{£960} \times 365 = 91.3$ days
Trade payables payment period	$\frac{£205}{£960} \times 365 = 77.9$ days
Interest cover	$\frac{£180}{£10} = 18.0$ times
Gearing ratio	$\frac{£100}{£1,450 + 100} \times 100 = 6.5\%$

Activity 7: Interpreting ratios

True	
False	✓

The irrecoverable debt is not the reason for the increase. In fact, a large debt write-off at the year end would decrease trade receivables and, thereby, receivables days.

Possible reasons (only **one** was required):

- Some customers have been allowed extended credit terms (for example, because they are so significant that the business needs to maintain good relations with them).

- Sales were unusually high just before the year end, or were increasing throughout the year. If this were the case, receivables at the year end would be high in relation to total sales for the year.

- Credit control procedures have not been applied during the last few months of the year.

Activity 8: Effect of revaluation

	True	False
Asset turnover is higher.		✓
Gearing is higher.		✓
Operating profit percentage is lower.	✓	
Return on capital employed is lower.	✓	

Revaluation of assets normally increases asset values. This means that the depreciation charge also increases. The revaluation surplus is taken to a revaluation reserve, which increases equity. There is no effect on sales.

As a result:

- Profit is reduced
- Capital employed is increased

This means that:

- Return on capital employed (ROCE) is lower
- Asset turnover is lower
- Operating profit percentage is lower

However, gearing is reduced, because assets and equity have increased and there is no effect on liabilities.

The company may appear to be less efficient and less profitable, but also less risky as an investment or as a loan creditor.

Activity 9: Benjamin Lens

Benjamin,

As requested, I have analysed the performance of Glass Ltd in relation to the industry. Based on my findings, I also provide advice on whether or not you should invest in the company.

(a) (i) Gross profit percentage

(1) This is slightly below the industry average, but not excessively so.

(2) This indicates that Glass Ltd has a slightly higher cost per sale, or a slightly lower selling price. It may be trying to reduce its prices to encourage sales volume, since its inventory sales appear to be slow (inventory days are long).

(3) Perhaps it has a slightly different sales mix.

(ii) Operating profit percentage

    (1) Glass Ltd is generating a much smaller operating profit than the industry.

    (2) This indicates that administration and distribution costs are higher, since the gross profit percentage is similar to the industry.

    (3) Perhaps it is offering discounts and free delivery to aid the increase of sales volume.

(iii) Return on capital employed

    (1) This is roughly four percentage points lower than the industry equivalent.

    (2) This means that Glass Ltd is not as efficient in using its resources as other companies.

    (3) This could be caused by old property, plant and equipment being less efficient or by new property, plant and equipment being purchased near year end and, therefore, not contributing to a year's worth of increased efficiency, perhaps only a few months.

(iv) Current ratio

    (1) The current ratio is very good, at just over two times.

    (2) This is significantly better than the industry average.

    (3) Glass Ltd appears to be able to pay its debts when they fall due.

    (4) The high current ratio could be driven by the large inventory holding.

    (5) It would be better to look at the quick ratio in these circumstances.

(v) Inventory holding period

    (1) This is very long – three months versus the industry average of one month.

    (2) It would appear that the inventory is not selling that well and this may be driving the increased expenses in the profitability section of this report.

    (3) Perhaps there is some obsolete inventory that should be written off and which is skewing this ratio.

(vi) Receivables collection period

    (1) The receivables collection period is in line with the industry average.

    (2) This confirms that the customers are paying their bills in a timely fashion and contributes to a good liquidity situation.

    (3) Management seem to be efficient at collecting their debts.

(vii) Interest cover and gearing

    (1) The interest cover is high and the gearing is low.

    (2) This is a good situation as it means that Glass Ltd has relatively little debt.

    (3) It could easily afford to take out a new loan if it so desired.

    (4) Perhaps it should take out a loan and replace some of the property, plant and equipment.

    (5) This may have the effect of reducing some of the inefficiency costs discussed under the operating profit percentage.

(b)
- Benjamin should not invest in this company.

- While the gross profit percentage is similar to the industry average, the operating profit percentage is poor.

- In addition, the return on capital employed is low and the inventory holding period is long.

- Management could secure additional financing, but this seems unlikely to assist with some of the weaknesses listed above.

Test your learning: Answers

CHAPTER 1 Introduction to limited companies

1

True	✓
False	

Limited liability means that the owners' liability is limited to the amount that they have paid for their shares.

2

True	
False	✓

Shares are stated in the statement of financial position at their nominal value, not their market value.

3

Accruals	
Drawings	
Loan stock	✓
Sales	

4

£40,000	
£52,500	✓
£66,000	
£126,500	

Working

	£
Profit from operations	140,000
Loan stock interest (150,000 × 9%)	(13,500)
Profit before tax	126,500
Tax	(74,000)
Profit for the year	52,500

Dividends are not deducted as an expense from profit for the year.

5 (a) **Hearts Ltd**

Statement of profit or loss for the year ended 31 December 20X2

	£000
Revenue	16,100
Cost of sales: 4,515 + 10,493 – 5,292	(9,716)
Gross profit	6,384
Operating expenses	(3,912)
Profit from operations	2,472
Finance cost	(105)
Profit before tax	2,367
Tax	(280)
Profit for the year	2,087

(b) **Hearts Ltd**

Statement of financial position as at 31 December 20X2

	£000	£000
Assets		
Non-current assets:		
Property, plant and equipment		5,852
Current assets:		
Inventories	5,292	
Receivables	3,578	
		8,870
Total assets		14,722
Equity and liabilities		
Equity:		
Share capital		840
Revaluation reserve		1,365
Retained earnings (3,955 + 2,087)		6,042
		8,247

	£000	£000
Non-current liabilities:		
Bank loan		2,100
Current liabilities:		
Trade payables	3,675	
Tax payable	280	
Bank overdraft	420	
		4,375
Total liabilities		6,475
Total equity and liabilities		14,722

6   **Journal**

Account name	Debit £	Credit £
Bank	160,000	
Share capital		100,000
Share premium		60,000

CHAPTER 2 The frameworks and ethical principles

1   The purpose of financial statements is to provide useful information about the financial performance and financial position of an entity to existing and potential investors, lenders and other creditors (providers of finance). These users are often external to the company and, therefore, they depend on financial statements for information about a company's performance and position.

Accounting standards and companies legislation ensure that financial statements actually do provide the information that users need to make decisions about providing finance to a company. Without regulation, preparers of financial statements would be able to adopt whatever accounting practices they chose. This would make it impossible for users to compare the financial statements of different entities in any meaningful way. It would also be impossible to compare the financial statements of the same entity over time.

Managers normally wish to show the performance of a company in the best possible light. At worst, without regulation, information might be deliberately presented in such a way as to mislead users.

2

To prepare and approve the annual accounts	
To file the accounts with the Registrar of Companies	
To keep accounting records that are neutral, complete and free from error	✓
To ensure that the accounts show a true and fair view	

The directors have a duty to keep adequate accounting records.

3

True	
False	✓

4   The objective of general purpose financial reporting is to provide financial information about the reporting entity that is useful to existing and potential investors, lenders and other creditors in making decisions about providing resources to the entity.

5

Employees	
Government	
Investors	✓
Lenders	✓

6

Accruals	
Consistency	
Going concern	✓
Reliability	

7

Consistency	
Going concern	
Relevance	✓
Timeliness	

8   Elements:

- Assets
- Liabilities
- Equity
- Income
- Expenses

9

True	
False	✓

Although the contract looks like a liability, it does not meet the definition in the *Conceptual Framework*. The business has an obligation to transfer economic benefit but only if the managing director actually does work for the business for the next five years. Therefore there is no **past** 'obligating event' that would result in a liability.

10

Current cost	
Fair value	
Historical cost	
Present value	✓

11

True	
False	✓

12

	✓
Enhance the reputation and standing of its members	✓
Limit the number of members that it has	
Make sure that its members are able to earn large salaries	

13

	✓
Say that you will get back to him when you have looked up the answer.	✓
Give him the contact details of a friend in your firm who knows all about accounting standards.	
Clarify the limits of your expertise with the client.	

14

	✓
It is in the public interest that employees who fail to comply with standards are prosecuted.	
It is in the public interest that services are carried out to professional standards.	✓

CHAPTER 3 The statement of financial position

1

True	
False	✓

If the end of the reporting period (year end) changes so that the financial statements are prepared for a different period, the entity should disclose the reason for the change, and the fact that the comparative figures are not entirely comparable.

2   Current assets:

- Inventories
- Trade and other receivables
- Cash and cash equivalents

3

Financial liabilities	
Investment properties	
Prepayments	✓
Trade and other payables	

4   **Statement of financial position as at ...**

	£000
ASSETS	
Non-current assets:	
Property, plant and equipment (W1)	11,407
Current assets:	
Inventories	3,061
Trade and other receivables (W2)	4,217
	7,278
Total assets	18,685
EQUITY AND LIABILITIES	
Equity:	
Share capital	3,000
Share premium	1,950
Revaluation reserve	525
Retained earnings	4,503
Total equity	9,978
Non-current liabilities:	
Bank loan	5,400
Current liabilities:	
Trade and other payables (W3)	1,375
Tax payable	1,458
Bank overdraft	474
	3,307
Total liabilities	8,707
Total equity and liabilities	18,685

Workings

(1) Property, plant and equipment

	£000
Land and buildings: Cost	7,724
Plant and machinery: Cost	6,961
Accumulated depreciation: Buildings	(468)
Accumulated depreciation: Plant and machinery	(2,810)
	11,407

(2) Trade and other receivables

	£000
Trade receivables	4,294
Allowance for doubtful debts	(171)
Prepayments	94
	4,217

(3) Trade and other payables

	£000
Trade payables	1,206
Accruals	169
	1,375

CHAPTER 4 The statements of financial performance

1

True	
False	✓

2

£147,000	
£215,000	
£223,000	✓
£239,000	

Working

	£000
General administrative expenses	155,000
Depreciation of office furniture	76,000
Prepayment (24,000 × 1/3)	(8,000)
	223,000

3   **Tarragona plc**
   Statement of profit or loss and other comprehensive income for the year ended 30 September 20X3

	£000
Revenue	33,202
Cost of sales (W)	(17,788)
Gross profit	15,414
Distribution costs	(6,165)
Administrative expenses	(3,386)
Profit from operations	5,863
Finance costs	(517)
Profit before tax	5,346
Tax	(1,333)
Profit for the period from continuing operations	4,013
Other comprehensive income	
Gain on revaluation of land (5,800 – 4,800)	1,000
Total comprehensive income for the period	5,013

Working

Cost of sales	£000
Opening inventories	8,570
Purchases	19,480
Closing inventories	(10,262)
	17,788

4 | Accounting policies | are the specific principles, bases, conventions, rules and practices applied by an entity in preparing and presenting financial statements.

5 **Statement of changes in equity for the year ended 31 December 20X5**

	Share capital	Share premium	Revaluation reserve	Retained earnings	Total equity
	£000	£000	£000	£000	£000
Balance at 1 January 20X5	1,000	300	0	700	2,000
Changes in equity for 20X5					
Total comprehensive income	0	0	150	300	450
Dividends	0	0	0	(50)	(50)
Issue of shares	100	20	–	–	120
Balance at 31 December 20X5	1,100	320	150	950	2,520

CHAPTER 5 The statement of cash flows

1

True	✓
False	

2

Bank current account in foreign currency	
Bank overdraft	
Petty cash float	
Short-term deposit	✓

Deposits must be repayable on demand to qualify as cash. A deposit is repayable on demand if it can be withdrawn without notice. A short-term deposit normally has a fixed maturity date and cannot be withdrawn earlier without incurring a penalty. However, depending on the term of the deposit, it could be part of cash equivalents.

3

Classification	Items
Operating activities	(d)
Investing activities	(c)
Financing activities	(b)
Increase/decrease in cash and cash equivalents	(a)

4 (a)

The direct method	✓
The indirect method	

(b)

True	
False	✓

IAS 7 allows either method.

5 (a)

Cash inflow of £5,600	
Cash outflow of £64,400	
Cash outflow of £94,400	✓
Cash outflow of £100,000	

Cash flows from investing activities:

	£
Payments to acquire property, plant and equipment (W)	100,000
Receipts from sale of property, plant and equipment	(5,600)
	94,400

Working

Property, plant and equipment: Cost	£
Opening balance	400,000
Disposals	(20,000)
Closing balance	(480,000)
Cash paid (balancing figure)	(100,000)

(b)

£6,000	
£18,000	
£26,000	
£30,000	✓

Working

Property, plant and equipment: Accumulated depreciation	£
Opening balance	68,000
Disposals (20,000 – 8,000)	(12,000)
Closing balance	(86,000)
Depreciation charge (balancing figure)	(30,000)

6 (a) **Reconciliation of profit before tax to net cash from operating activities for the year ended 30 June 20X5**

	£000
Profit before tax	270
Depreciation	305
Finance costs	62
Increase in inventories (1,009 – 960)	(49)
Increase in receivables (826 – 668)	(158)
Increase in trade payables (641 – 563)	78
Cash generated from operations	508
Interest paid	(62)
Tax paid	(53)
Net cash from operating activities	393

(b) **Statement of cash flows for the year ended 30 June 20X5**

	£000	£000
Net cash from operating activities		393
Investing activities:		
Purchase of property, plant and equipment (W)	(559)	
Net cash used in investing activities		(559)
Financing activities:		
Increase in long-term loan (610 – 460)	150	
Dividends paid	(59)	
Net cash from financing activities		91
Net increase (decrease) in cash and cash equivalents for the year		(75)
Cash and cash equivalents at the beginning of the year		100
Cash and cash equivalents at the end of the year		25

Working

Property, plant and equipment	£000
Property, plant and equipment at the beginning of the year	1,776
Depreciation	(305)
Property, plant and equipment at the end of the year	(2,030)
	(559)

Alternative working

Property, plant and equipment

	£000		£000
Balance b/f	1,776	Depreciation	305
Additions (bal fig)	**559**	Balance c/f	2,030
	2,335		2,335

7   There has been a decrease in cash of £238,000 and this has reduced the company's cash balance from £240,000 to only £2,000.

However, there are many positive signs:

- Cash generated from operations is more than £5,000,000 (compared with profit from operations of £4,214,000). If the company can regularly generate this amount of cash, it should be able to avoid serious cash flow problems. There are no signs of problems in managing working capital; only receivables have increased in the period.

- The main reason for the net cash outflow is that there have been asset purchases of nearly £3,000,000. This means that the company should be able to continue to generate profits and cash inflows in future periods.

- Cash has also been used to repay some of the company's loan stock. Therefore cash outflows to pay interest will reduce in future periods.

- The company still has a positive cash balance; it has not overdrawn its bank account.

Conclusion: the company is probably managing its cash flow well and there appear to be no liquidity problems.

CHAPTER 6 Property, plant and equipment

1

True	✓
False	

IAS 16 (para. 16, 17) states that, as well as its purchase price, the cost of an asset includes any further costs directly attributable to bringing the item to the location and condition necessary for it to be capable of operating in the manner intended by management.

2

True	✓
False	

This is routine maintenance expenditure and must be recognised as an expense in profit or loss in the period in which it was incurred. It cannot be added to the cost of the building (IAS 16: para. 16, 17).

3   (a)

True	
False	✓

IAS 16 (para. 29) states that where an item of property, plant and equipment is revalued, all assets of the same class should be revalued.

(b)

True	
False	✓

The company must keep the valuations up to date, but IAS 16 does not require annual revaluations. Revaluations should be carried out with sufficient regularity to ensure that the value at which an item is carried in the statement of financial position is not materially different from its actual fair value at the end of the reporting period.

(c) **Journal**

Account name	Debit £	Credit £
Freehold property: Cost/valuation	70,000	
Freehold property: Accumulated depreciation	30,000	
Revaluation reserve		100,000

4

True	
False	✓

IAS 16 does not prescribe a method of depreciation. Management should select a suitable method that reflects as fairly as possible the pattern in which the asset's economic benefits are consumed by the entity.

5

£20,000	
£24,000	
£30,000	✓

Depreciation must be based on the revalued amount. Therefore the charge for the year ended 31 December 20X6 is £30,000 (600,000 ÷ 20).

6

£48,500	
£50,000	✓
£102,500	
£181,250	

Gain on disposal:

	£000	£000
Sales proceeds		575
Less carrying amount		
Valuation	540	
Accumulated depreciation (540 × 1/36):	(15)	
		(525)
		50

CHAPTER 7 Intangible assets and inventories

1

Recognise expenditure on both projects in profit or loss	
Recognise expenditure on Project X in profit or loss Recognise expenditure on Project Y as an intangible asset	✓
Recognise expenditure on Project Y in profit or loss Recognise expenditure on Project X as an intangible asset	
Recognise expenditure on both projects as an intangible asset	

IAS 38 (para. 57) states that an intangible asset arising from development should be recognised, if an entity can demonstrate all of the following:

- The technical feasibility of completing the asset
- Its intention to complete the asset and its ability to use or sell it
- How the asset will generate probable future economic benefits
- The availability of adequate resources to complete the development
- Its ability to measure the expenditure reliably

Both projects appear to meet some of the IAS 38 conditions.

However, there is a possibility that adequate resources will not be available to complete Project X, as the company still has to obtain external funding. Therefore the expenditure must be recognised immediately in profit or loss.

Project Y is likely to be completed within the next few months and funding to complete the project appears to be available. On the basis of the information provided, all the conditions appear to be met. Therefore the company should recognise the expenditure as an intangible asset.

2

	True	False
An intangible asset may have an indefinite useful life.	✓	
An intangible asset should always be amortised over its useful life.		✓
Internally generated goodwill should never be recognised.	✓	
No internally generated intangible asset may be recognised.		✓

Intangible assets with an indefinite useful life are not amortised. Development expenditure should be recognised as an intangible asset if the project meets certain conditions.

3

True	
False	✓

IAS 36 states that most assets should be reviewed for impairment only where there is some indication that impairment has occurred. However, two types of assets must be reviewed at least annually: intangible assets with an indefinite useful life, and goodwill acquired in a business combination.

4   (a)   An impairment loss is the amount by which the carrying amount of an asset exceeds its recoverable amount.

(b)   The recoverable amount of an asset is the higher of its fair value less costs of disposal and its value in use.

(c)   An impairment loss should be recognised in other comprehensive income if the asset has previously been revalued upwards.

The loss is recognised in other comprehensive income (set against the revaluation reserve) until the carrying amount of the asset falls below depreciated historical cost; then the remainder of the loss is recognised in profit or loss.

5   (a)   Financial statements are prepared on an accruals basis. This means that the effects of transactions and other events are recognised when they occur and they are recorded in the accounting records and reported in the financial statements of the periods to which they relate. In addition, IAS 2 (para. 34) states that the carrying amount of inventories is recognised as an expense in the period in which the related revenue is recognised. Closing inventories are therefore recognised as an asset in the statement of financial position and carried forward to the next period, when they will be sold and the revenue will be recognised.

(b)   The cost of inventories comprises all costs of **purchase**, costs of **conversion** and other costs incurred in bringing the inventories to their present **location** and **condition**.

(c) Closing inventories are valued at the lower of cost and net realisable value.

(d) Inventories are an asset because:

- They are under the control of the entity (they can decide how to use them);

- They are the result of a past event (the purchase of goods); and

- The purchase of inventories gives rise to future economic benefits because it results in a future inflow of cash when the inventories are sold.

6

£2,170	
£2,225	
£2,295	✓
£2,670	

Gross profit for April (FIFO):

	£
Sales	5,000
Cost of sales	(2,705)
	2,295

FIFO

Closing inventories are £625 (25 × £25).

Cost of sales is £2,705 (3,330 – 625).

CHAPTER 8 Further accounting standards

1

Expense of £74,500; liability of £74,500	
Expense of £74,500; liability of £85,500	✓
Expense of £85,500; liability of £74,500	
Expense of £96,500; liability of £85,500	

Tax charge:

	£
Tax on profits for the year	85,500
Adjustments relating to previous years	(11,000)
	74,500

2

A finance lease	✓
An operating lease	

The note shows that leased assets have been capitalised (recognised as an asset).

3

£	57,600

Working

	Liability at 1 January £	Interest £	Repayment £	Liability at 31 December £
20X1	76,000	1,600	(20,000)	57,600
20X2	57,600	1,200	(20,000)	38,800
20X3	38,800	800	(20,000)	19,600
20X4	19,600	400	(20,000)	–
		4,000		

4 **Legal proceedings:**

Because the company will probably not be found liable, there is only a possible obligation to pay damages. Therefore the company should not recognise a provision.

However, there is a contingent liability, and information about the case should be disclosed unless the possibility that the company will have to pay damages is remote.

Staff retraining:

There does not appear to be any kind of obligation to carry out the retraining. The directors could still decide not to retrain the staff and to avoid the expense. Therefore no provision for training costs or loss of income should be made.

Because there is no obligation, there is no contingent liability.

5

Damage to inventory as a result of a flood	
Discovery of a fraud committed by one of the accounts staff	✓
Issue of new share capital	
Sale of a freehold property	

6   (a)   Revenue is the gross inflow of economic benefits during the period arising in the course of the ordinary activities of the entity (IAS 18: para. 7).

    (b)   An entity should recognise revenue from the sale of goods when **all** the following conditions have been satisfied:

- The entity has transferred to the buyer the significant risks and rewards of ownership of the goods.

- The entity retains neither continuing managerial involvement to the degree usually associated with ownership nor effective control over the goods sold.

- The amount of revenue can be measured reliably.

- It is probable that the economic benefits associated with the transaction will flow to the entity.

- The costs incurred or to be incurred in respect of the transaction can be measured reliably.

CHAPTER 9 Group accounts: the consolidated statement of financial position

1

C Ltd only	
B Ltd and C Ltd	
C Ltd and D Ltd	✓
All four companies	

The following are subsidiaries of A plc:

- C Ltd (majority of equity shares)
- D Ltd (a member and can appoint a majority of the directors)

B Ltd and E Ltd are not subsidiaries because the investor does not have a majority of voting rights. (Neither preference shares nor loan stock carry voting rights.)

2   (a)   A subsidiary is an entity that is controlled by another entity (IFRS 10: para. B2).

    (b)   An investor (a parent) controls an investee (a subsidiary) if, and only if, the investor has all the following:

- Power over the investee

- Exposure, or rights, to variable returns from its involvement with the investee

- The ability to use its power over the investee to affect the amount of the investor's returns

3 (a) Goodwill

£1,000,000	
£1,400,000	
£2,000,000	
£2,350,000	✓

	£000
Price paid	9,000
NCI at acqn. (5% × 5,000) + (5% × 2,000)	350
Less fair value of net assets acquired (5,000 + 2,000)	(7,000)
NCI share	2,350

(b) Consolidated retained earnings

£28,950,000	✓
£29,000,000	
£30,850,000	
£31,000,000	

	£000
Left plc	28,000
Right Ltd attributable to Left plc	
(95% × (3,000 – 2,000))	950
	28,950

(c) Non-controlling interest

£250,000	
£300,000	
£350,000	
£400,000	✓

	£000
Share capital attributable to NCI (5% × 5,000)	250
Retained earnings attributable to NCI (5% × 3,000)	150
NCI share	400

4   Why fair value adjustments should be made:

- The consolidated statement of financial position should reflect the assets and liabilities of the subsidiary at their cost to the group.

- If the subsidiary's assets and liabilities are not adjusted to fair value, goodwill will be overstated.

5

True	✓
False	

None of the goods remain in inventory at the year end, so there is no unrealised profit.

6 **Consolidated statement of financial position as at 31 March 20X7**

	£000
ASSETS	
Non-current assets:	
Intangible assets: Goodwill (W2)	1,200
Property, plant and equipment (8,000 + 6,000)	14,000
	15,200
Current assets:	
Inventories (2,400 + 1,440)	3,840
Trade and other receivables (2,640 + 2,400 − 960)	4,080
Cash and cash equivalents (480 + 360)	840
	8,760
Total assets	23,960

	£000
Equity and liabilities	
Equity attributable to owners of the parent:	
Share capital	5,000
Retained earnings (W3)	10,920
	15,920
Non-controlling interest (W4)	1,440
Total equity	17,360
Non-current liabilities (1,200 + 1,080)	2,280
Current liabilities:	
Trade payables (2,500 + 1,700 – 960)	3,240
Tax payable (860 + 220)	1,080
	4,320
Total liabilities	6,600
Total equity and liabilities	23,960

Workings

(1)   Group structure

Salt plc owns 80% (800,000/1,000,000) of the equity share capital of Pepper Ltd.

(2)

Goodwill	£000
Price paid	4,000
Non-controlling interest at acquisition	700
Net assets acquired: £1m + £2.5m	(3,500)
	1,200

(3)

Retained earnings	£000
Salt plc	7,960
Pepper Ltd attributable to Salt plc (80% × 6,200 – 2,500)	2,960
	10,920

(4)

Non-controlling interest at acquisition	£000
Share capital attributable to NCI (20% × 1,000)	200
Retained earnings attributable to NCI (20% × 2,500)	500
	700

(5)

Non-controlling interest at year end	£000
Share capital attributable to NCI (20% × 1,000)	200
Retained earnings attributable to NCI (20% × 6,200)	1,240
	1,440

CHAPTER 10 Group accounts: further aspects

1   The consolidated financial statements must reflect the operations of the group. If a company sells goods to another company in the same group, the group has not made a sale and no profit has been earned. Sales and profits should only be recognised when the goods are purchased by a customer external to the group.

Any purchases that are unsold at the year end will be included in inventories. The value of the inventory should be its cost to the group, not its cost to the individual group company that purchased it.

2

True	✓
False	

The parent sold goods to the subsidiary and therefore non-controlling interests are not affected by the provision for unrealised profit on inventories.

3

£1,250,000	
£1,340,000	
£1,450,000	✓
£1,540,000	

	£
Denston Ltd	950,000
Hawkedon Ltd	500,000
	1,450,000

4

£1,250,000	
£1,275,000	
£1,300,000	✓
£1,400,000	

Working

	£	£
Aldeburgh plc		800,000
Southwold Ltd		600,000
Adjustment: intra-group sale	(125,000)	
provision for unrealised profit	25,000	
		(100,000)
		1,300,000

5 Consolidated statement of profit or loss for the year ended 31 December 20X3

	£000
Revenue (W)	2,880
Cost of sales (W)	(1,380)
Gross profit	1,500
Other income	0
Operating expenses (360 + 180)	(540)
Profit before tax	960
Tax (240 + 120)	(360)
Profit for the year	600
Attributable to:	
Equity holders of the parent	564
Non-controlling interest (240 × 15%)	36
	600

Workings

Group structure

Thames plc owns 85% of the equity share capital of Stour Ltd.

Revenue	£000
Thames plc	2,280
Stour Ltd	1,200
Total inter-company adjustment	(600)
	2,880

Cost of sales	£000
Thames plc	1,320
Stour Ltd	660
Total inter-company adjustment	(600)
	1,380

CHAPTER 11 Interpreting financial statements

1

8%	
10%	✓
15%	
40%	

Operating profit percentage is $\dfrac{\text{Profit from operations}}{\text{Revenue}}$

Revenue is 80,000 (20,000 × 100/25)

Operating profit percentage is $\dfrac{20,000 - 12,000}{80,000} \times 100\% = 10\%$

2

True	
False	✓

ROCE = Operating profit percentage × asset turnover

Therefore asset turnover = $\dfrac{\text{ROCE}}{\text{Operating profit percentage}} = \dfrac{20\%}{10\%} = 2$ times

3 (a) Return on capital employed

$$\dfrac{\text{Profit from operations}}{\text{Total equity} + \text{non-current liabilities}} \times 100\%$$

(b) Acid test ratio

$$\dfrac{\text{Current assets} - \text{Inventories}}{\text{Current liabilities}}$$

(c) Inventory holding period (days)

$$\dfrac{\text{Inventories}}{\text{Cost of sales}} \times 365 \text{ days}$$

(d) Interest cover

$$\dfrac{\text{Profit from operations}}{\text{Finance costs}} \times 365 \text{ days}$$

4

40%	
60%	✓
80%	
150%	

Gearing ratio:

$$\frac{\text{Non-current liabilities}}{\text{Total equity} + \text{non-current liabilities}} = \frac{39,000}{26,000 + 39,000} \times 100\% = 60\%$$

5

| True | |
| False | ✓ |

6

	Formula (part (a))	Calculation (part (b))
Gross profit percentage	$\dfrac{\text{Gross profit}}{\text{Revenue}} \times 100\%$	$\dfrac{1,475}{4,100} \times 100\% = 36.0\%$
Inventory turnover	$\dfrac{\text{Cost of sales}}{\text{Inventories}}$	$\dfrac{2,625}{480} = 5.5$ times
Trade receivables collection period	$\dfrac{\text{Trade receivables}}{\text{Revenue}} \times 365$ days	$\dfrac{956}{4,100} \times 365 = 85$ days
Trade payables payment period	$\dfrac{\text{Trade payables}}{\text{Cost of sales}} \times 365$ days	$\dfrac{267}{2,625} \times 365 = 37$ days

7

| True | ✓ |
| False | |

Reducing administrative expenses will increase operating profit.

8 Comparisons between the ratios of different companies, even within the same industry sector, can be misleading.

- Companies may use different accounting policies. For example, some companies revalue non-current assets, while others carry them at historical cost. This can have a significant effect on key ratios.

- Ratios may not always be calculated according to the same formulae.

- Companies within the same industry can operate in completely different markets or adopt different strategies. This will affect ratios such as gross profit percentage and operating profit percentage.

9

REPORT

To: Michael Beacham

From: Accounting Technician

Subject: Interpretation of the ratios of Goodall Ltd

Date: October 20X3

As requested, I have analysed the financial performance and position of Goodall Ltd for 20X2 and 20X3. This analysis has been based on the ratios calculated by your financial adviser, which have been compared with industry averages.

Gearing ratio

This ratio is often used as a measure of the risk involved in investing in, or lending to, a business. The company's gearing has risen fairly sharply in 20X3 and is considerably higher than the industry average of 41%. Goodall Ltd has evidently taken out an additional long-term loan during the year, or increased an existing loan. The ratios show that the company is a much riskier investment than other businesses in its industry sector and that the position is deteriorating. It may be harder for the company to raise additional finance in the future, as potential lenders are normally reluctant to lend to a company that is already heavily in debt.

Interest cover

Interest cover has almost halved in the period, so that in 20X3 the company's profit from operations (profit before interest and tax) was only very slightly more than its interest payable. This is very low indeed compared with the industry average of 4.6.

This fall in interest cover has probably occurred partly because the company has increased its long-term loans and will now be paying more interest as a result. However, the ratio has deteriorated so sharply (compared to the rise in the gearing ratio) that there must be additional factors at work. Interest rates may have risen (lenders may be demanding higher rates because the company is now very heavily indebted). Alternatively, it is possible that profit from operations has fallen. A combination of lower profits and higher interest costs would be extremely worrying.

Quick ratio/Acid test

This ratio has decreased in the two-year period and it is now much lower than the industry average of 1.1. At its last year end, the company's current liabilities were twice as great as its 'quick' current assets. The industry average shows that Goodall Ltd does not operate in an industry where a low quick ratio is the norm.

A possible reason for the fall is that there have been high cash outflows during the year, either changing a positive cash balance to a bank overdraft, or increasing an existing overdraft. This worsening of the quick ratio suggests that the additional long-term loan has not been sufficient to meet the company's need for cash. Goodall Ltd does not have enough cash available to meet its current liabilities and it may have significant liquidity problems.

Return on equity

Return on shareholders' funds has fallen sharply over the period, suggesting that there is less profit available for equity shareholders. This means that they are unlikely to receive much immediate return on their investment (in the form of dividends) and that there is little profit available for reinvestment in the company to generate better returns in future. The return on shareholders' funds of Goodall Ltd is considerably lower than the industry average of 19%, which means that the company is much less likely to attract equity investors than other companies within the sector.

The increase in long-term loans will not have affected shareholders' equity. Therefore the lower return on shareholders' funds has probably been caused by increased interest costs, possibly combined with lower profit from operations.

Conclusion

Goodall Ltd is already very highly geared; its interest cover is deteriorating and it appears to be suffering liquidity problems. All these things suggest that there would be considerable risk in lending money to this company, unless the loan is almost certain to generate increased profits in the short term. It is quite possible that the company will be unable to meet its interest payments in future, as neither the profits nor the cash may be available. Return on shareholders' funds is very low, which means that the company is unlikely to be able to raise additional finance from investors. On the basis of the limited information provided, it would not be advisable to make a loan to this company.

Certain *Financial Statements of Limited Companies* assessment objectives will be tested in the AAT *Professional Diploma in Accounting* synoptic assessment. Therefore, at this stage in your studies, it is useful to consider the style of tasks you may see in the synoptic assessment.

However, it is recommended that the AAT *Professional Diploma in Accounting* synoptic assessment is only taken when all other units have been completed.

Relevant learning outcomes

Assessment objective 5	Analyse an organisation's decision making and control using ratio analysis.
Related learning objectives	**Accounting Systems and Controls** LO1 Demonstrate an understanding of the role and responsibilities of the accounting function within an organisation LO2 Evaluate internal control systems LO4 Analyse recommendations made to improve an organisation's accounting system **Financial Statements of Limited Companies** LO1 Demonstrate an understanding of the reporting frameworks and ethical principles that underpin financial reporting LO5 Interpret financial statements using ratio analysis **Management Accounting: Decision and Control** LO4 Use appropriate financial and non-financial performance techniques to aid decision making
Assessment objective 6	Analyse the internal controls of an organisation and make recommendations.
Related learning objectives	**Accounting Systems and Controls** LO1 Demonstrate an understanding of the role and responsibilities of the accounting function within an organisation LO2 Evaluate internal control systems LO3 Evaluate an organisation's accounting system and underpinning procedures LO4 Analyse recommendations made to improve an organisation's accounting system **Financial Statements of Limited Companies** LO1 Demonstrate an understanding of the reporting frameworks and ethical principles that underpin financial reporting

	Management Accounting: Budgeting
	LO3 Demonstrate how budgeting can improve organisational performance
	Management Accounting: Decision and Control
	LO4 Use appropriate financial and non-financial performance techniques to aid decision making
	LO5 Evaluate a range of cost management techniques to enhance value and aid decision making

Questions

1 You are the Assistant Accountant at Fontwell Ltd. The most recent statement of profit or loss and statement of financial position (with comparatives for the previous year) of Fontwell Ltd can be viewed by clicking on the buttons below:

Fontwell Ltd
Statement of profit or loss for the year ended 30 June 20X1

	£000
Continuing operations	
Revenue	89,463
Cost of sales	(51,279)
Gross profit	38,184
Loss on disposal of PPE	(39)
Dividends received	157
	38,302
Distribution costs	(11,389)
Administrative expenses	(15,126)
Profit from operations	11,787
Finance costs	(168)
Profit before tax	11,619
Tax	(2,712)
Profit for the period from continuing operations	8,907

Further information:

- The total depreciation charge for the year was £5,427,000.

- Property, plant and equipment with a carrying amount of £576,000 was sold in the year.

- All sales and purchases were on credit. Other expenses were paid for in cash.

- A dividend of £3,200,000 was paid during the year, and a further dividend of £1,300,000 was declared on 21 July 20X1 before the financial statements were authorised for issue.

Fontwell Ltd

Statement of financial position as at 30 June 20X1

	20X1 £000	20X0 £000
ASSETS		
Non-current assets		
Property, plant and equipment	47,835	32,691
Investments at cost	7,000	7,000
	54,835	39,691
Current assets		
Inventories	2,578	3,264
Trade receivables	7,964	9,325
Cash and cash equivalents	118	–
	10,660	12,589
Total assets	65,495	52,280

	20X1 £000	20X0 £000
EQUITY AND LIABILITIES		
Equity		
Share capital	22,500	18,000
Share premium	8,900	6,300
Retained earnings	23,307	17,600
Total equity	54,707	41,900
Non-current liabilities		
Bank loans	2,800	2,400
	2,800	2,400
Current liabilities		
Trade payables	5,198	4,726
Tax liabilities	2,790	3,180
Bank overdraft	–	74
	7,988	7,980
Total liabilities	10,788	10,380
Total equity and liabilities	65,495	52,280

(a) **Prepare a reconciliation of profit before tax to net cash from operating activities for Fontwell Ltd for the year ended 30 June 20X1.**

(b) **Prepare the statement of cash flows for Fontwell Ltd for the year ended 30 June 20X1.**

> **Note.** You don't have to use the workings boxes to achieve full marks on the task; however, data in the workings will be taken into consideration if you make errors in the proforma.

Your manager, the Chief Accountant of Fontwell Ltd, is putting you under pressure to give incorrect information to the company's internal auditors.

(c) **State the threat to your fundamental ethical principles identified by the situation and which safeguard against it you should take.**

Fontwell Ltd

Reconciliation of profit before tax to net cash from operating activities

		£000
▼		
Adjustments for:		
▼		
▼		
▼		
▼		
▼		
▼		
▼		
Cash generated from operations		
▼		
▼		
Net cash from operating activities		

Picklist:

Adjustment in respect of inventories
Adjustment in respect of trade payables
Adjustment in respect of trade receivables
Bank loans
Depreciation
Dividends received
Finance costs
Interest paid
Loss on disposal of PPE
Proceeds on disposal of PPE
Profit after tax
Profit before tax
Profit from operations
Purchase of investments
Purchases of PPE
Tax paid

Fontwell Ltd

Statement of cash flows for the year ended 30 June 20X1

	£000
Net cash from operating activities	
Investing activities	
▼	
▼	
▼	
Net cash used in investing activities	
Financing activities	
▼	
▼	
▼	
Net cash from financing activities	
Net increase/(decrease) in cash and cash equivalents	
Cash and cash equivalents at beginning of year	
Cash and cash equivalents at end of year	

Picklist:

Adjustment in respect of inventories
Adjustment in respect of trade payables
Adjustment in respect of trade receivables
Bank loans
Dividends paid
Dividends received
Proceeds of share issue
Proceeds on disposal of PPE
Purchases of PPE

Workings

Proceeds on disposal of PPE	£000
▼	
▼	
Proceeds on disposal of PPE	

Picklist:

Carrying amount of PPE sold
Depreciation charge
Loss on disposal of PPE
PPE at end of year
PPE at start of year

Purchases of PPE	£000
PPE at start of year	
▼	
▼	
▼	
Total PPE additions	

Picklist:

Carrying amount of PPE sold
Depreciation charge
Loss on disposal of PPE
PPE at end of year

Tax paid	£000
▼	
▼	
▼	
Tax paid	

Picklist:

Tax charge to profit/loss
Tax liability at end of year
Tax liability at start of year

2   You are the accountant for Miramar Ltd. The company makes a special type of binoculars for birdwatchers.

The following is a copy of the original budget and actual performance of the company for the last 12 months. You have been asked to prepare a flexible budget so that comparisons with the actual performance will be more useful.

Draft operating statement

	Original budget		Actual	
Sales volume units	50,000		60,000	
	£000	£000	£000	£000
Turnover		**15,000**		**16,500**
Material A	2,500		3,132	
Material B	990		1,557	
Material C	1,365		1,764	
Labour	2,700		2,980	
Energy	1,340		1,550	
Maintenance	745		987	
Rent and rates	940		945	
Administrative expenses	850		800	
Total expenses		**11,430**		**13,715**
Operating profit/(loss)		**3,570**		**2,785**

(a) Calculate the following budgeted prices and costs:

(i)   Selling price per unit

(ii)   Cost of material per unit for:

- Material A
- Material B
- Material C

(iii)   Cost of labour per unit

(iv)   Energy fixed cost for the year

(b) Calculate the following actual prices and costs:

(i)   Selling price per unit

(ii)   Cost of material per unit for:

- Material A
- Material B
- Material C

(iii)   Cost of labour per unit

Assumptions made when preparing the original budget:

- Material and labour costs are variable.

- Energy is a semi-variable cost. The variable cost per unit produced is £18.

- Maintenance is a stepped variable cost. For every £149,000 spent on maintenance, the company can produce 10,000 binoculars.

- Both rent and rates, and administrative expenses, are fixed costs.

- There were no opening or closing stocks.

- There were no purchases or sales of fixed assets during the year.

3   You are employed by Singh Ltd as a financial analyst. You have been asked to look at the profitability and interest cover of the company over the last two years.

You have calculated three key ratios for Singh Ltd in respect of its financial statements for the years 20X1 and 20X0, and an extract of the company's annual budget for 20X1 is also provided below.

Three key ratios:

	20X1	20X0
Gross profit %	31.6%	38.9%
Operating profit %	11.3%	9.2%
Interest cover	5.2 times	3.9 times

Singh Ltd – Extract of annual budget for 20X1

	£000
Revenue	940
Cost of sales	(630)
Gross profit	310
Operating expenses	(204)
Profit from operations	106
Finance costs	(23)
Profit before taxation	83

Prepare notes which include:

(a) **Comments on the relative performance of Singh Ltd in respect of the two years, giving possible reasons for any differences based upon the ratios calculated (the extract of the annual budget may also assist you in some aspects of this)**

(b) **THREE limitations of ratio analysis**

Solutions

1 (a) **Fontwell Ltd**

Reconciliation of profit before tax to net cash from operating activities

	£000
Profit before tax	11,619
Adjustments for:	
Depreciation	5,427
Loss on disposal of PPE	39
Finance costs	168
Dividends received	(157)
Adjustment in respect of inventories (2,578 – 3,264)	686
Adjustment in respect of trade receivables (7,964 – 9,325)	1,361
Adjustment in respect of trade payables (5,198 – 4,726)	472
Cash generated from operations	19,615
Tax paid (W)	(3,102)
Interest paid	(168)
Net cash from operating activities	16,345

(b) Fontwell Ltd

Statement of cash flows for the year ended 30 June 20X1

	£000
Net cash from operating activities	16,345
Investing activities	
Dividends received	157
Proceeds on disposal of PPE (W)	537
Purchase of PPE (W)	(21,147)
Net cash used in investing activities	(20,453)
Financing activities	
Bank loans	400
Proceeds of share issue	7,100
Dividends paid	(3,200)
Net cash from financing activities	4,300
Net increase/(decrease) in cash and cash equivalents	192
Cash and cash equivalents at beginning of year	(74)
Cash and cash equivalents at end of year	118

Workings

Proceeds on disposal of PPE	£000
Carrying amount of PPE sold	576
Loss on disposal of PPE	(39)
Proceeds on disposal of PPE	537

Purchases of PPE	£000
PPE at start of year	32,691
Depreciation charge	(5,427)
Carrying amount of PPE sold	(576)
PPE and end of year	(47,835)
Total PPE additions	(21,147)

Tax paid	£000
Tax liability at start of year	3,180
Tax charge to profit/loss	2,712
Tax liability at end of year	(2,790)
Tax paid	3,102

(c)

Ethical issue

Your situation represents an intimidation threat to your fundamental ethical principles and you should implement the safeguard of obtaining advice, for instance from your professional body.

2   (a)   (i)   **Budgeted selling price per unit** $= \dfrac{£15,000,000}{50,000 \text{ units}} = £300.00$

(ii)   **Budgeted cost of material A per unit** $= \dfrac{£2,500,000}{50,000} =$ £50.00

Budgeted cost of material B per unit $= \dfrac{£990,000}{50,000} =$ £19.80

Budgeted cost of material C per unit $= \dfrac{£1,365,000}{50,000} =$ £27.30

(iii)   **Budgeted labour cost per unit** $= \dfrac{£2,700,000}{50,000} = £54.00$

(iv) **Budgeted energy fixed cost**

	£000
Variable cost (50,000 × £18)	900
Total budgeted cost	1,340
Fixed cost	440

(b) (i) **Actual selling price per unit** = $\dfrac{£16,500,000}{60,000}$ = £275

(ii) **Actual cost of material A per unit** = $\dfrac{£3,132,000}{60,000}$ = £52.20

Actual cost of material B per unit = $\dfrac{£1,557,000}{60,000}$ = £25.95

Actual cost of material C per unit = $\dfrac{£1,764,000}{60,000}$ = £29.40

(iii) **Actual labour cost per unit** = $\dfrac{£2,980,000}{60,000}$ = £49.67

3 (a) (i) **20X1 gross profit percentage is worse.**

- Less gross profit is being generated by sales/lower gross profit margins on sales.

- Selling prices may have decreased.

- Cost of sales/purchase costs may have increased.

- The mix of products sold may have changed in 20X1.

- The annual budget anticipated a reduction of gross profit (to 33%) but the drop is greater than expected.

(ii) **20X1 operating profit percentage is better.**

- As the gross profit ratio has declined, the improvement is due to lower overhead costs.

- More operating profit is being generated from sales.

- The operating profit achieved is in line with the budget.

- As gross profit is lower than the budget, this indicates that costs are lower than planned.

(iii) **20X1 interest cover is better.**

- More profit is available to meet interest payments (less risky).

- May be caused by higher operating profits.

- May be caused by lower interest payments.

- May have paid off debt during the year.

- Interest rates may have declined.

- The improvement in interest cover was anticipated by the budget, but is better than expected.

(b) **Limitations of ratio analysis**

Note. Only **three** required.

- **Different accounting policies**

  The choices of accounting policies may distort inter-company comparisons.

- **Creative accounting**

  Companies may try to show a better financial performance or position.

- **Outdated information in financial statements**

  Financial statements are likely to be out of date and will not reflect the current position.

- **Changes in accounting policy**

  Changes may affect the comparison of results between different accounting years.

- **Ratios are not definitive measures**

  Ratios only provide clues to the company's performance or financial situation.

- **Historical costs not suitable for decision making**

  Ratios based on historical costs may not be very useful for decision making.

- **Interpretation of the ratio**

  It is difficult to generalise about whether a particular ratio is 'good' or 'bad'.

- **Price changes**

  Inflation renders comparisons of results over time misleading.

- **Changes in accounting standard**

  Change will affect the comparison of results over a number of years.

- **Impact of seasons on trading**

  Some businesses are affected by seasons and can choose the best time to produce financial statements so as to show better results.

- **Different financial and business risk profile**

  Businesses may operate within the same industry but have different financial and business risk.

- **Different capital structures and size**

  Companies may have different capital structures which makes comparison difficult.

Glossary of terms

It is useful to be familiar with interchangeable terminology including IFRS and UK GAAP (generally accepted accounting principles).

Below is a short list of the most important terms you are likely to use or come across, together with their international and UK equivalents.

UK term	International term
Profit and loss account	**Statement of profit or loss (or statement of profit or loss and other comprehensive income)**
Turnover or Sales	Revenue or Sales revenue
Operating profit	Profit from operations
Reducing balance depreciation	Diminishing balance depreciation
Depreciation/depreciation expense(s)	Depreciation charge(s)
Balance sheet	**Statement of financial position**
Fixed assets	Non-current assets
Net book value	Carrying amount
Tangible assets	Property, plant and equipment
Stocks	Inventories
Trade debtors or Debtors	Trade receivables
Prepayments	Other receivables
Debtors and prepayments	Trade and other receivables
Cash at bank and in hand	Cash and cash equivalents
Long-term liabilities	Non-current liabilities
Trade creditors or creditors	Trade payables
Accruals	Other payables
Creditors and accruals	Trade and other payables
Capital and reserves	Equity (limited companies)
Profit and loss balance	Retained earnings
Cash flow statement	**Statement of cash flows**

Accountants often have a tendency to use several phrases to describe the same thing! Some of these are listed below:

Different terms for the same thing
Nominal ledger, main ledger or general ledger
Subsidiary ledgers, memorandum ledgers
Subsidiary (sales) ledger, sales ledger
Subsidiary (purchases) ledger, purchases ledger

Bibliography

Association of Accounting Technicians (2016) *Financial Statements of Limited Companies sample assessment.* [Online]. Available from: www.aat-interactive.org.uk/elearning/Sample_assessments_AQ2016/ [Accessed 23 May 2016].

Association of Accounting Technicians (2016) 601/6551/0. *Level 4 Professional Diploma in Accounting Qualification Specification.* London, AAT.

Association of Accounting Technicians (2016) *Professional Diploma Synoptic assessment (PDSY).* [Online]. Available from: www.aat-interactive.org.uk/elearning/Sample_assessments_AQ2016/ [Accessed 23 May 2016].

Association of Accounting Technicians (2014) *AAT Code of Professional Ethics. Version 2.* [eBook] London, AAT. Available from: www.aat.org.uk /sites/default/files/assets/AAT_Code_of_Professional_Ethics.pdf [Accessed 27 April 2016].

International Accounting Standards Board (2010) Conceptual Framework for Financial Reporting. In *International Financial Reporting Standards* (2010). [Online]. Available from: http://eifrs.ifrs.org [Accessed 23 May 2016].

IFRS Foundation (2016) *IFRS* [Online]. Available from: http://eifrs.ifrs.org [Accessed 24 May 2017].

Index

Notes

REVIEW FORM

How have you used this Course Book?
(Tick one box only)

☐ Self study

☐ On a course_____

☐ Other _____

Why did you decide to purchase this Course Book? *(Tick one box only)*

☐ Have used BPP materials in the past

☐ Recommendation by friend/colleague

☐ Recommendation by a college lecturer

☐ Saw advertising

☐ Other _____

During the past six months do you recall seeing/receiving either of the following?
(Tick as many boxes as are relevant)

☐ Our advertisement in Accounting Technician

☐ Our Publishing Catalogue

Which (if any) aspects of our advertising do you think are useful?
(Tick as many boxes as are relevant)

☐ Prices and publication dates of new editions

☐ Information on Course Book content

☐ Details of our free online offering

☐ None of the above

Your ratings, comments and suggestions would be appreciated on the following areas of this Course Book.

	Very useful	Useful	Not useful
Chapter overviews	☐	☐	☐
Introductory section	☐	☐	☐
Quality of explanations	☐	☐	☐
Illustrations	☐	☐	☐
Chapter activities	☐	☐	☐
Test your learning	☐	☐	☐
Keywords	☐	☐	☐

	Excellent	Good	Adequate	Poor
Overall opinion of this Course Book	☐	☐	☐	☐

Do you intend to continue using BPP Products? ☐ Yes ☐ No

Please note any further comments and suggestions/errors on the reverse of this page. The BPP author of this edition can be emailed at: lmfeedback@bpp.com.

Alternatively, the Head of Programme of this edition can be emailed at: nisarahmed@bpp.com

REVIEW FORM (continued)

TELL US WHAT YOU THINK

Please note any further comments and suggestions/errors below